An African American Cookbook

An African American Cookbook

Traditional and Other Favorite Recipes

Phoebe Bailey

with the special assistance of
Christina G. Johnson and Kesha M. Morant

Good Books

Intercourse, PA 17534
800/762-7171
www.goodbks.com

Acknowledgments

A special thank you to the congregation of Bethel African Methodist Episcopal Church, ChurchTowne of Lancaster, Pennsylvania.

Thank you, too, to Saints Memorial Community Church, Willingboro, New Jersey, and to Mr. Jerald and Mrs. Dawn Davis.

All photographs by Merle Good, except those on pages 227 and 228.
Cover and Illustrations by Cheryl Benner
Design by Dawn J. Ranck

AN AFRICAN AMERICAN COOKBOOK
Copyright © 2002 by Good Books, Intercourse, PA 17534
International Standard Book Number: 1-56148-352-4 (paperback edition)
International Standard Book Number: 1-56148-381-8 (comb-bound paperback edition)
Library of Congress Catalog Card Number: 2002024136

Library of Congress Cataloging-in-Publication Data
Bailey, Phoebe.
    An African American cookbook : living the experience / Phoebe Bailey.
    p.cm.
    ISBN 1-56148-352-4
    1. African American cookery. I. Harambee Historical Services (Lancaster, Penn.) II. Title.

Tx715.B1613 2002
    641.59'296073--dc21   2002024136

To Mrs. Margaret M. Bailey, my mother,
a designer of recipes,
who gave her family and all who knew her
a wealth of wisdom and a strong example of faith.

The royalties from the sale of this book go to Bethel Harambee Historical Services and the Hopkins Research and Study Center. These two organizations are committed to the preservation, stories, and living history of African American traditions and culture in ChurchTowne of Lancaster, Pennsylvania.

Table of Contents

About This Cookbook 3

"Wade in the Water" *4*
Main Dishes..**5**
    Traditional 6
    Other Favorites 18

"Steal Away"..*40*
Meats **41**
    Traditional 42
    Other Favorites 48

"Swing Low" *90*
Vegetables **91**
    Traditional 92
    Other Favorites....................................100

"Go Down, Moses" *114*
Salads..**115**
    Traditional 116
    Other Favorites....................................118

"Let Us Break Bread Together" *128*
Breads **129**
    Traditional 130
    Other Favorites....................................136

"Follow the Drinking Gourd" *150*
Soups **151**
    Traditional 152
    Other Favorites....................................154

Bethel AME's Annual Cookout 164
Sweets **165**
    Traditional 166
    Other Favorites....................................169

A Newly Freed Man's Prayer 192
Cakes **193**
    Traditional 194
    Other Favorites....................................196

"We Are Climbing Jacob's Ladder" 214
Snacks and Appetizers............................**215**
    Other Favorites....................................216

Etc. **226**

Story and Song......................................**227**

About "Living the Experience" **229**

About Bethel Harambee Historical **230**
    Services and the Hopkins Research
    and Study Center

About ChurchTowne of Lancaster, ...**232**
    Pennsylvania

Index **233**

About the Author **248**

Introduction

Welcome reader! Here are mouth-watering recipes that are easy to prepare and that will make every meal a delight. And with the recipes comes a look into our family and cultural traditions and some lessons we've learned. You will find quotes from some famous and some not-so famous people. We heard about many of them for the first time while sitting at the dinner table. Some of our songs are here. We heard them while preparing meals— for they're more than church songs. They were born out of the enslaved Africans' battle for freedom.

This book is about more than just food. We believe that, as important as food is to our being, it is what happens around a meal that actually sustains us. It is in preparing a meal that we discover "If you do not have what you want, use what you have." And when we work within that attitude, we find that God sufficiently provides for all our needs. It is at mealtimes that we learn family traditions, manners, how to share, how to wait our turns, how to listen to others, and many other important life lessons.

We use this book ourselves at home. And we share it within our congregation, which is a part of the African Methodist Episcopal Church. We are known as AME's. I have discovered that AME also stands for "always eating and meeting." I can attest to the fact that this is true. So if you are in the neighborhood of ChurchTowne of Lancaster, Pennsylvania, please stop in and stay awhile. For at Bethel, it is always mealtime.

A special thanks to God for His many blessings, and to Phoebe, Christina, and Kesha who helped to make this cookbook a reality. Thanks to the Bethel African Methodist Episcopal Church family for their recipes, stories, prayers, support, and the down-home meals that inspired this book. Thanks to all the wonderful African American cooks who contributed their traditional and favorite recipes to create a cornucopia of dishes. Thanks to the Goods who patiently worked with us to bring this book to press, and to all and anyone else who helped us.

Thank you to whose "who had so little but did so much with the little they had." These are those who toiled in the heat of the day and complained not about their lot, who bore their crosses and marched on in Jesus' name. These are those who when they looked to the future they saw us. These are our heroes, our elders, our parents, our support. We bless your spirits and He who gave you the strength to provide us hope.

— *Reverend Edward M. Bailey*
Bethel African Methodist Episcopal Church, ChurchTowne of Lancaster, Pennsylvania

Wade in the Water

Wade in the water,
Wade in the water children.
Wade in the water,
God's gonna trouble the water.

See that host all dressed in white,
God's gonna trouble the water;
The leader look like the Israelite,
God's gonna trouble the water.

See that band all dressed in red,
God's gonna trouble the water;
Looks like the band that Moses led,
God's gonna trouble the water.

See that band all dressed in black
God's gonna trouble the water;
They come this far, and ain't turning back.
God's gonna trouble the water.

Spirituals carried code language for enslaved Africans. In this one, runaways are directed to go to the river. The water will cover the fleeing Africans' scent and tracks, to make it difficult for the bloodhounds to track them. The water also connects towns, cities, and states, leading the hearers to the conductor who will lead them to their next station or safe house. The song mentions three colors: red, white, and black. Fleeing Africans would look for someone wearing these colors at their next stop.

Main Dishes

Some of my fondest memories of my mother surround her ability to create a meal out of anything. Having to prepare supper for 15 children every evening required a lot of creativity and patience. Thankfully, my mother never ran short of either. She could make a simple meal a gourmet experience. I thank God that my mother had the ability to plan and prepare meals as she wanted to for us children.

Our ancestors who lived on plantations, however, did not have this luxury. Many mothers were in the fields working from sun-up to sun-down, planting and preparing the fields for harvest. These mothers' young children were often left back at the slaves' quarters, usually with an elder enslaved African, who because of illness or feebleness could no longer offer free field labor for the Massa.

Those mothers who worked in the Big House, the great house, the house that offered no comfort — these mothers who were separated from their babies — would try to sneak down to the slave quarters with some small morsel of food for their children, praying every step of the way not to be discovered.

— Phoebe Bailey

Main Dishes — Traditional

Gumbo Feast

Mary Alice Bailey

Makes 10 servings

1½ lbs. chicken legs and thighs
salt to taste
pepper to taste
1½ tsp. red pepper flakes
3 Tbsp. oil
1 lb. smoked pork sausage, kielbasa,
    or turkey sausage, cut into ½-inch
    pieces
1 large onion, chopped
3 cloves garlic, minced
2 qts. chicken stock
1 whole bay leaf
½ tsp. dried thyme leaves
1 bell pepper, chopped
2 ribs celery, chopped
¼ cup cornstarch
¼ cup cold water
1 bunch green onion tops, chopped
⅓ cup fresh chopped parsley

1. Season the chicken with salt, pepper, and red pepper flakes. Brown quickly in oil. Remove chicken from skillet and set aside.
2. Brown sausage in drippings. Remove sausage from skillet and set aside.
3. Add onions and garlic and stir into drippings. Cook, stirring constantly for about 4 minutes.
4. Add stock, seasonings, chicken, and sausage. Bring to a boil. Cook for 40 minutes, skimming the broth as needed.
5. Stir in chopped green pepper and celery ribs. Continue simmering another 20 minutes.
6. Make a smooth paste by mixing together cornstarch and cold water. Remove ½ cup stock from cooking pot and stir into paste. When smooth, stir into gumbo in stockpot. Continue stirring until broth thickens. Stir in green onion tops and parsley. Heat for 5 minutes.
7. Serve over rice.

Seafood Gumbo

Makes 6-8 servings

2 qts. beef stock or canned beef broth
1 cup chopped smoked ham
2 bay leaves
2 Tbsp. crushed red pepper
2 tsp. salt
6 Tbsp. bacon drippings
1/4 cup flour
3 Tbsp. vegetable oil
3 cups frozen or fresh okra
2 large onions, chopped
1 green bell pepper, minced
2 stalks celery, chopped
2 cloves garlic, minced
16-oz. can whole tomatoes
1/4 cup ketchup
1 Tbsp. hot pepper sauce
1 Tbsp. Worcestershire sauce
1/2 tsp. dried thyme
1 lb. raw shrimp, shelled and deveined
1 lb. crabmeat, or 6 hard-shell crabs, cooked and cleaned
12 oysters, shucked, with liquid
1 bunch scallions, chopped
1 Tbsp. gumbo file
6-8 cups cooked rice

1. Combine the stock, ham, bay leaves, red pepper, and salt in a large kettle. Bring to boil over high heat. Reduce to simmer. Cover and cook 60 minutes.

2. Meanwhile, heat bacon drippings in a skillet over medium heat. Stir in flour. Cook over very low heat, stirring constantly, until flour is dark brown and the roux smells nutty, about 25 minutes. Then stir into simmering beef stock until smooth and thickened.

3. Heat oil in skillet. Saute okra, onions, green pepper, celery, and garlic for 10 minutes, until vegetables are almost tender. Stir in tomatoes, ketchup, and seasonings and bring to boil.

4. Add vegetables to thickened stock.

5. Stir shrimp, crabmeat, oysters, scallions, and gumbo file into stew. Simmer, covered, for 5 minutes, or until shrimp are pink.

6. Serve immediately over 1-cup individual servings of rice.

We used to roast sweet potatoes in the fireplace before we had dinner. The only heat we had was from the fireplace and the cooking stove. Mother had made several quilts, so after getting ourselves situated and our feet warm, we were fine.
— Elizabeth McGill,
a member of Bethel AMEC,
Lancaster, PA

New Orleans Gumbo

Makes 8-10 servings

2 cups diced cooked chicken
2 cups diced cooked ham
2 cups diced cooked hot sausage
1/4 cup margarine
28-oz. can tomatoes
1/3 cup chopped onion
1 tsp. dried thyme
2 tsp. dried rosemary
1 tsp. dried basil
1 tsp. dried oregano
2 Tbsp. gumbo file
1 lb. jumbo shrimp, shelled and
    deveined
1 lb. crabmeat
2 Tbsp. chopped parsley

1. Place chicken, ham, and sausage in large pot.
2. Add margarine, tomatoes, onion, thyme, rosemary, basil, oregano, and gumbo file.
3. Cover and simmer 30 minutes.
4. Add shrimp and crabmeat. Continue to cook another 5 minutes.
5. Stir in parsley. Serve over hot rice.

Okra Gumbo

Lisa Jacobs

Makes 5-6 servings

4 slices bacon
1 medium onion, sliced thin
1 green pepper, chopped
2 celery ribs, sliced
2 10-oz. boxes frozen sliced okra,
    thawed and drained
16-oz. can sliced or stewed tomatoes,
    undrained
2 Tbsp. Worcestershire sauce
1/2 tsp. sugar
1/4 tsp. salt

1. Fry bacon until crisp. Drain and set aside.
2. Pour off half of drippings. Saute onion in drippings over medium heat until golden.
3. Stir in green pepper and celery. Saute until crisp-tender.
4. Add remaining ingredients, except bacon. Cover. Cook over low heat for 60 minutes, stirring every 15 minutes.
5. Crumble bacon over top before serving in soup bowls. Ladle into soup bowls or serve over rice.

Brunswick Stew

Mattie Mae Roche

Makes 6-8 servings

1 hog's head
1 lb. boneless stewing beef
1 lb. onions
3 lbs. white potatoes
1 qt. stewed tomatoes
1 qt. cream-style corn
1 pt. peas
2 Tbsp. salt
black pepper to taste
1 pt. lima beans
4 cups ketchup
1/2 cup Worcestershire sauce
1/2 cup apple cider vinegar
1/4 cup lemon juice
1 tsp. Tabasco sauce

1. In large stockpot cook hog's head and beef in water to cover until meat is tender and leaves the bone. Debone meat and reserve broth. Chop meat into small pieces and set aside.
2. Chop onions and cube or slice potatoes. Add to broth. Cook until just tender.
3. Stir in meat and other ingredients. Cook on low heat until vegetables are tender and stock thickens, about 2-3 hours.

Collard Greens

Betty Jean Joe, Carrie Alford

Makes 12 main-dish servings,
or 20 side-dish servings

large ham hock, or 1 lb. bacon, or 2
    lbs. neckbones
4 bunches collard greens
2 sticks butter
1 tsp. salt
1 Tbsp. sugar
1/2 cup vinegar

1. Cook meat. (Simmer ham hocks and neckbones until they are half-cooked or fry bacon.) Place in large stockpot.
2. Wash collard greens. Cut out stems. Cut greens into pieces. Wash again. Add to meat. Cover entirely with water.
3. Add butter, salt, sugar, and vinegar. Let boil 4-5 hours, or until meat and greens are tender.

Africans who found themselves on the shores of Pennsylvania at the beginning of the seventeenth century, with few exceptions, were not here to explore land or to practice the innovative socio-political ideology espoused by the end of the 18th century—"life, liberty, and the pursuit of happiness." These early forced African immigrants were transatlantic human cargo and became the foundation of the economic foothold in America.
— Dr. Shirley Parham

Collard Greens

Ann Beardan, Mrs. Dana Beardan Frierson

Makes 6-8 main-dish servings,
or 10-12 side-dish servings

2 smoked ham hocks, large turkey
   wings, or 1 lb. thickly sliced bacon
1½ qts. water
5 lbs. fresh collard greens
1 onion, chopped
1 tsp. salt
1 tsp. pepper
1 Tbsp. vinegar
1 pinch baking soda
hot pepper pods or hot sauce, optional

1. Place ham hocks or turkey wings in
Dutch oven or large stockpot. Add water.
Cook for 1½-2 hours. (If using bacon, fry
until crisp; then add to stockpot with
drippings. Add water and continue.)
2. Break off and discard collard green
stems. Wash leaves thoroughly. Slice into
bite-size pieces by rolling up several
leaves together and slicing in ¼-inch
strips.
3. Add collards, onion, salt, pepper,
vinegar, baking soda, and hot pepper
pods to pot. Cover and cook on medium
heat for an hour, or until vegetables are
tender.

Collard Greens with Ham Hocks

Makes 5 servings

1 smoked ham hock
4 cups water
2 lbs. collard greens
1 tsp. salt
1½ tsp. crushed red pepper flakes
1 Tbsp. sugar
¼ cup bacon drippings

1. Place ham hock in 5-quart pot. Add
water. Bring to boil. Cover. Reduce heat
and simmer for 45 minutes. Skim foam
from broth several times.
2. Cut away thick part of collards'
stems. Wash greens thoroughly. Drain.
Chop into small pieces. Add to ham hock
and broth.
3. Stir in salt, red pepper, sugar, and
bacon drippings. Cover. Cook at a lively
simmer for 20 minutes, or until greens
are tender.
4. Turn off heat. Cover pot and let sit
a few minutes before serving.

Quick(er) Collard Greens

Makes 4-6 main-dish servings

3 cups water
2 ham hocks
1-lb. bag frozen collard greens
1 Tbsp. sugar
1 tsp. salt
1/2 tsp. pepper

1. Place ham hocks in stockpot. Add water. Bring to boil over medium heat. Cover and simmer for 60 minutes, adding more water as needed.

2. Add collards, sugar, salt, and pepper to ham hocks and broth. Simmer for 30-45 minutes, or until meat and vegetables are tender

3. Remove meat from bone, stir into broth and vegetables, and serve.

> I love collard greens and rice. The way my mother cooked collard greens with fat back and cornbread . . . it was delicious.
> — Hattie McFadden,
> a member of Bethel AMEC,
> Lancaster, PA

Mustard Greens and Ham Hocks

Makes 8-10 servings

3 smoked ham hocks
3 qts. water
2 lbs. mustard greens
1 tsp. salt
1 tsp. freshly ground black pepper
1 tsp. sugar
1 tsp. dried thyme leaves
2 lbs. green cabbage
4 medium potatoes, peeled and cut into chunks

1. Place ham hocks in 4-quart saucepan. Cover with water. Cover pan and bring water to boil. Reduce heat to simmer and cook 90 minutes, or until meat is almost tender.

2. Wash mustard greens thoroughly. Drain. Remove thick part of stems. Coarsely chop leaves. Add to ham hocks.

3. Stir in salt, pepper, sugar, and thyme. Cook 30 minutes.

4. Cut cabbage into quarters. Remove core. Chop coarsely. Add cabbage and potatoes to pot. Cook 30 minutes, or until all vegetables are tender.

11

Cabbage and Smoked Neckbones

Makes 3-4 servings

3-4 smoked neckbones
1 head cabbage, chopped
1/2 tsp. salt
1/2 tsp. black pepper

1. Crack neckbones into pieces. Cover with water in large stockpot and cook slowly until done. Drain, leaving enough juice in pot to keep cabbage from sticking.
2. Add cabbage to pot with neckbones and broth.
3. Stir in seasonings. Cook slowly until cabbage is tender.

> The free African community, especially the churches, took leadership in the Underground Roadway. The Underground Railroad attests to the intellect, leadership, stamina, determination, and diligence of Africans in their efforts to freedom.
> — Dr. Shirley Parham

Turnip Greens and Cornmeal Dumplings

Carrie Alford

Makes 6-8 servings

1 ham hock
2 qts. water
1 bunch (about 3 lbs.) turnip greens with turnips attached
1 tsp. salt
1 cup cornmeal
1/2 tsp. salt
3/4 cup boiling water
1 egg, beaten

1. Place ham hock in Dutch oven. Add water and bring to boil. Cover. Reduce heat and simmer for an hour, or until meat is tender. Remove hock from oven; cut meat off bone. Set meat aside. Discard bone.
2. Peel turnips and cut in half. Clean greens and remove stems. Add turnips, greens, and 1 tsp. salt to ham broth.
3. Bring to boil. Cover. Reduce heat and simmer for 2 hours, or until greens and roots are tender. Stir ham back into greens and broth.
4. Combine cornmeal and 1/2 tsp. salt in mixing bowl. Stir in boiling water. Add egg. Mix well.
5. Drop dumpling batter by spoonfuls into boiling greens-ham broth. Cover. Boil for 20 minutes (don't lift the lid to look or stir). Reduce heat so that mixture simmers another 10 minutes.

Butter Beans
with Ham Hocks

Makes 4-6 servings

3 large ham hocks, or 1 meaty ham
   bone
3 cups water
1 1/2 lbs. fresh butter beans, or 2 16-oz.
   cans butter beans, drained
1 Tbsp. sugar
1/2 lb. okra, thinly sliced
1 1/2-2 tsp. salt
1/2-1 tsp. freshly ground pepper

1. Place ham hocks and water in large
stockpot. Cover and bring to boil. Reduce
heat and simmer 45 minutes.

2. Remove hocks from the cooking
pot. Cut meat from bone and shred it.
Return meat and bone to stockpot.

3. Add beans to pot. Heat to
simmering.

4. Stir in remaining ingredients.
Simmer for 25 minutes, or until beans
and okra are tender. Discard meat bones
and serve hearty soup.

Black-Eyed Peas
with Ham

Makes 4-6 servings

3/4 cups dried black-eyed peas
2 cups water
1/3 cup chopped, fully cooked, smoked
   ham
1 cup sliced okra
1 small onion, chopped
1/2 tsp. salt
2 cloves garlic, crushed
1/4 tsp. red pepper sauce
1 Tbsp. vegetable oil
1 Tbsp. chopped fresh cilantro
1 small tomato, seeded and chopped

1. Combine peas and water in
saucepan. Boil uncovered for 2 minutes.
Reduce heat.

2. Add ham. Cover. Simmer for 30-40
minutes, stirring occasionally, until beans
are tender. Drain.

3. Saute okra, onion, salt, garlic, and
pepper sauce in oil for 5 minutes, or
until onion is soft.

4. Stir in cilantro, tomato, peas, and
ham. Heat until heated through.

Boiled String Beans with Ham

Makes 4 servings

1 meaty smoked ham bone, or 8 pigs'
  tails
2$\frac{1}{3}$ lbs. fresh string beans
1 Tbsp. salt
1 tsp. freshly ground black pepper
1 tsp. sugar

1. Place meat in 6-quart stockpot. Fill
pot half-full of water. Bring to boil.
Cover. Simmer 45 minutes.
2. Snap stem end off each bean and
gently pull along length of bean to
remove string. Rinse under cold running
water. Drain.
3. Add beans, salt, pepper, and sugar
to meat. Simmer 15-30 minutes until
beans are very tender.
4. Remove meat from bone. Stir ham
back into vegetables and broth before
serving.

We lived in a house with no
ceiling and no water. It was normal
to look at the stars at night. My
mother used flour and parts of an
old catalog to make patches for
cracks in the walls, trying to keep
out the bitter cold air.
— Elizabeth McGill,
a member of Bethel AMEC,
Lancaster, PA

Red Beans, Sausage, and Rice

Makes 8 servings

1 lb. dried red beans
1 medium onion, chopped
4 garlic cloves, minced
8-oz. can tomatoes, drained
$\frac{1}{2}$ lb. salt pork, diced
1 lb. smoked sausage, sliced
red pepper or Tabasco sauce, optional

1. Cover beans with water and soak
overnight in large stockpot.
2. When ready to cook, add more
water if needed so that beans are
covered. Slowly bring to boil.
3. Add onion, garlic, and tomatoes.
Simmer until beans are tender, about
1$\frac{1}{2}$-2 hours.
4. Add salt pork, sausage, and red
pepper or Tabasco. Simmer until liquid is
thickened.
5. Serve over rice.

*Note: If you prefer a more tomato-y sauce,
add 3 more cups tomatoes or tomato juice in
Step 3. If adding juice, remove stockpot lid
for Step 4.*

Red Beans and Rice

Makes 12 servings

1 cup dried red kidney beans
5 cups water
1 smoked ham hock
2 Tbsp. salt
1/2 tsp. crushed red pepper flakes
1/2 tsp. crushed dried thyme
4 cups water
2 cups dry long-grain rice
1 cup water

1. Pour 5 cups water over beans. Soak in refrigerator overnight.

2. Drain beans and place in 5-quart pot. Add ham hock, salt, red pepper, thyme, and 4 cups water. Heat to boiling. Reduce to a low simmer. Cover and cook for 60 minutes, or until beans are almost tender

3. Stir rice and 1 cup water into beans. Heat to boiling. Reduce to simmer. Cover and cook about 25 minutes, until rice and beans are tender and liquid is absorbed.

4. Remove meat from ham hock. Chop and return to rice and beans.

Carolina Red Rice

Makes 8 servings

3/4 cup diced onion
1/3-1/2 cup diced green pepper
2 Tbsp. vegetable oil
1 1/2 lbs. cooked ham, finely chopped
2 8-oz. cans tomato sauce
2 cups water
1 1/3 Tbsp. sugar
1/2 tsp. salt
1/4 tsp. pepper
2 cups uncooked long-grain rice

1. Saute onion and green pepper in oil in a Dutch oven until tender.

2. Stir in ham. Cook over medium heat for 3 minutes.

3. Add tomato sauce, water, sugar, salt, and pepper. Stir well. Bring to boil.

4. Add rice. Reduce heat. Cover and simmer over low heat 15 minutes.

5. Cut a circle of brown paper, 2 inches bigger around than the circumference of the Dutch oven. Remove lid from Dutch oven and place paper over pot. Replace lid over paper. Continue to simmer over low heat 15-20 minutes.

New Orleans Red Beans and Rice

Michelle Akins

Makes 6 servings

6 slices bacon, cut into 1-inch pieces
2 onions, cut into ½-inch wedges
garlic clove, minced
14-oz. can beef broth
1 cup uncooked long-grain rice
1 tsp. dried thyme
1 tsp. salt, optional
½ cup diced green bell pepper
2 16-oz. cans red kidney beans

1. Fry bacon in skillet over medium heat until browned but not crisp. Remove from skillet. Reserve 2 Tbsp. drippings in pan.
2. Saute onion and garlic in drippings until onion is tender but not brown.
3. Add enough water to beef broth to make 2½ cups. Add to skillet. Bring to boil.
4. Stir in rice, bacon, thyme, and salt. Cover tightly and simmer 15 minutes.
5. Add green pepper. Cover and continue cooking for 5 minutes. Remove from heat.
6. Stir in beans. Cover and let stand for 5 minutes, or until all liquid is absorbed.

Dirty Rice

Makes 8 servings

1 lb. chopped chicken livers or giblets
1 lb. bulk sausage, crumbled
½ cup butter or margarine
1 cup chopped onion
½ cup chopped celery
1 bunch green onions, chopped
2 Tbsp. chopped fresh parsley, or dried parsley flakes
1 clove garlic, minced
½ tsp. dried thyme
½ tsp. dried basil
3 cups cooked rice
salt to taste
pepper to taste
hot sauce to taste
10¼ oz.-can chicken broth

1. Saute livers and sausage in butter or margarine until browned. Remove meat from skillet, reserving drippings.
2. Saute onion, celery, green onions, parsley, and garlic in butter until tender.
3. Stir in thyme, basil, rice, livers, and sausage. Mix well.
4. Add salt, pepper, hot sauce, and chicken broth.
5. Cook over medium heat until rice is hot, stirring frequently to avoid sticking.

Grits Souffle

Rebecca Carter

Makes 10-12 servings

4 cups boiling water
1½ cups grits
1½ tsp. salt
12 Tbsp. (1½ sticks) butter, at room
    temperature
6 eggs
1½ cups whole milk
1 cup grated sharp cheese, divided

1. Stir grits and salt into boiling water.
Cook until very thick.
2. Add butter. Mix well.
3. Beat eggs in mixing bowl. Add milk
and ½ cup cheese. Stir into hot grits.
4. Pour into greased 3-quart casserole
dish. Top with remaining ½ cup cheese.
5. Bake at 350° for 45 minutes.

Food was a part of a lot that we
did together at church — The
woman's auxiliary used to have
bake sales, and as part of our
Christmas parties we gave out
turkey baskets. We had chicken
and waffle dinners and coffee
klatches after the service. We had
fashion shows along with mother-
daughter banquets and teas. Every
Christmas we had the candlelight
service and food after that. We
made Easter candy and we
worked! We worked!

— Mary Boots,
a member of Bethel AMEC,
Lancaster, PA

Main Dishes — Other Favorites

Macaroni and Cheese, Home-style

Brothers and Sisters Cafe

Makes 4-6 servings

1 lb. dry macaroni
1 lb. sharp or extra sharp cheese, grated
1 stick (1/4 lb.) butter or margarine, at
    room temperature
12-oz. can evaporated milk
2 eggs, slightly beaten
salt to taste
pepper to taste

   1. Cook macaroni according to package
directions, until just soft. Drain.
   2. Gradually stir in cheese and butter until
well mixed.
   3. Fold in milk, eggs, and seasonings until
well blended. Pour into greased baking dish
   4. Bake at 350° for 45 minutes. Let set 10
minutes before serving.

*Note: You can use 1/2 lb. sharp yellow cheddar
cheese and 1/2 lb. sharp white cheddar cheese and
save a bit of each for garnishing the top of the
casserole before baking it.*

— *Cregg Carter*

Feather-Light Cheese Casserole

Nancy C. Hill

Makes 6-8 servings

2 Tbsp. margarine or butter
15 saltine crackers, crushed
1 1/2 cups (6 oz.) shredded cheddar cheese
1 1/2 cups milk
3 eggs, beaten
1/2 cup sliced fresh mushrooms, or canned
    mushrooms, drained

   1. Melt margarine or butter in 1 1/2-qt.
casserole.
   2. Combine crushed crackers, cheese,
milk, eggs, and mushrooms. Mix well. Pour
into casserole dish.
   3. Bake at 350° for 45-50 minutes, or until
puffy and set.

   Africans forced into American
slavery came from various African
specialty crafts and skills—griots
(African oral tradition), weavers,
silversmiths, bricklayers, glassmakers,
potters, seafarers, astronomers,
physicians, and mathematicians.
      — Dr. Shirley Parham

Fettucine and Mixed Fresh Vegetables

Carol Grassie

Makes 6-8 servings

¾ cup finely chopped onion
3 Tbsp. olive oil
1 large red bell pepper, cut into strips or minced
12 ozs. (5 cups) shitake, or similar, mushrooms, trimmed and thinly sliced
½ tsp. salt
⅛ tsp. pepper
1 lb. fettucine
¼ cup (½ stick) unsalted butter, cut in small pieces, at room temperature
½ cup finely chopped fresh parsley

1. Saute onion in oil, stirring occasionally, for 5 minutes or until softened.
2. Add red pepper, mushrooms, salt, and pepper. Cook, stirring occasionally, for 5-7 minutes, or until mushrooms are tender yet firm and have begun to give off liquid. Set aside.
3. Cook fettucine according to package directions. Drain. Toss with butter.
4. Add vegetable mixture and parsley. Toss.

Pasta Primavera

Gwen Jones

Makes 4 servings

1 large onion, diced
1 cup broccoli florets
½ cup diced carrots
½ cup fresh or frozen peas
1 cup diced zucchini
1 cup diced yellow squash
8-10 cups water
½ lb. whole wheat dry spaghetti
2 Tbsp. cornstarch
1 cup chicken stock or broth
¼ cup grated Parmesan cheese
1 small tomato, peeled and diced

1. Steam onion, broccoli, and carrots until crisp-tender. Set aside.
2. Steam peas, zucchini, and yellow squash until crisp-tender. Add to rest of cooked vegetables.
3. Boil spaghetti in water for 8-10 minutes. Drain.
4. Combine cornstarch with ¼ cup chicken stock and stir until smooth. Add remaining stock. Bring to boil. Reduce heat and stir constantly until thickened.
5. Add Parmesan cheese. Mix well. Pour over spaghetti, tossing thoroughly.
6. Add steamed vegetables. Garnish with diced tomato.

Primavera Pizza

Makes 10-12 servings

2 Tbsp. olive oil
1 tsp. garlic, minced
1 cup zucchini, thinly sliced
3/4 cup mushrooms, sliced
1 cup broccoli florets
1/4 cup black olives, sliced
1 pizza crust
2 cups provolone cheese, grated
8 tomato slices
3 Tbsp. fresh chopped basil
2 tsp. dried oregano
2 cups mozzarella cheese, grated

1. Heat oil in heavy skillet. Add garlic, zucchini, mushrooms, and broccoli. Cook until just soft.
2. Add olives. Set aside.
3. Top crust with provolone cheese. Top with tomatoes. Sprinkle on basil and oregano. Cover with cooked mixture. Top with mozzarella cheese.
4. Bake at 425° for 20-25 minutes, or until cheese begins to melt.

Linguini with Asparagus & Pesto

Rina Mckee

Makes 3-4 servings

8 ozs. dry linguini
1 tsp. olive oil
1 lb. fresh asparagus, cut into 1-inch lengths
3 fresh basil leaves
1/4 cup grated Parmesan cheese
1/4 cup chopped pecans or walnuts
1 small garlic clove
1/4 tsp. salt
3 Tbsp. olive oil

1. Cook and drain linguini. Add 1 tsp. oil. Toss. Set aside and keep warm.
2. Steam asparagus lightly until just tender. Set aside and keep warm.
3. Combine remaining ingredients in blender. Blend until smooth.
4. Stir asparagus into pesto sauce. Serve over linguini.

Fettuccine Alfredo

Makes 4 servings

12-oz. pkg. fettuccine noodles
1 cup half-and-half
4 Tbsp. butter or margarine
1/2 cup grated Parmesan cheese
1/4 tsp. salt
1/4 tsp. coarsely ground black pepper

1. Cook fettuccine according to package directions. Drain.
2. Return fettuccine to saucepan. Add remaining ingredients. Mix well. Heat over low heat and serve.

Note: To make this a complete meal, add cooked chicken breast and broccoli to the cooked fettuccine. Add remaining ingredients, heat through, and serve.

I loved Arco Starch. You wanted to get the really big hunks. I remember the little blue box said something about starch for clothing, but Arco Starch you could eat. I always wondered why all the adults had white mouth, but it was the Arco Starch.
— Barbara McFadden Enty,
a member of Bethel AMEC,
Lancaster, PA

Spinach Manicotti

Rina Mckee

Makes 8-10 servings

1 qt. and 1 cup spaghetti sauce with meat
1 1/2 cups water
15-oz. box ricotta cheese
10-oz. pkg. frozen chopped spinach, thawed and squeezed dry
1 cup shredded mozzarella cheese
1/4 cup grated Parmesan cheese
1 egg
2 tsp. minced fresh parsley
1/2 tsp. onion powder
1/2 tsp. pepper
1/8 tsp. garlic powder
8-oz. pkg. manicotti shells
1/2 cup shredded mozzarella cheese
1/2 cup shredded Parmesan cheese

1. Combine spaghetti sauce and water. Spread 1 cup diluted sauce in ungreased 9" x 13" pan.
2. Combine ricotta cheese, spinach, 1 cup mozzarella cheese, 1/4 cup Parmesan cheese, egg, parsley, onion powder, pepper, and garlic powder.
3. Stuff uncooked manicotti with spinach cheese mixture. Arrange over sauce in pan.
4. Pour remaining sauce over manicotti.
5. Sprinkle with 1/2 cup mozzarella cheese and 1/2 cup Parmesan cheese.
6. Cover and refrigerate overnight.
7. Remove from refrigerator 30 minutes before baking.
8. Bake uncovered at 350° for 40-45 minutes.

Note: To add zest to the flavoring, add 2 cloves minced garlic and 1 small chopped onion to the mixture in Step 2.

Risotto with Spring Veggies

Rina Mckee

Makes 8 servings

4 Tbsp. butter
2 leeks, thinly sliced
1/2 cup chopped onion
2 cups Arborio rice, uncooked
2 qts. vegetable stock
1 jar artichoke slices, drained
salt to taste
pepper to taste
2/3 cup fresh or frozen peas
2/3 cup peeled fava beans
1 Tbsp. finely chopped parsley
4 Tbsp. (1/2 stick) butter
Parmesan cheese, optional

1. In large saucepan, saute leeks and onions in 4 Tbsp. butter until onion is transparent.
2. Add rice. Stir to coat grains. When rice glistens and becomes opaque, add a ladleful of stock over high heat, allowing the rice to absorb the liquid. Stir rice and broth constantly so rice doesn't stick to bottom of pot. After stock is absorbed, add another ladleful, continuing to stir so the rice does not dry out.
3. After 5 minutes, fold in artichoke slices. Add salt and pepper.
4. A ladleful at a time, add as much of the rest of the simmering stock to the rice as is needed to make it tender but not mushy. Stir constantly.
5. When rice has become tender and creamy, add peas, fava beans, parsley, and 4 Tbsp. butter. Toss gently.
6. Shave Parmesan cheese over each serving.

Stuffed Yellow Squash with Cheese Sauce

Marlene Clark

Makes 6 servings

3 medium-sized yellow squash
2 cups water
1 tsp. salt
1 Tbsp. oil
1 clove garlic crushed
1/2 lb. ground beef
1/2 cup raw, long-grain rice
1 tsp. salt
pepper to taste
16-oz. can stewed tomatoes
1/2 cup water
2 Tbsp. butter or margarine
2 Tbsp. flour
1 cup milk
1 cup shredded sharp cheddar cheese

1. Wash squash. Cut off stems and discard. Cut squash in half lengthwise. Scoop out seeds.
2. In medium skillet, bring water and salt to boil. Add squash, cut side down. Cover. Cook over medium heat for 5 minutes, or until vegetables are tender but not mushy. Drain well.
3. Saute garlic and beef in oil until beef is no longer pink, about 10 minutes.
4. Add rice, salt, and pepper. Cook for 2 minutes, stirring constantly.
5. Add tomatoes and water. Cook, tightly covered, over low heat for 20 minutes, or until rice is cooked and liquid is absorbed.
6. Fill squash with rice mixture. Bake at 375° for 20-25 minutes.
7. Meanwhile, melt butter or margarine in saucepan. Stir in flour over low heat, contin-

uing to cook and stir for about 3 minutes to take away raw flour taste.

8. Whisk in milk and continue cooking and stirring until mixture comes to boiling point and begins to thicken.

9. Stir in grated cheese until smooth.

10. Pour cheese sauce over baked stuffed squash before serving, or pass cheese sauce separately so that your diners can serve themselves.

Italian Eggplant Parmigiana

Mrs. Margaret Bailey

Makes 8 servings

2 medium eggplants (about ½ lb. each),
   washed and stemmed
salt
1 cup chopped onion
2 Tbsp. oil
6-oz. can tomato paste
2¼ cups water
1 tsp. dried basil
½ tsp. dried oregano
1 tsp. salt
¼ tsp. pepper
1 cup flour
3 eggs, beaten
1 cup oil
¾ lb. mozzarella cheese, sliced
1 cup grated Parmesan cheese

1. Cut eggplants crosswise into ¼"-thick slices. Place in colander. Sprinkle with salt. Leave to drain for 30 minutes. Wipe dry with paper towel.

2. Saute onion in oil until tender.

3. Stir in tomato paste, water, basil, oregano, 1 tsp. salt, and pepper. Cook slowly, uncovered, for 20 minutes, stirring occasionally. Remove from heat.

4. Dust each eggplant slice with flour. Dip in beaten eggs. Fry on both sides in hot oil until soft and golden. Add more oil as needed. Drain.

5. Line a 2½-quart baking dish with a little of the tomato sauce. Arrange a layer of eggplant slices over it. Cover with a layer of mozzarella cheese. Add more sauce and a sprinkling of Parmesan cheese. Repeat layers until all ingredients have been used.

6. Bake at 350°, uncovered, for 30 minutes, or until eggplant is tender and golden on top.

Spanish Rice

Rina Mckee

Makes 2-4 servings

2 Tbsp. oil
1 cup uncooked, long-grain rice
1 cup chopped onion
2½ cups water
1½ tsp. salt
¾ tsp. chili powder
⅛ tsp. garlic powder
½ cup chopped green pepper
8-oz. can tomato sauce

1. Saute rice and onion in oil for 5 minutes, stirring frequently, until rice is golden brown and onion is tender.

2. Stir in remaining ingredients.

3. Heat to boiling. Reduce heat to low. Cover and simmer for 30 minutes, stirring occasionally, until rice is tender and liquid is absorbed.

Spanish Rice

Michelle Akins

Makes 6-8 servings

6 slices bacon, chopped
1/4 cup chopped onion
1/4 cup chopped green pepper
2 cups canned tomatoes
3 cups cooked rice
1 tsp. salt
1/8 tsp. pepper
1/4 cup grated cheese

1. Fry bacon until crisp. Remove from skillet and reserve drippings.
2. Add onions and pepper to drippings. Cook until onions are soft.
3. Add tomatoes, rice, salt, pepper, and bacon.
4. Pour into greased casserole. Sprinkle with cheese.
5. Bake at 350° for 30 minutes.

> We had nothing to eat but yams, which were thrown amongst us at random — and of these we had scarcely enough to support life.
> — Charles Ball

Pasta Mexicana

Makes 4-6 servings

2 medium onions, coarsely chopped
5 chili peppers, chopped
28-oz. can Italian-style plum tomatoes
2 cups of your favorite beef or turkey chili, or see *Two-Bean Beef Mix* on page 26.
1/2 lb. dry linguini, cooked

1. Place onion and chili peppers in heavy skillet or roasting pan. Cover. Cook over high heat for 8-10 minutes, until onions are browned and chili skins are charred.
2. Remove fresh chilies. Peel. Discard skin and seeds. Chop and return to pan.
3. Stir in tomatoes and beef or turkey chili. Cook over medium heat, stirring occasionally, for 15-20 minutes.
4. Serve sauce over linguini.

Note: You may substitute 2 4-oz. cans chopped green chilies for the 5 chili peppers. Stir them into the skillet (in Step 1) after the onions begin to brown. Skip Step 2 and go on to Step 3.

Baked Lasagna

Willie Jean Murray

Makes 10-12 servings

3 12-oz. cans tomato puree
1 can water
1 tsp. salt
1/4 tsp. pepper
garlic powder to taste
1 lb. bulk sausage
1 lb. ground beef
2 eggs, beaten
1 lb. ricotta cheese
1 1/2 lbs. cottage cheese
1/4 cup water
1/2 tsp. salt
1/8 tsp. pepper
1-lb. box lasagna noodles
salt
3 Tbsp. oil
1 lb. mozzarella cheese, thinly sliced
1/3-1/2 cup Parmesan cheese

1. Combine tomato puree, 1 can water, 1 tsp. salt, 1/4 tsp. pepper, and garlic powder in large saucepan. Bring to boil, then reduce heat to simmer.

2. Form sausage into small balls. Saute in skillet until slightly browned. Add to tomato mixture in saucepan.

3. Form ground beef into small balls. Saute until lightly browned. Remove from pan and add to tomato-sausage mixture in saucepan.

4. Simmer for 1 hour over low heat, stirring occasionally.

5. Combine eggs, ricotta cheese, cottage cheese, 1/4 cup water, 1/2 tsp. salt, and 1/8 tsp. pepper. Mix well and set aside until ready to assemble lasagna.

6. While tomato-meat sauce is simmering, cook lasagna noodles until al dente.

7. Grease lasagna baking dish (or a 9" x 13" baking pan) and cover bottom with a thin layer of tomato-meat sauce. Add a layer of noodles, a layer of cheese mixture, a layer of mozzarella cheese, and another layer of sauce. Repeat layers until all ingredients are used. Sprinkle with Parmesan cheese. Cover with foil.

8. Bake at 350° for 1 hour.

Stuffed Shells

Makes 6 servings

1 lb. ground beef
1 small onion, chopped
1 Tbsp. oil
dash of garlic powder
salt to taste
pepper to taste
8 ozs. mozzarella cheese, shredded
1/4 cup dry bread crumbs
1/4 cup chopped fresh parsley
1 egg, slightly beaten
1/3 cup water
18-20 giant shells, uncooked
1 qt. spaghetti or pizza sauce
1/2 cup grated Parmesan cheese

1. Brown beef and onion in oil. Drain.

2. Add garlic powder, salt, and pepper. Cool.

3. Stir in mozzarella cheese, bread crumbs, parsley, egg, and water.

4. Cook shells in boiling water for 15 minutes. Drain.

5. Stuff shells with meat mixture.

6. Spread half jar of sauce over bottom of greased 9" x 13" pan.

7. Add shells. Cover with remaining sauce. Sprinkle with Parmesan cheese.

8. Bake at 400° for 25 minutes.

Eggplant-Beef Medley

Marlene Clark

Makes 6-8 servings

3 Tbsp. bacon drippings
1 1/2 lbs. ground beef
1/3 cup chopped onions
1/3 cup chopped green peppers
3 small hot peppers, chopped
1 tsp. garlic, minced
1 1/2 tsp. salt
1/4 tsp. pepper
2 medium eggplants, peeled and chopped
1 1/2 cups rice, cooked
2 tsp. lemon juice

1. Heat drippings in skillet.
2. Stir in ground beef, onions, peppers, garlic, salt, and pepper. Stir constantly, cooking over medium heat for 5 minutes, or until the vegetables begin to become tender and the beef browns. Then stir in eggplant and continue cooking for about another 5 minutes, until the eggplant softens but does not lose its shape.
3. Stir in rice. Pour into greased baking dish.
4. Bake at 375° for 30 minutes. Remove from oven. Sprinkle with lemon juice.

Two-Bean Beef Mix

Cormylene Williams

Makes 10 servings

1 lb. ground beef
1/2 cup chopped onions
28-oz. can whole tomatoes
15-oz. can chili beans
15-oz. can kidney beans
15-oz. can tomato sauce
2 tsp. chili powder
1/4 tsp. garlic powder
1/8 tsp. red pepper
shredded cheddar cheese

1. Brown beef and onions in large stockpot. Drain.
2. Stir in remaining ingredients except cheese. Simmer 20-25 minutes.
3. Garnish with cheese.
4. Serve in soup bowls with sturdy bread alongside, or over cooked brown rice.

Baked Beans Brewster-Style

Debbie Brewster

Makes 10 servings

1/2 lb. ground beef
1 large onion, chopped
1 large can baked beans
2 cups barbecue sauce
1 tsp. brown sugar
hot sauce, optional
1/2-3/4 cup shredded cheddar cheese

1. Brown ground beef and onion together in skillet.
2. Mix together with remaining ingredients, except cheese, in large mixing bowl.
3. Pour into greased casserole dish.
4. Bake at 350° for 30-40 minutes, or until heated through and bubbly.
5. Garnish with shredded cheese and return to oven until cheese melts and browns.

Hamburger Casserole

Cregg Carter

Makes 6 servings

1 green pepper, chopped
1 cup diced onions
1 lb. ground beef, browned
2 cups dry macaroni
10 3/4-oz. can cream of chicken soup, undiluted
1/2 cup ketchup
1 cup grated cheese

1. Saute pepper, onions, and hamburger together in large skillet.
2. Meanwhile, cook macaroni until al dente.
3. In large mixing bowl combine ground beef, vegetables, and cooked macaroni.
4. Add soup and ketchup and blend well.
5. Pour into greased baking dish.
6. Sprinkle cheese over top.
7. Bake at 350° for 20-30 minutes, or until casserole bubbles.

> When I came to Bethel African Methodist Episcopal Church, I heard a sermon about the Queens of Farica and how beautiful and wise they was — Queen of Jeni, Queen of Sheba, Queen Mother Dira. Then I realized that my skin was not black, but sun-kissed, my lips weren't big, they's luscious, and my hair, my hair is naturally beautiful. That sermon helped me to love myself!
> — *Living the Experience*

Shepherd's Pie to Feed a Crowd

Makes 30-35 servings

10 lbs. ground beef
2 jumbo onions, chopped
1 qt. brown gravy
1 lb. 10-oz. box instant mashed potatoes
3 lbs. frozen peas
ground black pepper
paprika
1/2-1 cup butter, melted
3-4 cups brown gravy

1. Saute ground beef and onions in batches in large skillet until browned. Place browned meat and onions in large mixing bowl. Drain drippings from skillet after each batch is browned and discard.

2. Stir 1 qt. gravy into browned meat and onions. Pour into large greased casseroles or baking pans.

3. Make mashed potatoes according to directions on package. Spread on top of hamburger.

4. Spoon frozen peas over mashed potatoes.

5. Sprinkle with black pepper and paprika.

6. Top with melted butter.

7. Bake at 350° for 30-40 minutes.

8. Serve with additional gravy.

Corned Beef and Cabbage

Mary Alice Bailey

Makes 10 servings

5-lb. corned beef brisket
1 large onion, coarsely chopped
6 whole cloves
6 carrots, peeled and sliced
8 potatoes, peeled and cubed
1 tsp. dried thyme
1 small bunch of parsley
2 lbs. cabbage, cut into wedges
freshly ground black pepper

Sauce:
1/2 pint whipping cream
2 Tbsp. horseradish

1. Place beef in large pot. Cover with cold water and bring to boil. Reduce heat to simmer and cook for 2 hours. Skim fat as it rises to the top.

2. Add onion, cloves, carrots, potatoes, thyme, and parsley. Cook for another hour.

3. Remove parsley and whole cloves.

4. Add cabbage. Simmer 20 minutes.

5. Remove meat and slice. Place on center of large platter.

6. Strain vegetables. Season heavily with black pepper. Arrange vegetables around meat on platter.

7. Whip cream until it stands in peaks. Fold in horseradish. Serve with meat.

Ground Beef and Cabbage

Makes 6-8 servings

1 medium onion, sliced
1 Tbsp. oil
1 lb. ground beef
salt to taste
pepper to taste
1 medium head cabbage, shredded
2 Tbsp. oil
14½-oz. can stewed tomatoes
8-oz. can tomato sauce

1. Saute onion in oil until soft.
2. Add ground beef, salt, and pepper. Brown meat. Remove from pan but reserve drippings.
3. In pan, saute cabbage in drippings and oil until crisp-tender.
4. Add beef mixture, stewed tomatoes, and tomato sauce. Cover.
5. Simmer for 10 minutes.

Note: Add 2-3 Tbsp. brown sugar in Step 4, if you wish.

Chinese Beef with Broccoli

Linda Maison

Makes 4 servings

1 lb. round steak, thinly sliced
1 envelope dry meat marinade mix
1 cup water
½ tsp. ground ginger
1 lb. broccoli, peeled and cut up
2 Tbsp. oil

1. Place steak in bowl.
2. Combine meat marinade mix, water, and ground ginger. Pour over steak. Let stand 15 minutes.
3. Stir-fry beef and broccoli in oil in large skillet or wok for 5-8 minutes, until broccoli is crisp-tender.
4. Pour marinade over meat and vegetables and heat through. Serve over rice.

The front door of a white family's house was off-limits, unless you were cleaning that area. When you were doing housework in the South, you ate your food on the porch if there was a screen, or in the corner of the kitchen. You ate whatever was left over. You did not use the same dishes they used, unless it was a "good" white lady.

Young white children called grown black folks by their first names, but you had to call them "Mr." or "Miss."
— Elizabeth McGill,
a member of Bethel AMEC,
Lancaster, PA

Succulent Veal Stew

Doris Kelly

Makes 4 servings

1-lb. boneless veal shoulder, cut in 1-inch
    cubes
1 tsp. salt
1/4 tsp. ground ginger
1/4 tsp. garlic powder
3 Tbsp. flour
2 Tbsp. vegetable oil
1 1/4 cups chicken broth
1 Tbsp. cornstarch
2 Tbsp. water
1 Tbsp. dry sherry

1. Place salt, ginger, garlic powder, and
flour in clean paper bag. Add veal cubes.
Shake vigorously until all pieces are coated.
2. Heat oil in large skillet. Add seasoned
veal and brown on all sides. Reduce heat.
3. Add broth. Cover and simmer over low
heat for 60 minutes, or until veal is tender.
4. Combine cornstarch and water. Stir into
mixture. Cook for several minutes, until
liquid thickens and clears.
5. Stir in sherry.
6. Serve over pasta or rice.

> I can give but little hope that the
> infamous Slave Law will be declared
> unconstitutional. I can advise nothing
> better than that the subjects of it put
> themselves beyond reach.
> — Thaddeus Stevens, Esq., referring
> to the Fugitive Slave Law of 1850

Ham and Cabbage Dinner

Edna Hardrick

Makes 6-8 servings

1 cup prepared mustard—brown, spicy, or
    plain
1/2 cup light brown sugar
4-5-lb. precooked ham
1/2 lb. bacon, cut into 1-inch squares
half a head of cabbage, sliced
2 medium onions, sliced
1 1/2 cups water
4-5 medium-sized potatoes, sliced or cut
    into small chunks
red pepper to taste
salt to taste

1. Dissolve brown sugar in mustard to
make glaze.
2. Brush portion of glaze over ham.
3. Bake ham in 350° oven, uncovered, for
25 minutes per pound, brushing with glaze
periodically.
4. Meanwhile, brown bacon in Dutch
oven.
5. Add cabbage, onions, and small amount
of water to bacon. Stir and cook for 5
minutes.
6. Layer potatoes over cabbage. Steam
until potatoes are done.
7. Sprinkle with red pepper and salt.
8. Slice ham and wedge into Dutch oven
or serving platter, alongside vegetables.
Spoon juices over all.

Pork
Fried Rice

Makes 4 servings

1 small onion, chopped
1 green pepper, sliced
2 Tbsp. oil
1½ lbs. pork strips
4-oz. can bean sprouts, drained
2 cups cooked rice
2 Tbsp. soy sauce
salt to taste
2 eggs, beaten

1. Saute onion and green pepper in oil
until browned. Remove vegetables from oil.
2. Saute pork in oil just until cooked.
3. Add onion, green pepper, bean sprouts,
and rice to pork.
4. Stir in soy sauce and salt.
5. Add eggs and cook until eggs are set,
stirring often, about 5-10 minutes.

Pork Mu Shu
Burritos

Makes 4 servings

1½ cups canned chop suey vegetables
1½ Tbsp. oil
6 ozs. boneless pork chops, beef tips, or
    chicken or turkey breast, cut into ¼" x
    1½" strips
half a jar of hoisin sauce, divided
4 large flour tortillas, warmed

1. Drain vegetables. Rinse with cold water.
Drain. Cover with cold water for 10 minutes.
Drain very thoroughly.
2. Heat oil in wok or heavy skillet over
high flame. Add meat. Saute for 3 minutes,
until just done.
3. Add vegetables. Heat.
4. Add 4 Tbsp. hoisin sauce to pork-
vegetable mixture. Heat through.
5. Spread 1 Tbsp. hoisin sauce on each
tortilla. Fill with meat mixture. Roll up like a
burrito.

Cajun Cassoulet

Nancy Perkins

Makes 6-8 servings

1/4 lb. bacon
1 medium onion, diced
1 green bell pepper, diced
3 cloves garlic, minced
1 rib celery, diced
2 1/2 cups red beans, cooked from dried
    beans, or canned
1 Tbsp. tomato paste
2 cups chicken broth
1/2 lb. andouille or smoked sausage, sliced
    and lightly browned
1 cup bread crumbs
2 Tbsp. melted butter
1 tsp. Cajun seasoning

1. Saute bacon in heavy skillet. Remove
bacon but reserve drippings. Crumble and set
bacon aside.
2. Saute onion, pepper, garlic, and celery
in bacon drippings. Cook until soft.
3. Stir in beans, tomato paste, broth, and
bacon. Simmer 15 minutes.
4. Place sausage in greased casserole dish.
Top with bean mixture. Cover. Bake at 350°
for 30 minutes.
5. Toss together bread crumbs, butter, and
seasoning. Sprinkle over casserole. Bake
uncovered for 20 minutes, or until lightly
browned.

Cornbread Sausage Stuffing

Nanette Akins

Makes 6 servings

3 cups water
2 cups chopped celery
1 cup grated carrots
1 cup chopped onions
1 tsp. poultry seasoning
salt to taste
pepper to taste
1 lb. bulk sausage, browned and drained
3 cups crumbled cornbread
1 egg, lightly beaten

1. Make cornbread one day before you
make stuffing. (See page 130 for Cornbread
recipe.)
2. Combine water, celery, carrots, onions,
poultry seasoning, salt, and pepper in
saucepan. Cook over medium heat for
20 minutes. Remove from heat.
3. Stir in browned sausage, crumbled
cornbread, and egg. Mix well.
4. Pour into greased casserole dish. Cover.
5. Bake at 350° for 1 1/2-2 hours. Uncover
during last 20 minutes of baking time to
brown.

Cornbread Dressing

Makes 4-6 servings

10-oz. box cornbread mix
8 ozs. bulk pork sausage
3/4 cup (1 1/2 sticks) butter
1 cup chopped onion
1 cup chopped celery
1 cup sliced fresh mushrooms
1 Tbsp. poultry seasoning
3 cups herb-seasoned croutons
1/4 cup chopped parsley
3/4 cup chicken broth or milk

1. Bake cornbread according to directions on box. Break into pieces. Set aside.
2. In skillet, cook sausage until lightly browned. Transfer to large bowl.
3. Saute onion, celery, and mushrooms in butter until tender. Stir in poultry seasoning. Add to sausage. Mix well.
4. Toss cornbread, croutons, parsley, and chicken broth with sausage mixture.
5. Spoon into buttered baking dish. Cover with foil.
6. Bake at 325° for 30 minutes.

Sausage & Cheese Omelet

Makes 2-3 servings

8 turkey sausage links, removed from
    casings
6 eggs
freshly ground pepper
1 Tbsp. cold water
1 Tbsp. vegetable oil
1/3 cup shredded sharp cheddar cheese
3-oz. can chopped mushrooms, drained

1. Crumble sausage and cook in large skillet. When browned remove meat from skillet and set aside. Keep drippings in pan.
2. Beat together eggs, pepper, and water until combined but not frothy.
3. Pour egg mixture into meat drippings in skillet. Sprinkle with sausage, cheese, and mushrooms.
4. Cover. Cook until cheese starts to melt and omelet is golden brown. Fold in half. Serve immediately.

Hearty Sausage Bake

Makes 4 servings

1 lb. bulk sausage
8 potatoes
1/2 cup chopped celery
1/3 cup chopped onions
14 1/2-oz. can diced tomatoes, undrained

1. Brown sausage in skillet and set aside.
2. Cook and mash potatoes.
3. Mix together sausage and mashed potatoes. Add remaining ingredients.
4. Pour into greased baking dish.
5. Bake at 325° for 1 1/2-2 hours.

I remember my mother would sit down at the table in the wealthiest mansions and be asked what the menu should be for an upcoming affair. My mother would skillfully draft out a 12-course menu for the evening's event.
— Margaret Jamison

Chicken and Vegetables

Sonya Gibson

Makes 8-10 servings

2 medium onions, chopped
1/4 cup chicken broth
2 1/2 lbs. chicken breast, cut in pieces, skin
    removed
1 1/2 tsp. salt
1/2 tsp. pepper
1/2 tsp. curry powder
water
1 sweet red pepper, sliced
1 green pepper, sliced
6 medium tomatoes, peeled and coarsely
    chopped
1/2 lb. French-style fresh green beans, or
    19-oz pkg. frozen French green beans
        thawed to room temperature
1/2 lb. fresh mushrooms, sliced
2 leeks, sliced
half a medium cucumber, peeled and
    cubed
1 clove garlic, crushed
chopped fresh parsley

1. Cook onions in broth until soft.
2. Add chicken. Sprinkle with salt, pepper, and curry powder. Add water until covered. Simmer 30 minutes.
3. Add peppers, tomatoes, beans, mushrooms, leeks, cucumber, and garlic. Add more water if needed.
4. Cook 10-15 minutes, or until vegetables are tender.
5. Sprinkle with parsley just before serving.
6. Serve over rice.

Chinese Pot-Au-Feu

Doris Kelly

Makes 6-8 servings

2 cups water
8 dried Chinese mushrooms
3 1/2-lb. chicken with giblets, cut into 8 or
    more pieces
2 leeks, cut in 2-inch pieces
4 carrots, sliced thin
2 cloves garlic, minced
4 slices fresh ginger
1/4 cup dry sherry
1 Tbsp. light soy sauce
1 head Napa cabbage (Chinese celery),
    cored and cut in 2-inch pieces
1 lb. fresh spinach, washed, with stems
    discarded
salt to taste
pepper to taste

1. Bring water to boil. Remove from heat. Add mushrooms and soak for 15 minutes. Drain, reserving liquid.
2. Remove mushroom stems. Thinly slice mushrooms.
3. In large saucepan, combine chicken, giblets, mushrooms, leeks, carrots, garlic, ginger, sherry, and soy sauce. Add mushroom liquid and enough water so that all ingredients are covered.
4. Bring to boil. Skim off froth and fat.
5. Lower heat. Partially cover saucepan and simmer until chicken is tender, 45-60 minutes.
6. Add cabbage, spinach, salt, and pepper. Simmer 5 minutes. Discard ginger. Skim fat from liquid.
7. Serve chicken and vegetables on platter, accompanied by a tureen of stock and another of boiled white rice.

Wild Rice, Chicken, and Broccoli Bake

Channie Tyson

Makes 4-6 servings

2 cups cooked wild rice
1 lb. fresh broccoli, lightly steamed and
    drained
3-4 cooked chicken breast halves, cooked
    and cubed
1 can cream of chicken soup
1 cup milk
1/4 lb. mushrooms, sliced
1 tsp. lemon juice
1/2 tsp. curry powder
1 cup shredded sharp cheddar cheese

1. Place rice in greased casserole dish.
2. Arrange broccoli over rice.
3. Spread chicken over broccoli.
4. Combine soup, milk, mushrooms, lemon juice, and curry powder. Pour over chicken.
5. Sprinkle cheese over top. Cover.
6. Bake at 375° for 30 minutes.

Chicken Divan

Makes 8 servings

4 large whole chicken breasts, cooked
2 lbs. broccoli, cooked until just tender
2 Tbsp. butter or margarine
2 Tbsp. flour
1 cup chicken stock
1 egg yolk
1/4 cup Parmesan cheese
1 Tbsp. cooking sherry

1. Place chicken in shallow pan. Cover with broccoli.
2. Melt butter over low heat. Add flour. Stir in chicken stock and bring to boil.
3. Add a bit of hot mixture to egg yolk. Add egg to hot mixture. Mix well. Bring entire mixture to a boil until slightly thickened.
4. Remove from heat. Stir in Parmesan cheese and cooking sherry. Mix well.
5. Spread over chicken and broccoli. Place under broiler until slightly brown, about 8-10 minutes.

Roast Turkey with Oyster Cornbread Stuffing

Willie Jean Murray

Makes 10-14 servings

2 cups white, water-ground cornmeal
water
peanut oil
1 stalk celery, chopped
4 Tbsp. (½ stick) margarine or butter
1 large white onion, chopped
half a large loaf bread (about 12 slices),
   slices toasted
½ lb. (2 sticks) butter, melted
3 eggs
1½ tsp. salt
½ tsp. pepper
½ tsp. dried thyme
2 tsp. poultry seasoning
½ tsp. paprika
1 pt. oysters, drained and diced
liquid from oysters
12-lb. turkey

1. Combine cornmeal with enough water to make the consistency of a stiff biscuit dough.
2. Heat small amount of peanut oil in frying pan over low heat. Pat cornmeal dough over the entire bottom of pan. Cook over low heat until light brown. Turn and cook other side. (Don't worry if the cornmeal mixture crumbles as you turn it over.) Remove from pan. Cool in large mixing bowl. Crumble when cool.
3. Saute stalk of celery in 4 Tbsp. margarine or butter. Add onion and cook until tender.
4. Combine cornmeal mixture, celery, onion, bread, ½ lb. butter, eggs, salt, pepper, thyme, poultry seasoning, paprika, oysters, and liquid. Stuff into turkey.
5. Bake in large roaster at 325° for 20-30 minutes per pound. Tent with foil if turkey begins to become too brown or dry. Bake any extra stuffing that wouldn't fit into the bird in a greased casserole at 325° for 30 minutes.

Smoked Turkey & Black-Eyed Peas

Jean Townsend

Makes 10-12 servings

2 14½-oz. cans black-eyed peas
16-oz. can stewed tomatoes, undrained
1 medium onion, sliced
2 tsp. seasoning salt
1½ tsp. dried basil leaves
½ tsp. dried oregano
½ tsp. dried thyme leaves
½ tsp. ground cayenne red pepper
3 lbs. smoked turkey drumsticks
½-1 cup water, optional

1. Combine all ingredients in a 6-quart stockpot. Cover. Bring to a boil. Reduce heat and simmer for 30 minutes. If mixture seems to become dry, stir in water.
2. Remove drumsticks and slice meat from bones. Stir turkey back into vegetable mixture.
3. Serve over rice.

Jambalaya

Sonya Gibson

Makes 6-8 servings

½ cup chopped celery
one-quarter medium-sized green pepper, chopped
¼ cup chopped onions
2 Tbsp. oil
14-oz. can tomatoes
4 cups cooked rice
½ tsp. salt
¼-½ tsp. black pepper, according to your preference
1 cup chopped cooked ham
1 cup chopped cooked chicken
1 cup chicken stock
1 lb. fresh, medium-sized shrimp, shelled and deveined

1. In large stockpot saute celery, green pepper, and onions in oil until tender.
2. Stir in tomatoes and rice.
3. Season with salt and pepper.
4. Stir in ham, chicken, and stock.
5. Add shrimp. Stir gently.
6. Pour into greased 3-4-quart casserole.
7. Bake at 325° for 30 minutes.

Note: To create a spicier stew, add 2 chopped hot chili peppers in Step 1 and add 1 cup thinly sliced andouille or hot Italian sausage in Step 4.

Stuffed Bell Peppers

Mrs. Margaret Bailey

Makes 12 servings

½ cup (1 stick) butter or margarine
¼ cup finely chopped parsley
1 medium onion (about 1 cup), finely chopped
1 rib celery, finely chopped
½ lb. ground beef
2 lbs. shrimp, cooked, peeled, and deveined
1 loaf stale French bread, torn into ½-inch pieces
6 eggs
1 tsp. dried thyme
salt to taste
pepper to taste
6 large green bell peppers, cleaned and cut in half
¼ cup (½ stick) butter or margarine, melted
bread crumbs

1. Saute parsley, onion, and celery in ½ cup butter. Simmer for 20 minutes.
2. Add ground beef. Cook 15 minutes longer, stirring constantly. Stir in shrimp and cook an additional 5 minutes, continuing to stir.
3. Place bread in large baking pan. Pour water over until bread is dampened. Squeeze dry.
4. Add eggs. Mix well.
5. Add beef/shrimp mixture. Mix well.
6. Season with thyme, salt, and pepper.
7. Bake at 325° for 2 hours, stirring well every 30 minutes. Remove from oven. Cool and refrigerate.
8. Stuff peppers with cooled mixture. Top with bread crumbs. Brush with ¼ cup melted butter or margarine. Brown under broiler.

Green Pepper Surprise

Michelle Akins

Makes 4-6 servings

4 green peppers
1/2 cup chopped celery
2 Tbsp. chopped onion
1/2 cup (1 stick) butter
1 1/2-2 cups herb-seasoned stuffing
1/2 cup water
1 cup fresh or canned crabmeat
6-oz. can tomato sauce

1. Cut green peppers in half. Remove stems and seeds. Cook in boiling water for 2 minutes. Drain.
2. Saute celery and onion in butter until golden brown.
3. Add stuffing, water, and crabmeat. Mix well.
4. Fill pepper halves with crabmeat mixture.
5. Place in greased shallow baking dish
6. Bake at 350° for 30 minutes.
7. Heat tomatoes sauce to boiling point. Serve separately to pour over peppers.

Shrimp Stir-Fry

Nanette Akins

Makes 6-8 servings

3 Tbsp. margarine or oil
1 large onion, sliced or chopped
1 garlic clove, minced
1/4 jar sliced pimentos
1 green pepper, sliced or chopped
1 rib celery, sliced
8 ozs. fresh or canned mushrooms, sliced
1 lb. shrimp, cleaned and deveined
8 ozs. snow peas
8 ozs. fresh bean sprouts
1 Tbsp. Old Bay Seasoning
soy sauce to taste
8-oz. can water chestnuts

1. Stir-fry onions, garlic, pimentos, pepper, celery, and mushrooms in margarine for 2 minutes. Push vegetables aside.
2. Add shrimp and cook until just pink in color. Stir together all ingredients.
3. Add snow peas, bean sprouts, Seasoning, and soy sauce. Stir in water chestnuts. Cook for 2 minutes.
4. Serve over rice.

Shrimp Fried Rice

Makes 12-16 servings

8 cups cooked rice
¼ cup Italian dressing
1½ lbs. frozen shrimp, cooked
¼ cup (½ stick) butter
3 medium onions, chopped
3 cans small shrimp
7 eggs, lightly scrambled
large can bean sprouts, drained
3 Tbsp. soy sauce

1. Saute rice, dressing, and frozen shrimp in butter in large wok until rice browns. (If you don't have a wok, use a large iron skillet, working in batches.)
2. Stir in onions and canned shrimp. Saute lightly.
3. Add eggs, bean sprouts, and soy sauce. Mix well and heat just until warmed through.

Note: This recipe can be easily divided to serve a smaller group.

Herring & Rice

Allen Mitchell

Makes 6 servings

5-6 pieces fresh herring, about 3 lbs. total
half green pepper, chopped
1 small onion, chopped
1 tsp. vegetable oil
2 cups long-grain rice, uncooked
5 cups water
salt to taste
pepper to taste

1. Soak herring in cold water overnight.
2. Saute green pepper and onion in skillet.
3. Place rice and water in large stockpot, along with sauteed vegetables and cut-up herring. Cover. Cook slowly until rice is tender, about 45-60 minutes. Do not allow to cook dry.
4. Season with salt and pepper before serving.

> I was lying in a room, and this woman came in. She had new clothes in her hand, and I thought theys couldn't be for me, I ain't never had anything like them before. The touch of the soft cotton against my skin, made me think I done died and went to heaven.
> — *Living the Experience*

Steal Away!

Steal away, steal away, steal away to Jesus!
Steal away, steal away home, I have not long to stay here.

My Lord calls me.
He calls me by the thunder.
The trumpet sounds within my soul;
I have not long to stay here.

Green trees are bending,
Poor sinners are a trembling;
The trumpet sounds within my soul;
I have not long to stay here.

My Lord calls me,
He calls me by the lightning;
The trumpet sounds within my soul;
I have not long to stay here.

Here the escaping enslaved African is told that the time has come to leave. This song gives instructions and directions. The first instruction is to leave during a storm — "My Lord calls me, He calls me by the thunder." The song tells the African to meet at the river, near the willow tree, on the side where the moss grows, toward the North.

Meats

I remember my father bringing home deer meat for my
mother to prepare. By the time my mother was done
with it, not only was it tender, but we had forgotten that
we were eating deer meat. My first experience with steak tartare
was in my mother's kitchen. She was amazing in her kitchen.

During the enslavement period, the Africans were rarely given
any meat to eat. If they were given meat, it was usually the
undesirable parts of the hog. Yet they were able to create meals
that are still part of our culture today.

The saying, "living high on the hog," indicated that you were
eating the finer parts of the hog: ribs, pork chops, and ham. This
term came to represent economic and social status.

Africans who were brought to this country tried to recreate the
natural diet they maintained in their mother countries. In order to
supplement the protein in their diet, they incorporated game meat,
such as deer, squirrel, and rabbit, into their meals whenever
possible.

— Phoebe Bailey

Meats — Traditional

Fried Chicken

Makes 12-15 servings

2 3½-lb. frying chickens, each cut into
    8 pieces
salt to taste
fresh ground pepper to taste
2 cups flour
2 Tbsp. paprika
oil
1 Tbsp. paprika

    1. Trim fat and skin from chicken.
Sprinkle with salt and pepper.
    2. Combine flour and 2 Tbsp. paprika
in shallow bowl. Dredge chicken in flour
mixture until well coated. Shake off
excess flour.
    3. Pour 2″ oil into skillet. Heat to
375°.
    4. Fry chicken in oil, making sure
pieces do not touch each other. Turn
chicken until golden brown on all sides
and cooked through. Drain.
    5. Sprinkle pieces with paprika before
serving.

*Note: To adapt a traditional recipe to a more
modern convenience, pour ¼″ oil into an
electric frying pan and set it at 325°. Legs
and thighs will take about 30-40 minutes.
Large breast pieces will take about 45
minutes.*

— *Linda Maison*

Fried Chicken

Wanda Davis

Makes 6-8 servings

1 broiler chicken
1 tsp. salt
1½ cups flour
salt to taste
pepper to taste
paprika to taste
1½ cups shortening

    1. Wash chicken thoroughly. Soak in
bowl of cold water, with 1 tsp. salt
dissolved in it, for 20 minutes.
    2. Drain chicken. Cut into pieces.
    3. Season flour with salt, pepper, and
paprika.
    4. Heat shortening in frying pan.
    5. Dredge chicken in flour and place
in hot oil. Cook until golden brown on
both sides, about 30-40 minutes total.
    6. Remove to plate covered with paper
towels to drain.

Fried Chicken

Betty Jean Joe

Makes 3-4 servings

2-3 cups vegetable oil
6-7 pieces chicken
1/2 tsp. salt
3 tsp. poultry seasoning
1/2 tsp. garlic salt
1/2-3/4 cup self-rising flour

1. Heat oil in kettle.
2. Mix salt, poultry seasoning, garlic salt, and flour together in large bowl.
3. Dredge chicken, a piece at a time, in seasoned flour until well coated.
4. Place chicken in hot oil. Fry 10-20 minutes per side, depending on the size of the pieces.

Oxtails

Marilyn Parks

Makes 4-6 servings

4 oxtails, cut into 2" pieces
1 cup flour
salt to taste
pepper to taste
1 clove garlic, minced
oil
1 onion, chopped

1. Combine flour, salt, and pepper.
2. Trim fat from oxtails. Wash. Pat dry. Dredge in seasoned flour. Sprinkle with garlic.
3. Brown tails on all sides in hot oil. Drain off fat.
4. Add onion to tails and cover with water. Cook slowly until tender, about 2 hours.
5. Serve with rice, buttered lima beans, and salad.

> We had talked long enough; we were now ready to move. If not now, we never would be, and if we do not intend to move now, we had as well fold our arms, sit down, and acknowledge ourselves fit only to be slaves.
> — Frederick Douglass

Liver and Onions

Brothers and Sisters Cafe

Makes 4 servings

2 lbs. liver, sliced
salt to taste
pepper to taste
1/2 cup flour
2 Tbsp. oil
1/2-1 cup sliced onions

1. Season liver with salt and pepper. Roll in flour.
2. Fry in oil just until golden brown on both sides. Remove liver and keep warm.
3. Add onions to hot drippings. Cook for about 10 minutes, or until tender and brown.
4. Serve liver topped with onions.

A lot of times when we were hungry we'd go down to the ditches near our house out by the road. We would go down there and look in the water and see the crayfish crawling. We'd catch them. They have these little things on them that would pinch you if you didn't catch them across the back! Sometimes we'd take a little sack and drag it in the water and get the crayfish that way. We'd take them home and boil them in salt water for 15 minutes or so. We'd make Crayfish Dunk out of ketchup and horseradish and dunk the crayfish in that before we ate them.

— Frances Morant,
Bothers & Sisters Cafe

Pork Sausage and Gravy

Makes 6-8 servings

2 Tbsp. oil
1 1/2 lbs. country-style pork sausage links
1/3 cup flour
1 cup water
1 cup milk
1 cup heavy cream
salt to taste
pepper to taste

1. Fry sausage in oil for 15-20 minutes, turning often. Place sausage on serving plate and cover with foil. Place in warm oven.
2. Remove all but 1/3 cup of drippings in the skillet. Sprinkle flour over drippings. Stir quickly over medium heat.
3. Add water, a little at a time, stirring quickly to keep mixture from getting lumpy.
4. Stir in milk, cream, salt, and pepper. Bring to boil and continue stirring until gravy is thick and bubbly.
5. Serve gravy in tureen with browned sausage.

Talmadge Ham and Red-Eye Gravy

Rebecca Carter

Makes 2 servings

ham slice, 1/8″ thick
oil
1/2 cup hot water

1. Rinse ham. Pat dry.
2. Fry ham in oil in heavy skillet. Cut gashes in fat of ham to prevent curling. Fry over medium heat until fat is glazed, turning several times. Remove from skillet. Cover and keep warm.
3. Add 1/2 cup hot water to drippings in skillet. Cook, stirring, until gravy turns red.

My mother told me that my crib was a wooden fish box with a burlap sheet over the box for shade. When I was an infant my mother would take me in the field with her while she picked cotton. She'd take a little time to nurse me, put me back in the box, and keep picking cotton. She said many times she'd break down and cry because she couldn't just sit and hold her child.

— Elizabeth McGill,
a member of Bethel AMEC,
Lancaster, PA

Pig's Feet

Makes 6 servings

6 medium-sized pig's feet
1 cup apple cider vinegar
1 large onion, chopped
1 green pepper, sliced
1 clove garlic, minced
2 bay leaves
1/8 tsp. cayenne pepper, or 1 hot pepper
salt to taste
pepper to taste

1. Wash and clean pig's feet.
2. Simmer in water and vinegar for 2 hours.
3. Add onion, green pepper, garlic, bay leaves, cayenne pepper, salt, and pepper. Simmer for another 2 hours, or until meat is fork-tender.
4. Drain feet of liquid and serve with vegetables.

Cregg's Pigs Feet

Cregg Carter

Makes 4-6 servings

5 pig's feet split
1 cup vinegar
2 tsp. salt
1 tsp. whole peppercorns
3 bay leaves, broken in pieces
2 medium potatoes
3 carrots
1 medium onion

1. Place enough water to cover pig's feet in stockpot. Bring water to boil. Add pig's feet. Boil for 5 minutes. Discard cooking water and rinse feet in fresh hot water.

2. Again, place enough water to cover pig's feet in stockpot. Bring water to boil. Add vinegar, salt, peppercorns, and bay. Again, add pig's feet. Boil about 1 hour.

3. Cut potatoes into quarters. Add to kettle.

4. Slice carrots. Add to kettle.

5. Cut onion in quarters. Add to kettle.

6. Simmer until meat and vegetables are well done, about 2 hours.

7. Lift meat and vegetables out of liquid and serve.

Chitlins and Maw

Makes 6-8 servings

2 lbs. pork maw (hog's throat or mouth)
2 Tbsp. salt
2 tsp. crushed red pepper flakes
4 ribs celery, finely chopped
4 small onions, finely chopped
4 small green bell peppers, cored, seeded, and finely chopped
5 lbs. precooked chitlins (hog's small intestine)
salt to taste
pepper to taste

1. Wash pork maw several times in cold water. Drain well. Place in large pot. Fill cooking pot with cold water 2 inches above the meat.

2. Add 2 Tbsp. salt, red pepper flakes, and half the celery, onions, and green peppers.

3. Heat to boiling. Reduce to simmer. Cover and cook until tender, from 1½-3 hours. Remove maw to platter to cool. Reserve cooking broth.

4. Meanwhile, wash the chitlins several times in cold water. Drain well. Refrigerate until needed.

5. Place chitlins in large pot. Add enough of the maw cooking liquid to cover by 2 inches. Add remaining celery, onions, and green peppers.

6. Heat to boiling. Reduce heat to simmering. Cover and cook until tender, about 1½ hours.

7. Meanwhile, when maw is cool enough to handle, cut into 1" pieces.

8. When chitlins are tender, stir in maw pieces. Simmer together for 15 minutes. Season with salt and pepper.

Fried Fish

Makes 6 servings

6 pieces fresh catfish fillet
1 cup white cornmeal
1/2 cup flour
1 tsp. salt
1/2 tsp. pepper
oil

1. Rinse fish in cold water. Gently dry with paper towels.
2. Combine cornmeal, flour, salt, and pepper in paper bag. Shake to mix ingredients.
3. Put piece of fish in paper bag. Shake to coat. Lay fish on waxed paper. Continue until all fillets are coated.
4. Pour 1/2" oil into skillet. Heat until hot. Gently fry fish for 3-4 minutes on each side. Drain fried fish on paper towels.

Seafood Batter Dip

Linda Maison

Makes enough batter for 4-6 servings

1/2 cup self-rising flour
1/2 cup enriched cornmeal
1 tsp. salt
1/4 tsp. pepper
1 cup cold water
1 1/2 lbs. fish fillets or shrimp

1. Combine flour, cornmeal, salt, and pepper.
2. Add water. Mix well.
3. Dip fish into batter. Drain off excess.

4. Fry in 375° oil for 3-4 minutes. Drain on paper towels.

Basic Tempura

Dianne Prince

Makes 2 cups batter, enough to serve 6

1 cup ice water
1 egg
1 cup all-purpose flour
1 tsp. salt
1/4-1/2 tsp. black pepper, according to your preference
fresh vegetables
seafood
peanut oil

1. Combine water and egg. Mix well.
2. Add flour. Do not beat, but stir only until blended. Batter should be lumpy.
3. Dip well chilled vegetables and seafood into batter, a few pieces at a time.
4. Drop into 375° oil and fry until golden brown. Drain on tempura rack or paper towels. Serve immediately.

When I was small my uncle had a pig farm and he used to butcher. Then we'd make cracklins out of the skin and my grandmother would make cracklin bread and we used to eat that all the time . . . delicious cracklin bread.

— Mary Boots,
a member of Bethel AMEC,
Lancaster, PA

Meats — Other Favorites

Barbecued Chicken

Betty Jean Joe

Makes 3-4 servings

6-7 pieces of chicken
1/2 tsp. salt
1/2 tsp. garlic salt
1 Tbsp. poultry seasoning
1/2 tsp. salt
1 cup tomato sauce
1/4 cup prepared mustard
1/4 cup mayonnaise
1/2 cup honey
1/3 cup vinegar
2 tsp. brown sugar
1/4 tsp. black pepper

1. Place chicken in large pot. Cover with water. Add 1/2 tsp. salt. Bring to boil. Boil 3 minutes. Drain chicken.
2. Season chicken with garlic salt, poultry seasoning, and 1/2 tsp. salt. Place in baking pan.
3. Bake at 250° for 30 minutes. Turn chicken and bake another 30 minutes.
4. Combine remaining ingredients. Brush chicken with sauce.
5. Bake at 300° for 10 minutes.
6. Heat remaining sauce and serve with chicken.

Parmesan Baked Chicken Legs

Mrs. Margaret Bailey

Makes 12 servings

2 cups fine bread crumbs
3/4 cup Parmesan cheese
1/4 cup chopped parsley
1 clove garlic, minced
2 tsp. salt
1/2 tsp. black pepper
24 chicken legs
1 cup (2 sticks) butter, melted

1. Combine bread crumbs, Parmesan cheese, parsley, garlic, salt, and pepper in mixing bowl.
2. Dip each chicken leg into melted butter and then into crumb mixture.
3. Lay pieces in shallow roasting pan. Pour remaining butter over chicken.
4. Bake at 350° for 45-60 minutes, or until tender, basting frequently.

Sesame Fried Chicken

Mrs. Margaret Bailey

Makes 6 servings

1¼ cups flour
¼ cup sesame seeds
1½ tsp. salt
1½ tsp. poultry seasoning
½ tsp. paprika
freshly ground black pepper
2 2½ -3-lb. frying chickens, quartered
⅔ cup evaporated milk
½ cup (1 stick) butter
½ cup oil

1. Combine flour, sesame seeds, salt, poultry seasoning, paprika, and pepper in mixing bowl.
2. Dip chicken in milk. Roll in sesame seed mixture.
3. In large skillet saute chicken in butter and oil for 30 minutes, or until golden brown and tender.

Honey Buffet Chicken

Makes 10-12 servings

3 lbs. chicken legs and thighs
2 Tbsp. butter or margarine, melted
2 Tbsp. soy sauce
2 Tbsp. lemon juice
¼ cup honey
1 tsp. salt
¼ tsp. pepper

1. Arrange chicken in shallow baking pan.
2. Combine butter, soy sauce, lemon juice, honey, salt, and pepper. Mix well. Pour over chicken, turning pieces to coat.
3. Bake uncovered at 325° for 1 hour, or until chicken is tender. Turn oven to 375° and bake another 10 minutes to brown chicken.
4. Serve chicken and sauce with rice, pasta, or mashed potatoes.

> Every year around Thanksgiving we'd have a goose. I hated that time of year because we had to take goose grease and sugar for a tonic. Then they'd rub us down with it. We had to take it for the croup.
>
> — Nelson Polite, Sr.,
> a member of Bethel AMEC,
> Lancaster, PA

Honey Baked Chicken

Nancy Perkins

Makes 6 servings

3-lb. fryer, cut up
5⅔ Tbsp. (⅓ cup) butter or margarine,
   melted
⅓ cup honey
2 Tbsp. prepared mustard
1 tsp. salt
1 tsp. curry powder

   1. Arrange chicken in shallow baking pan,
skin side up.
   2. Combine butter, honey, mustard, salt,
and curry powder. Pour over chicken.
   3. Bake at 350° for 75 minutes, until
chicken is tender and browned.
   4. Serve with rice.

Lemony Chicken Thighs

Dianne Prince

Makes 2 servings

2 chicken thighs, deboned
salt to taste
pepper to taste
1 large carrot
1 large rib celery
2 Tbsp. butter, melted
¼ cup lemon juice

   1. Flatten each thigh and then sprinkle
with salt and pepper.
   2. Cut carrots and celery into strips, ¼"
thick and 4-5" long. Drop vegetables into
small amount of boiling water. Boil 2
minutes. Drain well.
   3. Arrange strips in center of each boned
thigh. Wrap chicken around strips and place,
seam-side down, in greased shallow baking
pan.
   4. Combine butter and lemon juice. Brush
over chicken.
   5. Bake at 350° for 30-45 minutes until
chicken is done, basting occasionally.

Orange Baked Chicken

Patricia Washington

Makes 4-5 servings

1/3 cup flour
1 tsp. salt
1/8 tsp. pepper
1 chicken, cut up and skin removed
1/3 cup shortening
1/2 tsp. celery seed
1/2 cup diced onions
3/4 cup orange juice
1 unpeeled orange, cut into 8 wedges

1. Combine flour, salt, and pepper in small bag. Add chicken. Shake thoroughly.
2. Fry chicken in shortening. Sprinkle with celery seed and onions. Place in greased casserole.
3. Bake at 350° until tender, about 45 minutes.
4. Pour orange juice over chicken. Top with orange wedges. Bake 30 more minutes.

Orange Ginger Chicken

Makes 4 servings

2 1/2-3-lb. chicken, cut up
salt to taste
pepper to taste
1/4 cup oil
1/2 cup barbecue sauce
2 Tbsp. flour
1 cup orange juice
2 Tbsp. packed brown sugar
1 Tbsp. chopped candied, or crystallized, ginger
dash of Tabasco sauce
1 unpeeled orange, sliced

1. Season chicken with salt and pepper. Brown in oil. Drain. Place in slow cooker.
2. Combine barbecue sauce and flour. Mix well.
3. Stir in orange juice, brown sugar, ginger, and Tabasco sauce. Mix well. Pour over chicken. Cover.
4. Simmer 30 minutes
5. Add orange slices. Simmer uncovered for 10 minutes, or until chicken is tender.
6. Arrange chicken and orange slices on serving plate. Serve with sauce.

Chicken Teriyaki

Makes 4-6 servings

2 Tbsp. butter or margarine
1 lb. boneless chicken breast, cubed
half a red pepper, sliced thin
half a green pepper, sliced thin
1/4 lb. (1 3/4 cups) mushrooms, sliced
1/2 lb. (2 1/2 cups) broccoli florets
1/2 tsp. salt

Sauce:
1/4 cup flour
5 Tbsp. teriyaki sauce (see next recipe)
seasoning salt to taste
pepper to taste
1 1/2 cups warm water

1. Melt butter in skillet. Add chicken and stir until brown. Stir in red pepper, green pepper, and mushrooms. Cook until vegetables are crisp-tender.
2. In separate saucepan steam broccoli in salted water. When crisp-tender, drain and set aside.
3. Combine flour, teriyaki sauce, seasoning salt, pepper, and warm water. Mix well.
4. Add all vegetables and sauce to chicken. Stir together gently. Simmer 10-15 minutes, or until sauce thickens.
5. Serve over cooked rice.

Teriyaki Sauce

Rina Mckee

Makes about 2 cups sauce

1 cup soy sauce
3/4 cup sugar
3 Tbsp. fresh ginger, grated
2 tsp. garlic, minced

1. Combine ingredients in saucepan. Simmer for 30 minutes.
2. Strain. Cool.
3. Refrigerate in airtight container, or pour over chicken legs and thighs and bake, basting chicken with sauce every 20 minutes while baking.

I remember when I was little we were blessed to have enough to eat, but for some reason I loved to eat grease sandwiches. I used to just lay my slice of bread down in the leftover grease in the frying pan, and then I'd get another slice of bread and make a sandwich, or just fold one slice in half.
— Barbara McFadden Enty,
a member of Bethel AMEC,
Lancaster, PA

Chicken In White Wine

Norine Dickter

Makes 4-6 servings

2-2½ lbs. chicken pieces
1 Tbsp. oil
½ lb. fresh mushrooms, sliced
½ lb. pearl onions, or 8 small white
   onions
1 cup dry white wine
1 cup water
1 chicken bouillon cube
1 garlic clove, chopped
¼ tsp. pepper
½ lb. fresh green beans, cut lengthwise
   into long strips

1. Brown chicken in oil. Remove chicken from pan; reserve drippings.
2. Saute mushrooms and onions in drippings until tender. Add more oil if needed.
3. Return chicken to pan. Stir in wine, water, bouillon cube, garlic, and pepper.
4. Heat to boiling. Reduce heat. Cover and simmer 45 minutes.
5. Add beans. Return to boiling. Reduce heat. Cover and simmer until beans are done, 15-20 minutes. Cover and refrigerate for 24 hours.
6. Twenty minutes before serving, spoon off fat. Heat chicken and vegetables to boiling. Reduce heat. Cover and simmer 10 minutes.
7. Garnish with parsley and serve.

Chicken Marsala

Willie Jean Murray

Makes 8 servings

3½-lb. chicken, cut into eight pieces
3 Tbsp. margarine or butter
12 small white onions, peeled
3 white turnips, pared and quartered
3 carrots, peeled and cut in 1½" pieces
2 ribs celery, cut in 1½" pieces
1 cup chicken stock, or canned chicken
   broth
½ cup dry Marsala wine
2 Tbsp. tomato paste
1 bay leaf
¼ cup chopped fresh parsley
¼ tsp. tarragon
salt to taste
pepper to taste

1. Melt margarine in large saucepan over medium heat. Brown chicken on all sides. Remove meat.
2. Drain all but 2 Tbsp. drippings from pan. Return chicken to saucepan. Add remaining ingredients. Stir to combine well.
3. Bring to boil. Cover pan and simmer gently until chicken and vegetables are tender, about 30-35 minutes.
4. Serve over couscous or rice, or with hearty bread.

Rosy Glazed Chicken

Makes 4-6 servings

2½-3-lb. broiler-fryer chicken, cut up
salt to taste
pepper to taste
8-oz. can tomato sauce
1 Tbsp. oil
7-oz. can whole cranberry sauce
2 Tbsp. brown sugar
1 Tbsp. lemon juice
¼ tsp. salt
1 lb. 13-oz. can yams, drained

   1. Sprinkle chicken with salt and pepper. Place in 9″ x 13″ baking dish.
   2. Bake at 375° for 30 minutes.
   3. Combine remaining ingredients, except yams, in saucepan. Heat and stir until smooth.
   4. Add yams to chicken. Pour sauce over all. Continue baking until chicken is tender, about 30 minutes, basting occasionally.

Chicken Piccata

Germaine W. Pickney

Makes 4 servings

2 whole chicken breasts, each flattened to
  ¼ -inch thick
⅛ tsp. salt
⅛ tsp. pepper
¼ cup flour
3 Tbsp. butter
1 Tbsp. olive oil
2 garlic cloves, peeled and minced
½ lb. mushrooms, thinly sliced
2 tsp. lemon juice
½ cup dry white wine
2 tsp. capers, drained, optional
3 Tbsp. minced parsley, optional
half a lemon, thinly sliced, optional

   1. Sprinkle chicken with salt and pepper. Dredge in flour. Shake off excess.
   2. Melt butter and olive oil in large skillet. Add garlic and saute briefly. Add chicken and saute until lightly browned. Remove chicken.
   3. Saute mushrooms for 1 minute.
   4. Return chicken to pan. Stir in lemon juice and wine. Simmer, covered, for 10 minutes, or until chicken is tender.
   5. Stir in capers. Heat well.
   6. Place chicken on platter. Spoon on juices and mushrooms. Garnish with parsley and lemon slices.

Smoked Almond-Crusted Chicken

Makes 4 servings

2 eggs, lightly beaten
3/4 cup milk
1 1/2 cups flour
salt to taste
pepper to taste
1 1/2 cups smoked almonds
3 Tbsp. olive oil
4 6-oz. boneless, skinless chicken breasts
barbecue sauce, warmed slightly

1. Combine eggs and milk.
2. Season flour with salt and pepper.
3. Puree almonds in food processor or blender.
4. Heat oil over medium flame.
5. Dip chicken in seasoned flour, then in egg mixture, and finally in almonds.
6. Place chicken in oil. Cook until browned on both sides, about 5-7 minutes.
7. Serve with warm barbecue sauce for dipping.

Lemon Barbecued Chicken

Carletha Akins

Makes 4 servings

1 1/2 lbs. skinless, boneless chicken breasts
dash of paprika
dash of cayenne pepper
3 Tbsp. lemon juice
1 Tbsp. honey
1 Tbsp. toasted sesame seed

1. Season chicken with paprika and pepper.
2. Combine lemon juice and honey. Set 2 Tbsp. aside.
3. Place chicken on broiler rack or charcoal grill. Broil 4-5" from heat for 15 minutes, basting occasionally with lemon honey mixture.
4. Turn chicken over. Baste with honey mixture and broil 15 additional minutes.
5. Combine sesame seeds and reserved lemon-honey mixture. Spoon over chicken just before serving.

> I resolved that, however long I might remain a slave in form, the day had passed forever when I could be a slave in fact.
> — Frederick Douglass

Chicken Lemonaise

Willie Jean Murray

Makes 6 servings

3 whole chicken breasts, halved, skinned,
  and boned
1/4 cup mayonnaise
1/2 cup fine dry bread crumbs
3 Tbsp. margarine
1/2 cup chopped onion
3 Tbsp. flour
1 1/2 cups water
3 chicken-flavored bouillon cubes
1/4 cup chopped parsley
3 Tbsp. lemon juice
1/2 cup mayonnaise

1. Brush chicken with 1/4 cup mayonnaise. Coat with bread crumbs.

2. Melt margarine in skillet. Cook chicken, 3 pieces at a time, for 15 minutes, or until tender. Keep warm.

3. Saute onion in pan drippings. Add more margarine if needed. Stir in flour until well blended. Gradually stir in water.

4. Add bouillon cubes, parsley, and lemon juice. Cook and stir until mixture boils.

5. Blend in mayonnaise. Cook until hot. Spoon sauce over chicken to serve.

Chicken Parmesan

Makes 4 servings

1/3 cup seasoned dried bread crumbs
1/4 tsp. pepper
2 Tbsp. milk
1 large egg
4 large skinless, boneless chicken breast
  halves
2 Tbsp. oil
14-16-oz. jar marinara sauce
8 ozs. mozzarella cheese, shredded

1. Combine bread crumbs and pepper on waxed paper.

2. Slightly beat milk and egg together in pie plate.

3. Dip chicken breasts in milk mixture and then in bread-crumb mixture, coating well.

4. Cook each chicken breast in hot oil for 3-4 minutes on each side, until golden brown.

5. Pour half of marinara sauce in 12" x 8" baking dish. Top with chicken breasts. Spoon remaining sauce over chicken. Sprinkle with cheese.

6. Bake at 350° for 20-30 minutes, until cheese melts and mixture is hot and bubbly.

Mexican Chicken

Makes 6 servings

6 medium-sized skinless, boneless chicken
   breast halves
1/2 lb. jalapeno Monterey Jack cheese
1 cup flour
1 1/4 tsp. salt
1 large egg
1/4 cup milk
3/4 cup cornmeal
3 Tbsp. salad oil
12-oz. jar thick and chunky hot salsa
8-oz. jar hot or mild taco sauce
1/3 cup water

1. Make 2 1/2" horizontal cut in the meatier
part of each chicken breast to make a deep
pocket.
2. Cut half of cheese into 6 slices. Shred
remaining cheese.
3. Place 1 slice of cheese in each pocket,
cutting cheese to fit.
4. Combine flour and salt on waxed paper.
5. Combine egg and milk in bowl.
6. Pour cornmeal on another sheet of
waxed paper.
7. Dredge each chicken breast in flour,
then dip into egg mixture, then dredge in
cornmeal.
8. Saute each breast in skillet in hot oil for
about 5 minutes, until browned on both
sides. Remove to plate.
9. When breasts are all browned, in same
skillet add salsa, taco sauce, and water. Heat
to boiling.
10. Arrange chicken in sauce. Reduce heat
to low. Simmer, uncovered, for 15 minutes.
11. Sprinkle with shredded cheese. Cover
and cook until cheese melts. Serve chicken in
sauce.

Champagne & Mushroom Chicken

Makes 4-6 servings

2 Tbsp. flour
1/2 tsp. garlic powder
1/4 tsp. white pepper
1/2 tsp. salt
1/4 tsp. paprika
4 chicken breast halves, skinned and
   boned
1 Tbsp. butter
1 Tbsp. oil
3/4 cup champagne or dry white wine
1/2 cup sliced fresh mushrooms
1/2 cup heavy cream
2 Tbsp. chopped parsley

1. Combine flour, garlic powder, white
pepper, salt, and paprika.
2. Lightly coat chicken in flour mixture.
3. Heat butter and oil in skillet over
medium heat. Add chicken. Brown 4 minutes
on each side.
4. Add champagne. Continue cooking over
medium heat until chicken is tender, about
10 minutes. Place chicken on platter. Keep
warm.
5. Add mushrooms and cream to skillet.
Cook over low heat, stirring constantly until
thickened. Return chicken to skillet. Spoon
sauce over chicken and heat until warmed
through.
6. Garnish with parsley just before
serving.

Sunshine Chicken

Makes 2 servings

1 1/2 Tbsp. butter
2 chicken breast halves, skinned & boned
1 pkg. dry onion soup
2 tsp. cornstarch
1 cup orange juice
2 tsp. honey

1. Melt butter in small baking dish.
2. Add chicken to dish, turning to coat both sides.
3. Combine soup mix, cornstarch, orange juice, and honey. Pour over chicken. Cover with foil.
4. Bake at 350° for 15 minutes. Flip chicken. Bake an additional 15 minutes.
5. Serve topped with sauce.

Hawaiian Chicken

Makes 6-8 servings

6-8 chicken breast halves
21-oz. can pineapple chunks
1 pkg. dry onion soup mix
1/2 cup (1 stick) butter or margarine
2 tsp. lime juice
1 tsp. cornstarch

1. Place chicken in ungreased baking dish.
2. Drain pineapple, reserving juice. Distribute pineapple chunks over chicken.
3. Sprinkle onion soup mix over chicken and fruit.
4. Melt butter in skillet. Stir in lime juice and reserved pineapple juice. Heat for 5 minutes. Stir in cornstarch to thicken sauce. Pour over chicken.
5. Bake at 350° for 45 minutes.

Fargo a Portuguese

Nancy Perkins

Makes 6 servings

3 whole boneless chicken breasts
2 Tbsp. oil
1/2 cup water or chicken stock
1 cup chopped onions
1 clove garlic, minced
14 1/2-oz. can diced tomatoes
2 Tbsp. flour
1 Tbsp. salt
1/2 tsp. pepper

1. Cut chicken into small bite-sized pieces.
2. Brown chicken in oil.
3. Add water or stock, onions, and garlic to chicken. Cook until onions begin to soften.
4. Add tomatoes, flour, salt, and pepper. Mix well. Bring to boil.
5. Serve over rice.

With 14 children, my mother was very creative with her cooking. She'd take whatever was left over from breakfast and make supper. She didn't waste anything. We didn't have a lot of cooking pots, so Mama just put it all together. White folks would call what she made a "casserole." Back then it was just a meal.

— Frances Morant,
Brothers & Sisters Cafe

Sweet N' Sour Chicken

Makes 6-8 servings

1/2 cup pancake/waffle mix
10¾-oz. can condensed chicken broth
1⅓ cups water, or more
1/2 tsp. salt
dash of pepper
1 lb. boneless chicken, cut into 1-inch
   pieces
oil
1 large green pepper, cut into 1-inch pieces
1 large onion, cut into 12 wedges
8-oz. can pineapple chucks
2 Tbsp. cornstarch
1/2 cup maple syrup
1/4 cup vinegar
1 Tbsp. soy sauce
1 medium tomato, cut into wedges
hot cooked rice

1. Combine pancake mix with chicken broth, water, salt, and pepper. Mix well.
2. Add chicken. Mix until well coated.
3. In large skillet, heat 1" oil to 375°. Fry 10-12 pieces of chicken at a time for 3-4 minutes, or until crisp and golden brown. Place on absorbent paper until well drained. Place chicken on rack in shallow baking pan. Keep warm in 250° oven.
4. Drain all but 2 tsp. drippings from skillet.
5. Saute green peppers and onion in hot drippings. Remove vegetables from skillet.
6. Drain pineapple, reserving 1/4 cup juice. Combine juice with cornstarch and mix until smooth.
7. Combine syrup, vinegar, and soy sauce. Pour into skillet. Bring to boil, gradually stirring in pineapple juice-cornstarch mixture. Simmer for 1 minute, or until thick and clear.
8. Add pineapple chunks. Simmer 1 minute.
9. Stir in chicken, green pepper, onion, and tomato.
10. Cook 1-2 minutes until thoroughly heated.
11. Serve over hot rice.

Grilled Chinese Five-Spice Skewered Chicken

Rina Mckee

Makes 3-4 servings

1 lb. boneless, skinless chicken breast
1/2 cup soy sauce
1/4 cup white wine
2 Tbsp. rice wine vinegar
1½ tsp. sugar
1 tsp. five-spice powder

1. Cut chicken into long, thin strips.
2. Combine remaining ingredients. Pour over chicken. Toss well. Cover and refrigerate for 2 hours.
3. Weave chicken strips onto bamboo skewers. Brush with sauce; then grill 3-4 minutes. Brush with sauce and turn chicken over. Grill another 3-4 minutes.

Sweet & Sour Chicken

Makes 4-6 servings

2 lbs. boneless chicken, cut in cubes
2 Tbsp. oil
1 clove garlic, minced
1 cup green pepper strips
1 cup carrot matchsticks
1½ cups chicken broth
¼ cup soy sauce
3 Tbsp. vinegar
8 Tbsp. brown sugar
½ tsp. ground ginger
8-oz. can pineapple chunks with juice
⅓ cup teriyaki sauce
1½ cups minute rice

1. Brown chicken in oil.
2. Add garlic, green pepper, and carrots. Saute briefly.
3. Add broth, soy sauce, vinegar, sugar, ginger, pineapples with juice, and teriyaki sauce. Bring to full boil.
4. Stir in rice. Cover. Remove from heat and let stand a few minutes. Stir before serving.

I have seen hundreds of escaped slaves, but I never saw one who was willing to go back and be a slave. I think slavery is the next thing to hell.
— Harriet Tubman

Buffalo Chicken Drumsticks

Makes 6 servings

3 Tbsp. flour
12 medium-sized drumsticks
2 Tbsp. oil
1 medium onion, minced
¾ cups cayenne pepper sauce
1 tsp. cornstarch
celery stalks
blue cheese salad dressing

1. Place flour in sturdy plastic bag. Toss drumsticks, a few at a time, in flour.
2. Heat oil in skillet over medium heat. Cook drumsticks until browned on all sides. Remove to plate.
3. In drippings, saute onion until golden, about 5 minutes. Return chicken to skillet.
4. Combine cayenne pepper sauce and cornstarch. Pour over drumsticks. Heat to boiling. Reduce heat to low. Cover and simmer 25 minutes, basting occasionally, until chicken is tender.
5. Arrange drumsticks on platter. Spoon pepper sauce over chicken. Serve with celery and blue cheese dressing.

Buffalo Wings

Tammy Lynn Oatis

Makes 3-4 servings

2½ lbs. chicken wings (12-15 wings)
¼ cup red hot sauce
½ cup (1 stick) butter or margarine, melted

1. Split wings at joint. Discard tips.
2. Deep fry at 400° for 12 minutes, or until completely cooked and crispy. Drain.
3. Combine hot sauce and butter. Dip wings in sauce until coated.
4. Serve with celery and blue cheese dressing.

Note: You can bake the wings in a 425° oven for 35 minutes, instead of deep-frying them.

Barbecued Chicken Wings

Brenda Fowlerberry

Makes 6 servings

¼ cup oil
3 medium onions, diced
3 cups tomato sauce
1½ cups packed brown sugar
¾ cup white vinegar
3 Tbsp. Worcestershire sauce
4 Tbsp. chili powder
2 Tbsp. salt
¼ tsp. dry mustard
2½ lbs. chicken wings (about 24 wings)

1. Saute onions in oil until tender, about 5 minutes.
2. Add tomato sauce, brown sugar, vinegar, Worcestershire sauce, chili powder, salt, and dry mustard. Heat to boiling, stirring constantly. Reduce heat and simmer 30 minutes, stirring occasionally.
3. Split wings at joint. Discard tips. Place in baking pan. Cover with sauce.
4. Bake at 400° for 60 minutes.

Note: This sauce also works well over chicken legs and thighs.

Italian-Style Fried Chicken Wings

Makes 3-4 servings

15 chicken wings
1 cup Italian-style bread crumbs
1 cup flour
1 Tbsp. black pepper
1 Tbsp. garlic powder
2 Tbsp. seasoned salt
2 eggs
2 cups cooking oil

1. Combine bread crumbs, flour, pepper, garlic powder, and seasoned salt in large plastic bag.
2. Beat eggs.
3. Wash and dry chicken wings. Dip each in eggs. Drop 3-4 wings into bag at a time and shake to coat.
4. Fry in hot oil until cooked.

Note: Follow the same procedure through Step 3, then bake wings in oven at 400° for 35-45 minutes, or until done.

Use chicken legs instead of wings and follow same procedure through Step 3, then bake legs in oven at 350° for 45-60 minutes, or until done.

Wings Teriyaki

Linda Maison

Makes 4 servings

1 lb. chicken wings
1 tsp. ground ginger
1 clove garlic, minced
1/3 cup soy sauce
1/4 cup sherry
1 tsp. sugar

1. Cut wings into pieces at joints. Place in a single layer in a shallow roasting pan.
2. Roast uncovered at 375° for 30 minutes, or until skin is crisp.
3. Combine remaining ingredients and pour over wings.
4. Cover pan tightly with foil and bake another 30 minutes, or until wings are browned and tender, but not dry.

Hot Chicken Salad

Makes 6-8 servings

7 chicken breast halves, cooked and chopped
1 cup chopped celery
4-5 hard-boiled eggs
1/4 cup finely chopped onions
1/2 cup chopped red bell peppers
1/2 cup sweet relish
1/2 tsp. garlic powder
1/2 tsp. onion powder
1/8 tsp. cayenne pepper
1 1/2 to 1 3/4 cups salad dressing
10 1/2-oz. can cream of chicken soup
1/4 cup (1/2 stick) margarine
1 roll butter crackers, crushed

1. Combine chicken, celery, eggs, onions, red peppers, relish, garlic powder, onion powder, and cayenne pepper.
2. Stir in enough salad dressing for mixture to hold together.
3. Fold in chicken soup.
4. Spoon into greased casserole dish.
5. Melt margarine in 8″ skillet. Add crackers. Stir to mix. Spread on top of chicken mixture.
6. Bake at 350° for 20-25 minutes, or until lightly browned.

We never had hand lotion. We always had to use lard.
— Barbara McFadden Enty, a member of Bethel AMEC, Lancaster, PA

Chicken Cobbler

Elena Helmuth

Makes 6 servings

1/4 cup (1/2 stick) butter or margarine,
  melted
2 cups milk
1 cup cooked rice
2 cups diced, cooked chicken
1 cup flour
2 tsp. baking powder
1 tsp. salt
1 Tbsp. sugar
1 cup milk

1. Pour butter into 1 1/2-qt. casserole.
2. Combine 2 cups milk, rice, and chicken.
Spoon into casserole.
3. Sift together flour, baking powder, salt,
and sugar. Add 1 cup milk. Mix well. Spread
over chicken-rice mixture.
4. Bake at 350° for 50 minutes. Let stand 5
minutes before serving.

Turkey Scallopini Piccata

Willie Jean Murray

Makes 6-8 servings

7-lb. turkey breast, skinned
3/4 -1 cup flour
2 tsp. salt
1 tsp. pepper
1/2 tsp. dried thyme
1/2 tsp. dried marjoram
1/2 cup (1 stick) margarine or butter
2 cloves garlic, minced
juice of 1 lemon
1/2 cup chicken broth
1/2 cup dry white wine
3 Tbsp. chopped fresh parsley

1. Slice turkey meat off bone, as thinly as
possible. Reserve carcass for making stock.
2. Place individual slices of turkey
between sheets of waxed paper. Pound each
slightly.
3. Season flour with salt, pepper, thyme,
and marjoram.
4. Dredge turkey slices in flour mixture,
one at a time.
5. Saute turkey slices in batches, each in
about 2 Tbsp. margarine, for about 2 minutes
per side. Remove from pan and keep warm.
Reserve drippings.
6. When finished, saute garlic in drippings.
Add cooked turkey slices, lemon juice, broth,
and wine. Simmer for 5 minutes.
7. Sprinkle with parsley and serve
immediately.

Turkey Wings and Gravy

Makes 4 servings

6 turkey wings
2 ribs celery, sliced ½" thick
1 small onion, thinly sliced
1 medium green bell pepper, thinly sliced
1½ tsp. poultry seasoning
2 tsp. salt
¼ tsp. fresh ground pepper
½ cup flour
½ cup water
2 tsp. Gravy Master

1. Cut each wing into 3 pieces. Place wing pieces, celery, onions, and green pepper in large pot. Cover with cold water.
2. Add poultry seasoning, salt, and pepper. Heat to boiling. Reduce heat and simmer until wings are very tender, about 75 minutes. Adjust seasoning if needed.
3. Combine flour and water until smooth. Slowly stir flour mixture into simmering turkey liquid until it is smooth and thickened. Stir in Gravy Master.
4. Serve wings and gravy with mashed potatoes or rice.

Baked Turkey Wings

Ann M. Bearden

one wing per person
salt to taste
pepper to taste
¼ cup (½ stick) margarine, melted
¼ cup water
onion halves, according to your preference
celery sticks, according to your preference
¼ cup water

1. Season wings with salt and pepper. Place in roasting pan.
2. Pour butter over wings. Add a little water.
3. Bake at 350°, turning and basting until browned, about 60 minutes.
4. Add onions, celery, and water to pan. Cover. Continue baking until tender.

The laws of this country do not protect us, and we are not bound to obey them. You whites have a country and may obey its laws, but we have no country.

— William Parker

Turkey Supreme

Marlene Clark

Makes 6 servings

1 cup herb-seasoned stuffing mix
1-lb. pkg. frozen string beans, cooked
  lightly
1/4 cup slivered, blanched almonds
2 cups cooked turkey, cut in large pieces
10 1/2-oz. can condensed cream of
  mushroom soup
1/2 cup milk

Topping:
1 cup herb-seasoned stuffing
2 Tbsp. melted butter
1/4 cup water

1. Layer 1 cup stuffing mix, string beans, almonds, and turkey in greased baking dish.
2. Combine soup and milk. Pour over casserole.
3. Combine topping ingredients. Spread over casserole.
4. Bake at 400° for 25-30 minutes until browned and bubbly.

Turkey Loaf

Marlene Clark

Makes 8-10 servings

2 eggs, slightly beaten
4 Tbsp. (1/2 stick) butter, melted
1 pkg. (4 cups) herb-seasoned stuffing mix
1 1/2 cups turkey or chicken broth
2 cups cooked and cut-up turkey or
  chicken
2 Tbsp. minced parsley
1 Tbsp. minced onion
2 Tbsp. minced green peppers

Sauce:
10 1/2-oz. can condensed cream of celery
  soup
3/4 cup milk

1. Combine eggs, butter, stuffing mix, broth, turkey, parsley, onion, and green peppers. Spoon into greased 9" x 5" loaf pan.
2. Bake at 375° for 30-40 minutes, or until firm.
3. Combine sauce ingredients in saucepan. Simmer for 2 minutes.
4. Slice loaf and pour sauce over slices just before serving.

Turkey Croquettes

Nanette Akins

Makes 4 servings

1 1/2 cups cooked turkey, finely chopped
10 1/2-oz. can condensed cream of chicken
  soup
1 cup herb-seasoned stuffing mix
2 eggs, slightly beaten
1 Tbsp. minced onion
flour
oil

Sauce:
10 1/2-oz. can condensed cream of
  mushroom soup
1/3-1/2 cup milk

1. Combine turkey, 2/3 can of soup, stuffing mix, eggs, and onion. Pour into shallow dish. Refrigerate for 2-3 hours until firm and chilled.
2. Divide mixture into 8 equal parts. Form into log shapes. Lightly dust with flour.
3. Deep-fry in oil until golden brown.
4. Combine sauce ingredients. Simmer in saucepan for 2 minutes. Serve over croquettes.

Leiths Roast Duck

Doris Kelly

Makes 8 servings

2 5-lb. ducks
1 Tbsp. vinegar
1/2 cup chicken stock
2 oranges, juiced, and zest grated
3 Tbsp. brandy
2 small onions, finely chopped
2 celery ribs, finely chopped
1 tsp. salt
1 tsp. pepper
3 ozs. sliced almonds
2 whole oranges, unpeeled and sliced in
  rounds
2 bunches watercress

1. Prick ducks all over with fork. Place in roaster, breast side down.
2. Roast at 400° for 30 minutes. Turn breast side up and roast another 30 minutes. Test that ducks are tender; pierce to see if juice runs clear. If not, turn ducks over again and roast another 20 minutes. Test again. Continue baking, checking every 15 minutes, until they are done.
3. Remove ducks from roaster. Drain well. Remove skin and cut into pieces. Place in clean roaster.
4. Combine vinegar, chicken stock, orange juice, orange zest, and brandy. Pour over ducks.
5. Return to oven and heat, basting occasionally, for about 20 minutes more, until ducks are heated through. Remove meat to an ovenproof platter and keep warm.
6. Skim sauce to remove fat. Strain sauce into saucepan. Add onions and celery. Boil for 5 minutes, or until vegetables just begin to soften. Add salt and pepper. Serve sauce separately.

7. Brown almonds over low heat, stirring constantly. Scatter over ducks.

8. Garnish with sliced oranges and watercress.

Roast Duck with Orange Sauce

Makes 8 servings

5-5½-lb. duckling
salt
8 ozs. (1 cup) currant jelly
1 qt. orange juice
1 pt. concentrated orange juice mix
stock

1. Rub salt over duckling. Place on wire rack in roasting pan.

2. Roast at 350° for 2 hours.

3. Prepare orange sauce while duckling is roasting. Boil jelly and 1 qt. orange juice until reduced to half original amount. Add stock to make amount of gravy desired. Bring to boil. Boil for a few minutes until slightly reduced. Stir in concentrated orange juice. Heat through.

4. Remove duckling from oven. Drain off drippings. Pour orange sauce over duckling.

The workings of the human heart are the profoundest mystery of the universe. One moment they make us despair of our kind, and the next we see in them the reflection of the divine image.

— Frederick Douglass

Roast Cornish Hens with Melon Sauce

Makes 6-8 servings

4 2-lb. fresh Cornish hens, split
2 Tbsp. margarine or butter, melted
salt to taste
pepper to taste
3 cups chicken stock or canned chicken broth
2 carrots, coarsely chopped
2 ribs celery, coarsely chopped
1 medium onion, coarsely chopped
2 cloves garlic, peeled
2 Tbsp. dried tarragon
1 ripe cantaloupe

1. Place the hens, skin-side up, in a single layer in one or two baking pans. Brush with melted margarine. Season with salt and pepper.

2. Roast at 350° for about an hour, or until juices run clear.

3. Meanwhile, combine chicken stock, carrots, celery, onion, garlic, and tarragon in saucepan.

4. Cut cantaloupe in half. Scoop out seeds into a piece of cheesecloth. Tie cheesecloth into bag with string. Add bag to saucepan.

5. Bring to boil. Lower heat and simmer 30 minutes. Remove and discard seed bag.

6. In food processor or blender, puree vegetables with half of stock. Return puree to saucepan.

7. Dice cantaloupe into ½" cubes. Add to sauce and heat slowly.

8. Transfer hens to heated serving platter. Spoon portion of sauce over hens. Serve with remaining sauce on the side.

Chuck Wagon Roast

Makes 10 servings

5-lb. chuck roast
1/2 cup vegetable oil
1 cup beer or ale
2 Tbsp. lemon juice
2 cloves garlic, crushed
3/4 tsp. salt
2 bay leaves
1/2 tsp. pepper
3/4 tsp. dry mustard
1 tsp. dried basil
1 tsp. dried oregano

1. Place steak in deep bowl.
2. Combine oil, beer, lemon juice, and seasonings. Pour over steak. Cover and refrigerate for several hours.
3. Place roast in roasting pan. Baste with marinade.
4. Bake at 425° for 2 1/2 hours. Slice and serve.

Pepper Steak

Makes 5 servings

1 1/2-lb. round steak
3 green peppers, diced
1 large onion, chopped
14-oz. bottle ketchup
1/2 cup water
1 Tbsp. Worcestershire sauce
salt to taste
pepper to taste

1. Place meat in skillet or greased baking dish.
2. Combine remaining ingredients. Pour over steak.

3. Cover and simmer on top of stove for 1 1/2-2 hours, or bake covered at 350° for 1 1/2 hours. Uncover and continuing cooking or baking 30 minutes longer, or until tender.

Mexican-Style Pot Roast

Makes 6 servings

2 Tbsp. flour
1 tsp. chili powder
2 tsp. paprika
1 tsp. salt
3 1/2-lb. chuck blade roast
2 Tbsp. butter or margarine
2 medium onions
10 whole cloves
2 cinnamon sticks,
    or 1/2 tsp. ground cinnamon
1/2 cup water

1. Combine flour, chili powder, paprika, and salt.
2. Dredge meat in mixture.
3. Brown in butter in heavy kettle or Dutch oven.
4. Stud each onion with 5 cloves.
5. Add onions, cinnamon, and water to meat.
6. Bring to boil. Cover and simmer for 2 1/2 hours, or until meat is very tender, turning several times. Remove meat to hot platter and slice.
7. Discard onions and cinnamon sticks. Skim off fat.
8. Add more water if needed to make gravy of right consistency. Heat. Pour over meat and serve.

Chuck Roast with Vegetables

Makes 8 servings

4-lb. boneless chuck roast
salt to taste
pepper to taste
4 potatoes, quartered
4 carrots, sliced
5 small onions
1 pkg. dry onion soup mix
10½-oz. can mushroom soup

1. Place large sheet of heavy-duty foil in baking pan.
2. Season roast with salt and pepper. Place in baking pan.
3. Place vegetables around meat.
4. Sprinkle with dry soup mix. Pour mushroom soup over top.
5. Seal foil tightly.
6. Bake at 350° for 3-3½ hours, or until meat and vegetables are tender.

> My kids every year had to line up and take castor oil to clean them out in the springtime.
> — Nelson Polite, Sr.,
> a member of Bethel AMEC,
> Lancaster, PA

Pot Roast

Rev. Roger Bowman

Makes 10-12 servings

1-2 garlic cloves
4-5-lb. boneless chuck roast
1 Tbsp. oil
1 pkg. dry onion soup mix
pepper to taste
2-4 carrots, cut into chunks
2 bay leaves
1 cup water

1. Cut garlic cloves into slivers. With a sharp knife, cut slits on all sides of roast. Insert clove slivers into meat.
2. Brown roast in oil in Dutch oven.
3. Sprinkle with onion soup mix, pepper, carrots, and bay leaves.
4. Pour in water. Cover.
5. Bake at 300-325° for 3-3½ hours, or until meat and vegetables are tender.
6. Skim off excess fat and remove bay leaves. Thicken pan juices for gravy.

Oven-Baked Pot Roast

Makes 8 servings

3-4 lb. chuck roast
1 envelope dry onion soup mix
3-4 medium potatoes, cut in quarters
1 large rib celery, cut into pieces
4 carrots, cut into chunks

1. Place roast in baking dish or casserole with lid.
2. Sprinkle soup mix over roast. Cover.
3. Bake at 350° for 2-2½ hours.
4. Add vegetables. Continue baking for 60 more minutes.
5. Slice meat and serve surrounded with vegetables. Ladle broth over all.

We used to live on a sharecropper's farm. At the end of the harvest season, when we'd gathered our last crop, the man that owned the farm would make a big pot of catfish and serve it over rice. There'd be music and we would be dancing and celebrating that it was the end of the season. Each year we looked forward to this big festivity.

The difference between slavery and sharecropping was that when you were a sharecropper, they didn't whip you and they paid you a little bit of money for working for them. But you were still depending on them for your food and the things you needed. But you could move off their farm if you wanted to. You didn't have to stay there, like when you were enslaved.
— Frances Morant,
Brothers & Sisters Cafe

Beef Stroganoff

Doris Kelly

Makes 4 servings

1 lb. beef tenderloin or sirloin steak, cut ½-inch thick
⅛ tsp. pepper
½ lb. fresh mushrooms, sliced
1 medium onion, sliced
1 Tbsp. oil
2 Tbsp. flour
2 bouillon cubes
2 cups water
¼ cup tomato paste
½-1 tsp. dry mustard
½ tsp. dried oregano
½ tsp. dried dill
¼ cup sherry
1 cup yogurt

1. Cut meat into thin strips, about 2″ long. Sprinkle with pepper.
2. Saute mushrooms and onion in oil in heavy skillet. Remove with slotted spoon. Set vegetables aside.
3. Add flour to oil in skillet.
4. Dissolve bouillon cubes in boiling water. Gradually add to skillet and simmer, stirring constantly until thickened.
5. Add tomato paste, mustard, oregano, dill, and sherry. Mix until smooth.
6. Stir in beef, mushrooms, and onions. Cover. Simmer 2-3 minutes, or until beef is cooked through.
7. Five minutes before serving, stir in yogurt. Heat, but do not boil.
8. Serve over cooked rice.

Sweet and Sour Short Ribs

Makes 4 servings

½ cup flour
1 tsp. salt
¼ -½ tsp. pepper
2-3 lbs. short ribs, trimmed and cut into
    serving-size pieces
2 Tbsp. oil
1 cup sliced onions
1 clove garlic, minced
1½ cups hot water
⅓ cup ketchup
1 bay leaf
3 Tbsp. brown sugar
¼ cup wine vinegar
½ tsp. salt
hot buttered noodles

1. Combine flour, 1 tsp. salt, and pepper in plastic bag. Add ribs. Shake to coat. Set aside any leftover seasoned flour.
2. In skillet, brown ribs on all sides in oil. Reserve drippings. Place ribs in Dutch oven.
3. Saute onions and garlic in skillet. Cook until slightly browned. Pour over ribs.
4. Combine hot water, ketchup, bay leaf, brown sugar, wine vinegar, and ½ tsp. salt. Pour over ribs. Cover.
5. Cook for 2-3 hours, until tender. Remove ribs to serving dish. Keep warm.
6. Pour off excess drippings. Stir in leftover flour until smooth. Add enough water to make a gravy-like consistency. Cook until desired thickness.
7. Serve with hot buttered noodles.

Steak Tartare

Mrs. Margaret Bailey

Makes 1 generous full serving, or
4 appetizer servings

⅓ lb. finely ground fillet of beef or lean
    steak
salt to taste
pepper to taste
1 egg yolk
1 tsp. Dijon mustard
1 Tbsp. olive oil
1 tsp. lemon juice
pinch of cayenne pepper
2 Tbsp. minced onion
1 Tbsp. capers
1 Tbsp. minced parsley
1 tsp. Worcestershire sauce
1 egg yolk
2 Tbsp. minced onion
¼ cup minced parsley
¼ cup drained capers

1. Season meat with salt and pepper.
2. Add egg yolk, mustard, oil, lemon juice, cayenne pepper, 2 Tbsp. minced onion, 1 Tbsp. capers, 1 Tbsp. minced parsley, and Worcestershire sauce.
3. Shape into mound on serving dish. Make a depression in center. Put remaining egg yolk in depression.
4. Surround mixture with small mounds of minced onion, parsley, and capers.
5. Serve with thinly sliced dark bread and a cup of hot consomme.

Meat Loaf

Betty Jean Joe

Makes 12-16 servings

3-4 lbs. ground beef
2 cups seasoned bread crumbs
4 eggs
1/2 cup chopped onion
1/2 cup chopped green pepper
1/2 tsp. pepper
1 cup tomato sauce
6-oz. can tomato paste
1 tsp. salt

1. Combine all ingredients.
2. Form into loaf and place in baking pan.
3. Bake at 350° for 90 minutes.

Indian Meat Loaf

Nancy Perkins

Makes 6-8 servings

1 lb. ground beef
1/2 lb. ground pork
1 egg
1/2 cup cornmeal
1 tsp. salt
1/4 tsp. pepper
1/2 tsp. dried sage
1/2 cup chopped onions
1/4 cup chopped green pepper
1/2 cup cream-style corn
1 1/4 cups canned tomatoes

1. Combine all ingredients. Mix well.
2. Pack into 9" x 5" loaf pan.
3. Bake at 350° for 75 minutes.

Stately Meat Loaf

Michelle Akins

Makes 8 servings

2 lbs. ground beef
1/2 tsp. salt
1 tsp. pepper
1 tsp. chopped parsley
1 medium onion, minced
1/3 cup ketchup
2 egg whites, slightly beaten
1/4 cup ice water
2 Tbsp. prepared mustard
1 Tbsp. ketchup
3 cups coarsely shredded carrots
8 medium-sized, fresh mushrooms, sliced

1. Combine beef, salt, pepper, parsley, and onion.
2. Gradually add ketchup, egg whites, and water, working all ingredients together thoroughly. Shape mixture into loaf. Place meat in baking dish large enough to accommodate the meat and its bed of carrots (to be added later).
3. Bake at 375° for 30 minutes.
4. Combine mustard and ketchup. Spread over loaf.
5. Surround loaf with shredded carrots. Place mushrooms on top. Bake an additional 30 minutes.

Italian Meat Loaf

Nanette Akins

Makes 6 servings

1 medium onion chopped
2 Tbsp. butter or margarine
1 egg, slightly beaten
1/2 cup milk
1/2 cup herb-seasoned stuffing mix
1 lb. ground beef
2 Tbsp. chopped parsley
1 Tbsp. salt
1/4 tsp. pepper
6-ozs. tomato sauce
1/4 tsp. dried oregano

1. Saute onion in butter over low heat until golden.
2. Mix together sauteed onion, egg, milk and stuffing mix. Let stand 5 minutes.
3. Add beef, parsley, salt, and pepper. Mix lightly but thoroughly.
4. Shape meat into loaf in shallow baking dish.
5. Bake at 375° for 30 minutes.
6. Pour tomato sauce over meat. Sprinkle with oregano. Bake 30 minutes longer.
7. Remove from oven and let sit 5-10 minutes before slicing.

Sweet and Sour Meatballs

Susan Dyen

Makes 8 servings

2-2 1/2 lbs. ground veal or beef
2 eggs, slightly beaten
2 cups unsalted crackers, crushed fine
minced garlic to taste
1 Tbsp. Italian seasoning

Sauce:
1 large jar homestyle marinara sauce
1 jar all-fruit black cherry jelly

1. Combine meat, eggs, crackers, garlic, and Italian seasoning. Form into meatballs.
2. Combine sauce and jelly in large baking dish. Add meatballs.
3. Bake at 350° for 60-75 minutes, until cooked through and browned.

Braised Veal in Cider

Doris Kelly

Makes 6-8 servings

3 lbs. boneless veal, cut in 2" cubes
1 Tbsp. sweet Hungarian paprika
salt to taste
pepper to taste
2 Tbsp. margarine or butter
2 Tbsp. oil
2 onions, thinly sliced
2½ cups apple cider
½ cup chicken broth
1 bunch carrots, peeled and cut in
    1" pieces

1. Season veal with paprika, salt, and pepper.
2. Heat margarine and oil over medium heat in Dutch oven. Brown veal on all sides. Drain meat and return to Dutch oven.
3. Add onions, cider, and broth. Bring to boil.
4. Cover and bake at 325° for 45 minutes.
5. Add carrots. Continue to bake 20-25 minutes, until veal and carrots are tender.

Note: You may substitute pork cubes for the veal cubes.

Cajun Chops

Makes 4 servings

1 Tbsp. paprika
1 tsp. seasoned salt
1 tsp. dried sage
½ tsp. cayenne pepper
½ tsp. black pepper
½ tsp. garlic powder
4 pork chops, ½-inch thick
2 Tbsp. butter or margarine

1. Combine paprika, seasoned salt, sage, cayenne pepper, black pepper, and garlic powder.
2. Coat chops on both sides with seasoning mixture.
3. Heat butter until it starts to brown.
4. Cook chops until done, 45-60 minutes.

You have seen how a man was made a slave; you shall see how a slave was made a man.

— Frederick Douglass

Individual Baked Pork Chop Dinner

Jim Johnson

Makes 4 servings

2 Tbsp. oil
4 pork chops or steaks
black pepper to taste
1 small onion, thinly sliced
2 medium potatoes, thinly sliced
4 fresh or frozen ears of corn on the cob
1 tsp. dillweed
¼ cup (½ stick) margarine or butter
4 (16" x 12") rectangles heavy-duty
    aluminum foil

1. Brown pork chops in oil. Season with pepper.
2. Place one pork chop in center of each piece of foil.
3. Place one-fourth of onions and one-fourth of potato slices on top of each chop.
4. Place one ear of corn next to each pork chop.
5. Sprinkle each chop with ¼ tsp. dillweed. Dot each top with 1 Tbsp. margarine.
6. Fold aluminum foil around pork chop and corn. Seal top and sides securely. Place on jellyroll pan.
7. Bake at 350° for 60 minutes.

Pork Chops and Rice

Lee Williams

Makes 5-6 servings

5-6 center pork chops
¼ cup oil
1 onion chopped
1 can beef bouillon
1 can water
1 cup regular rice

1. Brown chops in oil. Remove chops and keep warm.
2. Saute onion in meat drippings until tender.
3. Pour rice into 9" x 13" pan. Pour in soup and water. Add browned onion. Mix well. Lay pork chops on top. Cover with foil.
4. Bake at 350° for 45 minutes. Remove foil and bake an additional 15 minutes, allowing meat and rice to brown slightly.

Orange Baked Pork Chops

Sonya Gibson

Makes 4 servings

4 pork chops, cut about ½" thick
seasoning salt to taste
¼ cup orange juice
½ tsp. dried mustard
2 tsp. brown sugar

1. Sprinkle chops with seasoning salt. Place on rack in baking pan.
2. Bake at 350° for 20 minutes.
3. Combine remaining ingredients. Baste chops.
4. Continue baking for 15 more minutes. Turn chops. Bake another 10 minutes. Baste frequently throughout baking time.

Cranberry Pork Chops

Makes 4 servings

4 1"-thick pork chops
1 tsp. salt
pepper to taste
2 Tbsp. oil
½ cup dry red wine
½ cup honey
1 cup fresh cranberries

1. Season pork chops with salt and pepper. Brown in hot oil, about 2 minutes on each side.
2. Combine wine and honey. Pour over chops. Cover and simmer for 50 minutes.
3. Add cranberries. Cook 10 minutes longer.

Stuffed Pork Chops

Makes 6 servings

6 1½"-thick, loin-end pork chops
salt to taste
pepper to taste
1 cup herb-stuffing mix
½ cup chopped unpeeled apples
2 Tbsp. raisins
2 Tbsp. butter or margarine, melted
2 Tbsp. orange juice
½ tsp. salt
⅛ tsp. ground cinnamon

1. Make a pocket along thickest side of each chop. Season inside and outside with salt and pepper.
2. Combine stuffing mix, apples, and raisins.
3. Combine butter, orange juice, ½ tsp. salt, and cinnamon. Gently mix into stuffing and fruit mixture.
4. Stuff chops. Hold pockets shut with toothpicks. Place in shallow baking dish.
5. Bake at 350° for 90 minutes. Cover during the last 30 minutes if chops become too brown or begin to dry out.

Herbed Pork Roast

Makes 8 servings

4-lb. boneless top loin roast
1 clove garlic, cut into halves
1 tsp. dried sage
1/2 tsp. dried marjoram
1/2 tsp. dried thyme leaves
salt to taste
pepper to taste

1. Rub roast with cut sides of garlic.
2. Combine remaining ingredients.
Sprinkle over roast. Place roast, fat side up,
on rack in shallow roasting pan. Insert meat
thermometer so that tip is in center of
thickest part of pork.
3. Roast uncovered at 325° until
temperature reaches 170°, about 2-2 1/2 hours.
Allow to sit 15-20 minutes before carving.

I can remember when we needed a
physic our mother would send us up
to the drugstore to get a mix of castor
oil and cherry soda. I can't drink
cherry soda to this day because of
that!

— Doris Johnson,
a member of Bethel AMEC,
Lancaster, PA

Barbecued Spareribs

Willie Jean Murray

Makes 6-8 servings

1 tsp. minced garlic
2 medium onions, chopped fine
1/4 cup vegetable oil
6-oz. can tomato paste
1/2 cup white vinegar
1 tsp. salt
1 tsp. dried basil or thyme
1/2 cup honey
1/4 cup Worcestershire sauce
1 tsp. dry mustard
1/2 can beef stock
4 lbs. ribs

1. In skillet saute garlic and onions 3-4
minutes in oil without letting onion brown.
2. Combine tomato paste and vinegar. Add
to skillet.
3. Stir in salt, basil or thyme, honey,
Worcestershire sauce, mustard, and beef
stock. Mix well. Simmer over low heat,
uncovered, for 10-15 minutes. Remove from
heat.
4. Place ribs, fat side up, on rack in
shallow roasting pan. With pastry brush,
cover ribs with sauce.
5. Bake at 400° for 45-60 minutes. Baste
frequently. When brown and crisp, cut into
individual portions and serve.

Spareribs

Makes 6-8 servings

6 lbs. pork spareribs
1 tsp. salt
1 tsp. freshly ground black pepper
6-oz. can tomato juice
1 medium onion, finely chopped
½ cup cider vinegar
½ cup firmly packed dark brown sugar
¼ cup vegetable oil
1 Tbsp. Worcestershire sauce
1 tsp. dry mustard

1. Season ribs with salt and pepper. Place in a large, flat (17" x 12" is an ideal size) roasting pan.
2. Combine remaining ingredients. Mix well. Pour over ribs, coating well.
3. Cover with heavy duty aluminum foil. Refrigerate 3-8 hours.
4. Uncover and bake at 350° for 60 minutes. Tent with foil near end of baking time if ribs begin to get too brown.
5. Cut ribs into 2-3 rib sections before serving. Serve with sauce from pan.

Spicy Ribs

Makes 15-18 servings

8 lbs. spareribs
water
2 Tbsp. vinegar
3 8-oz. cans tomato sauce
½ cup chicken stock or broth
½ cup minced onion
3 Tbsp. Worcestershire sauce
3 Tbsp. packed brown sugar
2 Tbsp. honey
1 Tbsp. lemon juice
1 garlic clove, minced
2 tsp. dry mustard
1½-3 tsp. chili powder
1 tsp. salt

1. Place spareribs in large stockpot. Cover with water, mixed with 2 Tbsp. vinegar. Simmer for about 15 minutes. Set aside until sauce is ready.
2. Meanwhile, combine all other ingredients in saucepan. Bring to boil. Reduce heat. Simmer uncovered for 30 minutes.
3. Brush ribs with sauce. Grill 45 minutes or until tender, basting and turning frequently.
4. Separate ribs into serving portions with scissors.
5. Serve with remaining basting sauce.

Note: Ribs may also be prepared in the oven. Place parboiled ribs on rack over baking sheet. Brush with sauce. Bake at 425° for 45-60 minutes, basting and turning frequently.

Baked Ham

Carletha Akins

Makes 30 or more servings

8-10-lb. precooked ham
whole cloves
12 maraschino cherries
1 cup light brown sugar
1-lb. can sliced pineapples, drained (juice
   reserved)
20-oz. bottle ginger ale

1. If ham has a skin, use a sharp knife to cut around edge of skin; then pull it off gently. Place meat in shallow roaster.
2. Score ham in diamond pattern. Insert whole clove at each juncture.
3. Cover ham with pineapple slices. Place one cherry in center of each slice. Secure each cherry with a toothpick.
4. In small saucepan, dissolve brown sugar in pineapple juice. Cook, stirring constantly, until smooth. Spoon half over ham.
5. Add half bottle of ginger ale. Cover meat with foil.
6. Bake at 300° for 70 minutes, basting often with remaining juice and ginger ale.
7. Remove foil. Bake an additional 20 minutes, continuing to baste.
8. To serve, cut ham lengthwise and then cut each half in slices. Serve with basting broth.

Grilled Lamb Chops

Makes 6-8 servings

6-8 thickly cut lamb chops
1 tsp. dried oregano
1/4 cup olive oil
1/4 -1/2 tsp. cayenne pepper
salt to taste
1 Tbsp. dried mint
2 lemons, juiced
2 Tbsp. white wine
1 tsp. soy sauce

1. Trim fat from lamb chops. Wash and pat dry. Place in deep dish.
2. Combine remaining ingredients. Pour over lamb chops, coating lamb on all sides. Cover and refrigerate at least 1 hour.
3. Grill or broil lamb chops for 2-3 minutes on each side. Lamb should be tender, but not pink.

Grecian Lamb

Carletha Akins

Makes 6 servings

1 tsp. dried thyme
1 tsp. salt
2 tsp. dried oregano
2 Tbsp. finely chopped fresh dillweed
2 bay leaves, crushed
1 small hot red pepper, crushed
3-4 cloves garlic, crushed
1/4 cup finely chopped green pepper
1 1/4-1 1/2 cups finely chopped onion
6-oz. can tomato paste
1 cup dry white wine
6 rib lamb chops

1. Combine all ingredients except chops.
Mix well.
2. Place chops in shallow baking dish.
Brush sauce over chops. Marinate 8-10 hours.
3. Bake at 375° for 45-50 minutes.

Marinated Lamb Chops

Clara Green

Makes 4 servings

2 Tbsp. French dressing
1 Tbsp. Worcestershire sauce
1/4 tsp. garlic powder
1/4 tsp. black pepper
1/4 tsp. dried thyme
4 shoulder lamb chops

1. Combine all ingredients except lamb
chops.
2. Brush on chops.
3. Cover and refrigerate for at least 8 hours.
4. Broil until done.

Garlic Herb Lamb Kabobs

Rina Mckee

Makes 4-6 servings

2-lb. boneless leg of lamb, cut into 1"
   cubes
1 Tbsp. minced garlic
2 tsp. dried oregano
2 tsp. dried rosemary
1/4 cup olive oil
1/4 cup lemon juice
3/4 cup red wine
onions, peeled and quartered
mushrooms
bell peppers, cut into squares

1. Combine lamb, garlic, oregano,
rosemary, olive oil, lemon juice, and red wine
in large, heavy plastic bag. Close tightly and
knead until well mixed. Refrigerate for 8
hours, turning often.
2. Remove meat from bag. Alternate meat
and vegetables on skewers.
3. Broil or grill lamb and vegetables for 12-
15 minutes, turning and basting often.

Broiled Shrimp Au Porto

Doris Kelly

Makes 6-8 servings

2 lbs. large shrimp
1½ cups white port wine
3 Tbsp. olive oil
juice of 1 lemon
2 shallots, minced
1 clove garlic, minced
1 Tbsp. Worcestershire sauce
½ tsp. salt
¼ tsp. dried oregano
pinch of dried thyme
pinch of cayenne pepper

1. Split shrimp down the back but do not peel. Remove and discard the black vein.
2. Combine remaining ingredients. Pour over shrimp. Marinate in refrigerator for 8 hours.
3. Place shrimp in single layer in broiler pan. Broil 2-3 minutes on each side, until they just turn pink. Serve shrimp in shells.

Garlic Shrimp

Makes 3-4 main-dish servings

¾ lb. large shrimp, peeled and deveined
3 Tbsp. olive oil
1½ tsp. garlic, minced
⅛ tsp. crushed red pepper flakes
dash salt
chopped parsley

1. Cook shrimp in oil until just pink.
2. Add garlic, crushed pepper, and salt.
3. Remove skillet from flame and let sit for 4 minutes, allowing shrimp to absorb the flavor of the seasonings.
4. Return pan to medium-low burner. Reheat for 2 minutes.
5. Garnish with parsley.

Their routes were many and varied, they often traveled in disguise, through woods and farms, by wagon, boat and train, hiding in stables and attics and storerooms, and fleeing through secret passages, but the destination they sought was always freedom.

— Charles Blockson, *Hippogreen Guide to the Underground Railroad*

Shrimp Bake

Makes 4-6 servings

2½ lbs. unpeeled large or jumbo shrimp
2 lemons, thinly sliced
2 onions, thinly sliced
⅔ cup (10⅔ Tbsp.) butter or margarine,
    melted
⅓ cup lemon juice
½ cup Worcestershire sauce
2 tsp. salt
½ tsp. coarsely ground pepper
¾ tsp. dried rosemary
pinch of ground red pepper
1-2 tsp. hot sauce, according to your
    preference
3 garlic cloves, minced
fresh rosemary sprigs

1. Rinse shrimp with cold water. Drain
well.
2. Layer shrimp, lemon slices, and onion
slices in ungreased 9″ x 13″ baking dish.
3. Combine butter, lemon juice,
Worcestershire sauce, salt, pepper, dried
rosemary, red pepper, hot sauce, and garlic.
Pour over shrimp.
4. Bake uncovered at 400° for 20-25
minutes, or until shrimp turn pink, basting
occasionally with juices.
5. Garnish with rosemary sprigs.

Sweet & Sour Shrimp

Makes 6-8 servings

21-oz. can cherry pie filling
3 Tbsp. firmly packed brown sugar
3 Tbsp. vinegar
1 tsp. ground ginger
1 green pepper, sliced in thin strips
8-oz. can sliced water chestnuts, well
    drained
1 lb. peeled and cooked medium shrimp
hot cooked rice

1. Combine pie filling, brown sugar,
vinegar, and ginger. Mix well.
2. Add green pepper, water chestnuts, and
shrimp. Mix just to combine.
3. Cover with waxed paper. Microwave 4-5
minutes on high, stirring 2-3 times.
4. Pour over rice in serving dish.

Frog legs! We used to catch frogs.
Those legs are expensive now, but
back then we were just eating!
— Frances Morant,
Brothers & Sisters Cafe

Shrimp and Mushrooms with Paprika Sauce

Sonya Gibson

Makes 4 servings

1/2 lb. fresh mushrooms, sliced thin
3 Tbsp. finely chopped shallots
salt to taste
pepper to taste
2 Tbsp. butter
1 tsp. paprika
3/4 cup dry cooking sherry
1 cup heavy cream
1/4 tsp. dried hot red pepper flakes
24 large shrimp (about 1 1/2 lbs.), peeled
    and deveined
1/4 cup sour cream
juice from half a lemon

1. Saute mushrooms, shallots, salt, and pepper in butter. Sprinkle with paprika. Cook, stirring for 1 minute.
2. Add sherry. Cook over relatively high heat for 5 minutes, stirring constantly until sherry is almost evaporated.
3. Stir in cream. Cook for 1 minute.
4. Add pepper flakes and shrimp. Cook, stirring gently for 1 minute.
5. Stir in sour cream and lemon juice. Bring to boil. Remove from heat and let stand 5 minutes before serving.
6. Serve over cooked pasta.

Shrimp Newburg

Addison Lockett

Makes 3-4 servings

2 Tbsp. butter
2 Tbsp. flour
1/2 cup milk
2 hard-boiled eggs
salt to taste
pepper to taste
1/4 cup sherry
2 cups cooked shrimp

1. In saucepan, melt butter. Stir in flour until smooth. Over low heat, stir in milk until smooth, continuing to stir until mixture thickens.
2. Cut up egg whites finely. (Use yolks in another dish.) Add chopped whites to milk sauce.
3. Stir in salt, pepper, sherry, and shrimp.
4. Serve over hot rice.

Chafing Dish A La Newburg

Bernadette Dabney

Makes 12-16 servings

6 Tbsp. butter
6 Tbsp. flour
3 egg yolks
3 cups milk
salt to taste
red pepper to taste
1 lb. small shrimp, cooked
1 lb. crabmeat, flaked
1 lb. lobster meat, cut up and cooked

1. Melt butter in double boiler.
2. Add flour and eggs. Mix well.
3. Stir in milk and seasonings. Cook over medium heat until thickened.
4. Stir in seafood. Heat until warm.
5. Serve over melba toast, patty shells, or rice.

> My train never ran off the track, and I never lost a passenger.
> — Harriet Tubman, the woman called "Moses"

Oven-Fried Fillets of Sole

Rev. Walter Price

Makes 4 servings

1 lb. fresh sole or other mild white fish fillets
1 Tbsp. vegetable oil
4 Tbsp. oven frying mix

1. Rinse fish. Pat dry. Lightly coat both sides with oil.
2. Sprinkle oven frying mix on shallow platter. Coat oiled fish with crumbs. Arrange in single layer on shallow nonstick baking pan or greased cookie sheet.
3. Bake at 425° for 8-10 minutes.

Oven Frying Mix:
1 1/2 cups unseasoned bread crumbs
1/2 cup flour
1/2 tsp. pepper
2 tsp. celery salt
2 tsp. onion salt
2 tsp. paprika

Combine ingredients. Store in airtight container.

Mushroom-Stuffed Flounder

Makes 4 servings

2 lbs. flounder
salt to taste
pepper to taste
1/4 cup chopped scallions or onions
1 cup chopped mushrooms
1 tsp. oil
1/8 tsp. thyme
1 Tbsp. chopped parsley
1 tsp. lemon juice
1/2 tsp. lemon zest
2 tsp. oil

1. Sprinkle flounder on both sides with salt and pepper.
2. Saute onions and mushrooms in 1 tsp. oil for 5 minutes.
3. Stir in thyme. Spread mixture over flounder.
4. Roll fish up jelly-roll fashion. Fasten with toothpicks. Sprinkle with parsley, lemon juice, and zest, and 2 tsp. oil.
5. Bake at 400° for 15-20 minutes.

Baked Flounder Fillets in Cheese Sauce

Makes 6 servings

10 1/2-oz. can condensed cheddar cheese
   soup
1 soup can of milk
1/4 cup chopped fresh parsley, or 2 Tbsp.
   dried parsley
1 Tbsp. capers
1 Tbsp. paprika
6 flounder fillets, or any other white fish
2 Tbsp. butter

1. Combine soup, milk, parsley, capers, and paprika.
2. Pour into shallow baking dish. Top with flounder. Dot with butter.
3. Bake at 375° for 25 minutes.

Grilled Salmon with Lemon and Herb Butter

Rina Mckee

Makes 4 servings

3 Tbsp. butter, softened
1 tsp. lemon juice
1/2 tsp. lemon zest
1 tsp. chopped fresh chives
1 tsp. chopped fresh parsley
2 12-oz. salmon fillets

1. Place butter, lemon juice, zest, and herbs in food processor. Pulse until well blended. Place in parchment paper or plastic wrap. Shape into log and roll up. Refrigerate for at least 30 minutes.
2. Cut each salmon fillet into two portions. Grill.
3. Cut butter "log" into 4 slices.
4. Divide salmon among 4 plates. Immediately top each with a butter circle and serve.

Baked Salmon

Makes 3-4 servings

14¾-oz. can red salmon
½ cup bread crumbs, divided
½ Tbsp. grated or finely chopped celery
½ Tbsp. grated or finely chopped onion
3 Tbsp. butter
2 tsp. flour
½ cup milk

1. Drain salmon of juice and remove skin and bones.
2. Crumble half the salmon into an 8″-square greased baking dish. Top with a layer of half the bread crumbs. Repeat those two layers.
3. Sprinkle onions and celery over the top.
4. Melt butter in small saucepan. Stir in flour. Add milk and heat until thickened. Pour over casserole.
5. Bake at 350° until brown, about 20-30 minutes.

Salmon or Tuna Loaf

Makes 4-6 servings

1 Tbsp. lemon juice
1-lb. can salmon
¾ cup medium white sauce (see below)
½ cup milk
½ tsp. salt
1 egg, beaten
½ cup chopped celery
1 cup dry bread crumbs

1. Flake salmon with fork. Combine with lemon juice.
2. Mix together remaining ingredients. Add to salmon.
3. Form into loaf and place in greased loaf pan.
4. Bake at 350° for 30 minutes, until browned.

Medium White Sauce
1½ Tbsp. butter or margarine
1½ Tbsp. flour
scant ¼ tsp. salt
¾ cup milk

1. Melt butter. Stir in flour and salt and mix together until smooth.
2. Cook until mixture bubbles.
3. Slowly whisk in milk, stirring constantly until smooth and thickened.

Salmon Loaf

Nancy Perkins

Makes 6-8 servings

2 lbs. canned salmon
2 cups soft bread crumbs
1/2 cup finely chopped celery
1/3 cup chopped parsley
2 eggs, slightly beaten
1/2 cup evaporated milk
1/3 cup fresh or bottled lemon juice
1/4 cup melted butter
1 tsp. salt
1 tsp. Worcestershire sauce
parsley sprigs
hard-boiled eggs

1. Drain and flake fish.
2. Combine all ingredients except parsley and eggs. Pat into 9" x 5" loaf pan or 1½-qt. casserole.
3. Bake at 375° for 35-40 minutes, or until firm.
4. Garnish with parsley sprigs and sliced eggs.

Crab Cakes

Makes 4 servings

1 lb. crabmeat
1 egg, slightly beaten
1/2 cup bread crumbs
1 Tbsp. finely chopped green pepper
1 Tbsp. chopped onion
1/4 cup mayonnaise, or more if needed to
    hold ingredients together
1 Tbsp. prepared mustard
1 Tbsp. lemon juice
salt to taste
pepper to taste
butter or margarine

1. Slightly flake crabmeat.
2. Add remaining ingredients.
3. Form into cakes and brown on both sides in butter or margarine.

> Sing! I say they did sing. Sing about the cooking and about the milking and sing in the field.
> — Hannah Hancock
>
> *We raise the wheat,*
>   *they give us the corn;*
> *We bake the bread,*
>   *they give us the crust;*
> *We sift the meal,*
>   *they give us the skin;*
> *And that's the way*
>   *They take us in . . .*
>
> — song lyric

87

Deviled Crab

Minnie Wilson

Makes 4-6 servings

4 Tbsp. (1/2 stick) margarine or butter
2 Tbsp. flour
1 Tbsp. chopped parsley
2 tsp. lemon juice
1 tsp. prepared mustard
1/2 tsp. horseradish
1 tsp. salt
2 cups crabmeat
2 hard-boiled eggs, cut up fine
6 crab shells
1/2 cup buttered bread crumbs

1. Melt margarine in saucepan. Stir in flour until smooth. Add remaining ingredients except shells and bread crumbs. Mix well.
2. Divide mixture among crab shells. Sprinkle each with bread crumbs.
3. Bake at 400° for 10 minutes.

Baked Oysters Italian Style

Nancy Perkins

Makes 6 servings

2 bunches green onions, tops and bottoms finely chopped
1 1/4 cups cracker crumbs
3/4 cup grated Parmesan cheese
1/3 tsp. salt
1/2 cup olive oil or less
1 qt. oysters, drained and patted dry

1. Coat bottom of baking dish with thin layer of olive oil.
2. Combine onions, cracker crumbs, cheese, and salt. Generously sprinkle a portion over bottom of pan.
3. Place layer of oysters over crackers. Sprinkle with crumb mixture. Repeat until oysters and crumbs are used up, ending with crumbs on top. Stream olive oil over entire top.
4. Bake at 375° for 45 minutes, or until juices are thickened and casserole is golden brown.

Ham Barbecue

Marian L. Mosser

Makes 4 sandwiches

1/4 cup vinegar
2 Tbsp. water
2 Tbsp. grape jelly
1/2 tsp. paprika
2 Tbsp. light brown sugar
dash of pepper
half a standard-sized bottle of ketchup
1/2 tsp. dry mustard
1 lb. chipped boiling ham

1. Combine all ingredients except ham. Cook for 2 minutes.
2. Stir in ham. Heat to boiling.
3. Serve on buns.

Grilled Meat Sticks

Nancy Perkins

Makes 4-6 servings

12-oz. can luncheon meat
1/3 cup honey
1/2 cup vinegar
1/4 cup salad oil
1 tsp. dry mustard
1/2 tsp. ground cloves

1. Cut luncheon meat into six finger-shaped sticks. Put in single layer in small dish.
2. Combine remaining ingredients. Mix well. Pour over meat. Refrigerate at least 2 hours, turning meat several times.
3. Grill over hot coals until browned on all sides, basting frequently.

Run away from Joseph Coleman in the Great Valley in Chester County, a Negro Man, named Tom, aged about 30 years, of middle stature, HE SPEAKS VERY GOOD ENGLISH, having on a white Shirt, Stockings and Shoes, a great riding Coat tyed round him with blew Girdles.
— *The American Weekly Mercury* (Philadelphia), July 11, 1723

To be Sold, Three Very likely Negro Girls being about 16 years of age, and a Negro Boy about 14, SPEAKING GOOD ENGLISH, enquire of the Printer hereof.
— *The American Weekly Mercury* (Philadelphia), June 20, 1723.

A likely Negro Boy about 14 Years of Age, country born, CAN SPEAK DUTCH OR ENGLISH, to be sold: Enquire of Printer hereof.
— *The New York Gazette,* revived in the *Weekly Post-Boy,* Feb. 26, 1750

RAN - AWAY from Luykas Joh. Wyngaard, of the City of Albany, Merchant, a certain Negro Man named Simon, of a middle size, a slender spry Fellow, has a handsome smooth Face, and thick Legs; SPEAKS VERY GOOD ENGLISH: Had on when he went away a blue Cloth Great Coat.
— *The New York Gazette,* revived in the *Weekly Post-Boy,* Feb 25, 1750

Swing Low

Swing low, sweet chariot,
Coming for to carry me home,
Swing low, sweet chariot,
Coming for to carry me home.

I looked over Jordan, and what did I see,
Coming for to carry me home?
A band of angels coming after me,
Coming for to carry me home.

If you get there before I do,
Coming for to carry me home,
Tell all my friends I'm coming too,
Coming for to carry me home.

I'm sometimes up, I'm sometimes down,
Coming for to carry me home;
But still my soul feels heavenly bound,
Coming for to carry me home.

This spiritual was a favorite of Harriet Tubman. She reportedly sang this song on her deathbed.

Vegetables

Gardening was my mother's favorite pastime, and ours, because we knew that soon the garden would be bursting with fresh tomatoes on the vine (my favorite — a tomato in one hand and a salt shaker in the other), cucumbers, carrots, turnips, string beans, melons, and strawberries, just to name a few. My mother loved a bountiful harvest, and she would often sing when she worked, not unlike the enslaved Africans who labored in the fields, stables, and the Big House.

Singing was medicine to get through the misery and the pain. It was also a way to pace oneself while working. Most importantly, singing allowed open communication from African to African, sharing stories, giving valuable information. "Swing low, sweet chariot . . . I ain't got long to stay here."

— Phoebe Bailey

Vegetables — Traditional

Black-Eyed Peas

Makes 6-8 servings

1 lb. dried black-eyed peas
skin from a smoked ham, or 2-oz. slab
    bacon, diced
1/4 cup pork-ribs drippings, fried
    chicken drippings, or bacon
    drippings
3/4-1 tsp. salt
1/4-1/2 tsp. black pepper
1/2 tsp. sugar

1. Pick over peas to remove stones and
dirt. Rinse well. Soak in cold water for
20 minutes. Drain well.
2. Combine all ingredients in large
pot. Add cold water to cover peas by 1
inch.
3. Heat to simmering. Cover. Cook
about 1½ hours, until peas are tender
but still hold their shape. Add more
water if needed.
4. Remove ham skin, if used, before
serving.

Hoppin John

Carrie Alford

Makes 4-6 servings

1 cup dried black-eyed peas
1/2 lb. salt pork, cut into 1/2" cubes
half an onion, chopped
half a hot red pepper, seeded and
    coarsely chopped
1 cup uncooked long-grain rice
1 tsp. salt
1/8 tsp. pepper

1. Sort and wash peas. Place in Dutch
oven. Cover with water 2 inches above
peas. Let soak overnight. Drain peas and
return to Dutch oven.
2. Add salt pork, onion, and red
pepper to peas. Add enough water to
cover ingredients. Cover cooking pot and
bring to boil. Reduce heat and simmer 1
hour.
3. Stir in remaining ingredients. Bring
to boil. Reduce heat and simmer 20
minutes.
4. Check if mixture is creamy in
texture. If it is drier than that, add 2 cups
water so rice has enough liquid to cook
tender.
5. Continue cooking another 10
minutes. When rice and peas are both
tender, remove from heat and serve with
cornbread and collard greens.

Hominy Grits

Makes 8 servings

4 cups water
1 cup quick grits
2 eggs, separated
1/2 cup heavy cream
1 tsp. salt
1/4 tsp. pepper

1. Bring water to boil. Pour grits into boiling water. Cover. Cook over low heat for 5 minutes. Set aside to cool.
2. Pour 2 cups cooked and cooled grits into large bowl. Beat with wooden spoon until smooth.
3. Beat egg yolks with wooden spoon. (Reserve egg whites.) Stir into grits.
4. Add cream, salt, and pepper.
5. Whip eggs whites until they form stiff peaks, approximately 5 minutes. Gently fold into grits mixture until well blended. Spoon mixture into greased casserole dish.
6. Bake at 375° for 90 minutes, or until golden brown.

Southern Cooked Green Peas

Carrie Alford

Makes 6 servings

3 cups shelled, fresh green peas, cleaned (about 3 lbs. unshelled)
1 cup water
1/4 lb. salt pork
1/2 tsp. salt
2 Tbsp. butter, optional

1. Combine green peas, water, salt pork, and salt in a small saucepan. Bring to a boil.
2. Reduce heat. Cover and simmer 25 minutes, or until peas are tender. Drain.
3. Add butter, if desired, and toss lightly.

For racism to die, a totally different America must be born.
— Kwame Ture
(Stokely Carmichael)

Peas and Okra

Brothers and Sisters Cafe

Makes 8-10 servings

4 cups field peas
4-5 cups water
1 Tbsp. salt
¼ tsp. black pepper
¼ lb. salt pork
1 tsp. sugar, optional
8-10 small, tender, fresh okra, each
  about 2"-4" long

1. Combine all ingredients, except okra, in large stockpot. Bring to boil. Reduce heat to simmer. Cook 15 minutes.
2. Add okra. Cook 15 minutes longer.

> As a people, our most cherished and valuable achievements are the achievements of spirit.
> — Molefikete Asante

Fried Okra

1 lb. okra, tender and each about
  2"-4" long
4 Tbsp. vegetable oil, divided
2 tsp. salt, or to taste
2 tsp. black pepper, freshly ground

1. Wash okra in cold water and drain. Remove stems and cut okra into ½-inch chunks.
2. Heat 2 Tbsp. oil in large heavy skillet over medium heat. Add half the okra and spread evenly over the bottom of the skillet with a spatula. Sprinkle with salt and pepper. Fry, turning the okra with a metal spatual to cook evenly, until tender, crispy, and well browned, about 10 minutes.
3. Remove okra and drain on paper towels, keeping warm until ready to serve.
4. Repeat with remaining oil and okra. Serve hot.

Pan-Fried Okra

Carrie Alford

Makes 4-6 servings

1 pound okra, tender and each 2"-4"
   long, cleaned
3/4 cup cornmeal
1/2 tsp. salt
vegetable oil

1. Cut okra crosswise into 1/2-inch slices; set aside.
2. Combine cornmeal and salt.
3. Dredge sliced okra in cornmeal mixture.
4. Cook in 1/2 inch oil over high heat until lightly browned, stirring occasionally.
5. Drain. Serve immediately.

Batter-Fried Okra

Carrie Alford

Makes 4-6 servings

1 pound small fresh okra, cleaned
   with stems removed
1 tsp. salt
1/4 tsp. pepper
4 eggs, beaten
2 1/2 cups fine, dry bread crumbs
vegetable oil

1. Cut okra into 2-inch-chunks and place in medium saucepan. Cover with water. Bring to boil. Reduce heat, cover, and simmer for 5 minutes. Drain well.
2. Sprinkle okra with salt and pepper.
3. Dip in egg. Roll in bread crumbs.
4. Deep-fry in hot oil until golden rown. Drain well on paper towels.

Southern Cooked Butter Beans

Carrie Alford

Makes 2-3 servings

2 cups shelled fresh butter beans
2 cups water
2 Tbsp. butter or margarine
1 Tbsp. bacon drippings
1/2 tsp. salt

1. Combine all ingredients in saucepan. Cover.
2. Cook over medium heat for 45 minutes, or until tender, but with beans still holding their shape.

Dry Lima Beans

Edna Hardrick

Makes 6-8 servings

1-lb. pkg. dry lima beans
3 pig knuckles
1 medium onion, chopped
1/4 tsp. dill weed
salt to taste
pepper to taste

1. Soak beans as directed on package.
2. Cover pig knuckles with water and cook in large stockpot for 45 minutes.
3. Drain beans of their soaking water and add beans, onions, and dill to knuckles and broth. Cook until beans are soft, adding water as needed.
4. Season with salt and pepper.
5. Serve with cornbread.

Southern Cooked Dried Lima Beans

Carrie Alford

Makes 6 servings

2 cups dried lima beans (soaked and
    drained)
4½ cups water
¼ lb. salt pork, sliced
1 tsp. salt
½ tsp. pepper

   1. Combine all ingredients in large
saucepan. Bring to boil.
   2. Reduce heat. Cover and simmer for
2½ hours, or until beans are tender.

Fried Sweet Potatoes

Carrie Alford

Makes 6 servings

4 medium-sized sweet potatoes,
    cleaned and peeled
water
½ tsp. salt
⅓ cup bacon dripping
2 Tbsp. sugar

   1. Slice potatoes into slices ¼ inch
thick. Place in bowl, cover with water,
and stir ½ tsp. salt into water. Let soak
for 30 minutes, then drain.
   2. Heat bacon drippings in large
skillet. Add potato slices. Cook until
tender and golden brown, turning once.
Drain on paper towels.
   3. Sprinkle with sugar.

Candied Yams

Makes 10 servings

2 lbs. fresh yams, peeled and sliced
    ¼" thick
1 cup water
1 tsp. vanilla extract
4 Tbsp. (½ stick) unsalted butter,
    softened
½ cup granulated sugar, or more to
    taste
½ cup brown sugar, or more to taste
½ tsp. ground cinnamon
½ tsp. allspice
1 cup raisins
2 cups pineapple chunks, drained

   1. Place the yams in a greased 12" x
12" baking pan.
   2. Combine water and vanilla. Pour
over yams.
   3. Combine butter, sugars, cinnamon,
and allspice. Sprinkle over yams.
   4. Cover tightly. Bake at 400° for 45
minutes.
   5. Sprinkle raisins and pineapple
chunks over yams. Baste with the juices
in the pan. Cover.
   6. Continue baking about 20 minutes,
or until yams are tender and juices are
bubbling. Serve hot.

Fried New Potatoes

Carrie Alford

Makes 4 servings

4 slices bacon
1 lb. new potatoes, scrubbed, peeled,
  and cooked until just tender
1/2 tsp. salt
dash of pepper

1. Cook bacon in a large skillet until crisp. Remove bacon from skillet, reserving drippings. Drain bacon on paper towels, then crumble and set aside.
2. Cook potatoes in bacon drippings for 10 minutes, or until browned, turning frequently. Drain.
3. Place potatoes in serving dish. Sprinkle with salt, pepper, and crumbled bacon.

Fried Cabbage and Bacon

Makes 8-10 servings

1/2 lb. sliced bacon
3-lb. cabbage head
1/2 cup water
1 Tbsp. sugar
1 1/2 tsp. salt
1/4 tsp. freshly ground black pepper

1. In 4-quart stockpot, cook bacon over medium heat until crisp. Remove bacon and drain, but reserve drippings.
2. Cut cabbage into 1-inch-thick wedges. Add to bacon drippings. Cook for about 3 minutes, stirring constantly, until cabbage begins to brown.
3. Add water, sugar, salt, and pepper. Cover and cook about 10 minutes, until cabbage is tender.
4. Crumble bacon onto cabbage. Serve warm.

Note: Reduce the amount of bacon to 3-4 slices. You'll benefit from the bacon flavoring, but with fewer calories.

Fried Green Tomatoes

Makes 4 servings

2 large green tomatoes, unpeeled
1 egg, beaten with 1 Tbsp. water
3/4 cup dry bread crumbs, lightly
    salted
3 Tbsp. bacon fat or vegetable oil

1. Cut tomatoes into slices that are a little over 1/4 inch thick.
2. Dip tomato slices in egg-water mixture. Coat with bread crumbs.
3. Fry in hot oil over medium heat until golden brown on both sides and tender throughout.
4. Drain on paper towels.

If the white people can give festivals to raise funds for the relief of suffering soldiers, why should not the well-to-do colored people go to work to do something for the benefit of the suffering blacks? I made a suggestion in the colored church, that a society of colored people be formed to labor for the benefit of the unfortunate freedmen . . . and in two weeks "the Contraband Relief Association" was organized with forty working members.
— Elizabeth Keckley

Pan-Fried Green Tomatoes

Carrie Alford

Makes 4 servings

1/2 cup flour
1/2 tsp. salt
1/4 tsp. pepper
2 large green tomatoes, cut into
    1/2"-thick slices
1/4 cup (1/2 stick) butter or margarine
2 Tbsp. plus 2 tsp. brown sugar,
    divided

1. Combine flour, salt, and pepper.
2. Dredge tomato slices in flour mixture.
3. Melt butter in large skillet. Fry tomato slices on one side until browned. Remove from skillet, and place in 9" x 13" x 2" baking dish, browned side down.
4. Top each tomato slice with 1 tsp. brown sugar. Broil 3 inches from heat for 5 minutes, or until browned and bubbly.

Southern Cooked Rutabagas

Carrie Alford

Makes 4-6 servings

2-lb. rutabaga, peeled and cubed
3 cups water
1/4 lb. salt pork, rinsed and sliced
1 tsp. sugar
1/2 tsp. salt
1/8 tsp. pepper
additional pepper

1. Combine rutabaga, water, salt pork, sugar, and salt in large saucepan. Bring to a boil. Reduce heat. Simmer, uncovered, for 35 minutes, or until rutabaga is tender.
2. Drain. Remove and discard salt pork.
3. Add 1/8 tsp. pepper to rutabaga and mash to desired consistency. Sprinkle with additional pepper.

Glazed Honey Carrots

Nanette Akins

Makes 6-8 servings

3/4 tsp. salt
1 1/2 cups water
5-6 cups sliced carrots
1/2 cup honey
3 Tbsp. butter
1 1/2 tsp. lemon juice

1. Add salt to water and bring to boil.
2. Add carrots. Return to boil.
3. Add remaining ingredients. Reduce heat and cook until carrots are tender.

Harvard Beets

Carrie Alford

Makes 2-4 servings

1 lb. fresh beets
3 Tbsp. sugar
1 Tbsp. cornstarch
1/2 cup water
1/4 cup vinegar
1 Tbsp. butter or margarine
1/2 tsp. salt
fresh parsley sprigs

1. Trim beets and cut into chunks if large. Simmer over medium heat in a small amount of water until soft. Dice.
2. Combine sugar and cornstarch in medium saucepan. Mix well. Gradually add water, or liquid from cooking beets, stirring until smooth.
3. Add vinegar and butter. Constantly stir over medium heat until butter melts and sauce is thickened.
4. Stir in beets and salt. Cook for 5 minutes until thoroughly heated.
5. Garnish with parsley sprigs.

Vegetables — Other Favorites

Corn Pudding

Makes 6-8 servings

3 eggs, well beaten
2 cups corn, fresh or frozen
2 Tbsp. butter, melted
1 cup milk
1 cup cream
1/4 cup flour
1/2 tsp. salt
1/4 tsp. pepper

1. Fill 9" x 13" baking pan with an inch of water. Set in oven. Preheat oven to 325°.
2. Combine all ingredients. Pour into greased casserole dish. Place in baking pan of water in oven.
3. Bake uncovered for 75 minutes, or until knife inserted in center of casserole comes out clean.

Note: Substitute fat-free half-and-half for cream if you like.

Succotash

Makes 4-6 servings

10-oz. pkg. frozen baby lima beans
10-oz. pkg. frozen whole-kernel corn
16-oz. can tomatoes
1/2 cup chopped onions
2 Tbsp. margarine
salt to taste
pepper to taste
10-oz. pkg. frozen cut okra

1. Combine lima beans, corn, tomatoes, onions, margarine, salt, and pepper in 2-quart saucepan. Bring to a boil. Reduce heat and simmer 20 minutes.
2. Add okra and cook 10 minutes more.

My grandmother would can all week in the Mason jars. Tomatoes, green beans, peaches, and when she'd get them done she'd line them along the cellar way. You could smell it all outside when she'd be cooking.
— Sandra Polite Simms,
a member of Bethel AMEC,
Lancaster, PA

Collard Greens Sauteed

Makes 8-10 servings

3-4 lbs. collard greens
2 Tbsp. bacon drippings
large onion, chopped
half a firm ripe tomato, diced
salt to taste
pepper to taste
pinch of nutmeg

1. Trim stems off collards and discard. Wash leaves thoroughly. Slice into 1/4-inch strips. Blanch in boiling water for 30 minutes. Drain well.
2. In large skillet or saucepan, saute onion in drippings until tender.
3. Stir in tomato and cook until just tender.
4. Add collard greens. Stir until well coated. Cook until tender.
5. Stir in pinch of nutmeg.

Cheese Garlic Grits

Makes 6-8 servings

3 cups water
1 cup quick grits
1 tsp. salt (or less)
3 Tbsp. butter
1 cup shredded sharp cheddar cheese
2 large cloves garlic, pressed
2 eggs, beaten
1/4 cup milk
1/2 cup shredded sharp cheddar cheese

1. Bring water to boil in saucepan.
2. Add grits and salt. Reduce heat to simmer. Cook and stir for 4-5 minutes until thickened.

3. Stir in butter, 1 cup cheese, and garlic. Remove from heat.
4. Stir until butter and cheese are melted.
5. Stir in eggs and milk.
6. Pour into 1-qt. greased casserole. Sprinkle with remaining 1/2 cup cheese.
7. Bake at 350° for 45 minutes, or until set.

Mashed Sweet Potatoes

Makes 4-6 servings

2 lbs. sweet potatoes
2 Tbsp. butter, softened
8-oz. carton pineapple yogurt, pineapple orange yogurt, or mandarin orange yogurt, at room temperature
2 Tbsp. honey, optional
1/2 tsp. salt
dash of white pepper

1. Boil sweet potatoes in their skins until tender, about 45 minutes. Peel while potatoes are still hot.
2. Cut into chunks. Add butter. Mash until smooth.
3. Stir in yogurt, honey, salt, and pepper.
4. Serve.

101

Sweet Potato Pancakes

Mrs. Margaret Bailey

Makes 3 servings, or about 12 pancakes

1 cup sifted flour
1 tsp. baking powder
2 Tbsp. sugar
dash of cinnamon
dash of ground cloves
2/3 cup cooked, mashed sweet potatoes
1 Tbsp. margarine or butter, softened
1 egg, beaten
1-1 1/4 cups skim milk

1. Sift together flour, baking powder, sugar, cinnamon, and cloves.
2. In separate bowl combine sweet potatoes, margarine, egg, and milk until smooth and thoroughly blended. Add to dry ingredients. Mix until just blended.
3. For each pancake drop about 2 Tbsp. batter onto greased griddle. Cook until undersides are browned. Turn and brown on other side.
4. Serve with maple syrup or applesauce.

Our grandfathers had to run, run, run. My generation's out of breath. We ain't running no more.

— Kwame Ture
(Stokely Carmichael)

Horseradish Mashed Potatoes

Rina Mckee

Makes 6 servings

4 large potatoes
4 Tbsp. (1/2 stick) butter, softened
3/4 cup (or more) milk
salt to taste
white pepper to taste
1 1/4 Tbsp. prepared horseradish

1. Peel potatoes. Cut into pieces. Place in large saucepan and cover with water. Cook until soft. Drain and place in electric mixer bowl.
2. Add butter and half the milk. Whip on low. Gradually add remaining milk. Increase mixer speed and beat until smooth.
3. Add horseradish. Mix well.

Potatoes Pizziola

Nancy Perkins

Makes 6 servings

1" boiling water
1 tsp. salt
2 lbs. medium-sized potatoes, peeled
2 Tbsp. olive oil
2 Tbsp. tomato paste
2 1/2 cups chopped tomatoes
1 tsp. salt
1 tsp. dried basil
1 tsp. dried oregano
1/2 tsp. ground black pepper
1/4 tsp. garlic powder

1. Combine water and salt in saucepan. Bring to boil.

2. Add potatoes. Parboil for 15 minutes. Drain and cut into ⅛-inch slices. Set aside.

3. Heat olive oil. Stir in tomato paste, tomatoes, and seasonings. Cook 5 minutes.

4. Add potatoes. Cook 8-10 minutes, or until potatoes are tender.

5. Serve hot.

Oak Hill Potatoes

Rina Mckee

Makes 4 servings

1½ lbs. (4-5 medium-sized) potatoes
½ tsp. salt
2 hard-boiled eggs, peeled and sliced
small onion, diced
1 tsp. salt
¼-½ tsp. pepper
2 Tbsp. butter or margarine
4 Tbsp. flour
2 cups milk
1 Tbsp. butter or margarine
3 Tbsp. dried bread crumbs

1. Peel and dice potatoes. Place in large saucepan and cover with cold water. Add ½ tsp. salt. Bring to boil. Reduce heat to low and cook 20-25 minutes, or until potatoes are tender. Drain.

2. Combine potatoes, eggs, onion, salt, and pepper in lightly greased 1½-quart casserole.

3. Melt 2 Tbsp. butter in medium saucepan. Add flour and milk. Mix well. Cook, stirring constantly, until thickened. Add to ingredients in casserole. Blend lightly.

4. Melt remaining tablespoon of butter. Add bread crumbs. Mix well. Sprinkle over casserole.

5. Bake at 350° for 30 minutes, uncovered.

Scalloped Potatoes

Marlene Clark

4-6 servings

4 medium-sized potatoes
grated nutmeg
salt to taste
pepper to taste
flour
milk
grated cheese

1. Peel and thinly slice potatoes. Place a thin layer in buttered casserole dish.

2. Sprinkle with nutmeg, salt, pepper, and flour. Repeat until casserole is three-quarters full.

3. Pour enough milk down side of dish to just cover potatoes (pouring it directly in the center will make the flour float to the top).

4. Bake at 350° for 1 hour, or until potatoes are soft. Sprinkle with grated cheese. Return to oven for 15 minutes, uncovered.

Potato Pancakes

Makes 4-6 servings

2 lbs. raw potatoes, peeled and grated
1 onion, grated
1 cup boiling water
2 eggs
1 tsp. salt
½ tsp. freshly ground pepper
¼ cup flour, matzo meal, or
    cracker crumbs
½ cup oil
2 Tbsp. butter

1. Place potatoes and onions in strainer over bowl. Pour boiling water over them. Mix briefly to press out some moisture. (The boiling water will keep the potatoes from discoloring.)

2. Drain water from bowl, but leave starch from potatoes in bottom of bowl.

3. Beat eggs in separate bowl. Add potatoes, starchy sediment, salt, pepper, and flour (or meal or crumbs).

4. Place oil and butter in skillet. When hot, drop in potato mixture by heaping tablespoonfuls. Keep temperature of skillet low enough that pancakes cook through, but high enough that they get brown and crispy. When brown on one side, flip and brown other side.

5. Keep potatoes hot in 300° oven until all batter is used. Serve with applesauce as a side dish.

Flavorful Cooked Brown Rice

Mrs. Margaret Bailey

Makes 4-6 servings

1 cup brown rice
1 cup chicken broth
1 cup water

1. Combine ingredients. Bring to boil, stirring occasionally.

2. Reduce heat to simmer. Cover tightly and simmer 45-50 minutes, until liquid is absorbed. Fluff with fork before serving.

Easy Pilaf

Mrs. Margaret Bailey

Makes 6 servings

4-oz. can portabella, or regular,
    mushrooms, undrained
1 small carrot, shredded
3 Tbsp. minced onion
1 Tbsp. raisins
pinch of curry powder
pinch of cumin seeds
2 cups Flavorful Cooked Rice (above),
    or any cooked rice

1. Combine all ingredients except rice. Cover and simmer 3-4 minutes.

2. Add rice. Cover and place over low heat until heated through. Stir frequently to prevent rice from sticking to bottom of pan.

Bombay Rice Dressing

Mrs. Margaret Bailey

Makes 8 servings

3 cups Flavorful Cooked Rice (facing
  page), or any other cooked rice
1 unpared apple, shredded
1/2 cup chopped onions
1/2 cup finely minced celery
3 Tbsp. chopped parsley or cilantro
2 tsp. cumin seeds
1 tsp. curry powder
pinch of ground cinnamon
pinch of ground ginger
pinch of allspice
1/4 cup apple juice

1. Combine all ingredients except apple juice. Mix lightly.
2. Place in casserole. Pour apple juice over mixture and then cover.
3. Bake at 375° for 25 minutes.

Note: This can be used as a side dish, or as stuffing for roasted chicken.

Now I realize that my mother kept the family going with her prayer, much prayer. She used to have the three of us around her feet while she told stories about the Old Times. She'd read to us from a Little Red Riding Hood book and from the Bible. Of course, we didn't understand the "thee" and "thou," but we surely got the difference in living right or living wrong.
— Elizabeth McGill,
a member of Bethel AMEC,
Lancaster, PA

Glazed Carrots and Turnips

Makes 6 servings

3 Tbsp. butter
1 lb. white turnips
2 medium-sized carrots
1 cup chicken broth
1/2 tsp. salt, optional
1/4 tsp. white pepper
2 Tbsp. sugar
2 Tbsp. chopped parsley

1. Melt butter in large skillet.
2. Peel turnips and carrots. Slice both into julienne strips. Add to butter. Stir until coated.
3. Pour in broth. Cover and cook over medium heat 6 minutes.
4. Season with salt and pepper.
5. Increase heat to high. Cook uncovered 10 minutes, or until vegetables are tender and liquid is reduced and syrupy.
6. Sprinkle sugar over vegetables. Reduce heat to medium.
7. Stir the vegetables gently to distribute the sugar. Cover and cook for another minute. Remove from heat. Vegetables should be glazed and shiny.
8. Garnish with parsley.

Broccoli Casserole

Jean Townsend

Makes 6-8 servings

2 10-oz. pkgs. frozen broccoli, either spears
   or chopped
1/4 lb. (1 stick) butter, melted
1 lb. cottage cheese
2 eggs, beaten
5 Tbsp. flour
1/2 cup grated Swiss cheese
1/2 tsp. salt
pepper to taste

1. Steam broccoli until just tender. Place in 9" x 9" baking dish.
2. Combine butter, cottage cheese, eggs, flour, Swiss cheese, salt, and pepper. Pour over broccoli.
3. Bake at 350° for 45-60 minutes, or until edges are brown.

Broccoli Casserole

Lisa Bowman

Makes 8 servings

2 10-oz. pkgs. frozen chopped broccoli
2 eggs, well beaten
1 cup mayonnaise
1 medium-sized onion, chopped
dash of salt
dash of pepper
10 3/4-oz. can cream of mushroom soup
8-oz. can sliced water chestnuts
1 cup grated cheddar cheese
4 Tbsp. (1/2 stick) butter or margarine,
   melted
2/3 cup seasoned bread crumbs or stuffing
   cubes

1. Cook and drain broccoli. Set aside.
2. Combine eggs, mayonnaise, onion, salt, pepper, soup, and water chestnuts. Add broccoli and mix well. Pour into long greased baking dish.
3. Sprinkle with cheese.
4. Combine butter and crumbs. Spread over ingredients in pan.
5. Bake at 350° for 40-45 minutes.

Broccoli and Rice Casserole

Mattie Mae Roche

Makes 4-6 servings

10-oz. pkg. frozen chopped broccoli
3/4 cup chopped onions
3/4 cup chopped celery
4 Tbsp. (1/2 stick) butter or margarine
1 1/2 cups cooked rice
10 3/4-oz. can mushroom soup
8-oz. jar cheese spread

1. Cook broccoli until just tender. Drain.
2. Saute onions and celery in butter until clear.
3. Combine all ingredients. Pour into greased casserole dish.
4. Bake at 350° for 30 minutes.

I remember we ate sour grass. It had little leaves on it. And we used to eat white carrots. I don't know if they were really called carrots but they looked like carrots.

— Janet Gantz

Creamed Spinach Casserole

Dianne Prince

Makes 4-6 servings

2 10-oz. pkgs. frozen chopped spinach
10¾-oz. can cream of mushroom soup
4 Tbsp. (1/2 stick) butter
2 tsp. garlic salt
bread crumbs or cracker crumbs

1. Cook spinach according to package directions. Drain thoroughly.
2. Combine soup, butter, and salt in skillet. Cook for 3 minutes.
3. Add spinach. Mix well. Pour into greased casserole.
4. Top with bread or cracker crumbs.
5. Bake at 375° for 20-30 minutes, until heated through and lightly browned.

Stir-Fry Cabbage

Nanette Akins

Makes 4-6 servings

2 strips bacon, cut into squares
1/2 cup chopped onions
1/2 cup chopped green peppers
1 firm head white cabbage
1/2 tsp. garlic powder
1/4-1/2 tsp. black pepper, according to your taste preference
1/4-1/2 tsp. five-spice powder, according to your taste preference
2/3 cup water
2 Tbsp. soy sauce

1. Cook bacon in Dutch oven until soft.
2. Stir in onions and green peppers. Saute until clear.

3. Cut up cabbage coarsely. Rinse and drain. Add to Dutch oven. Mix well.
4. Sprinkle with garlic powder, pepper, and five-spice powder. Mix well.
5. Increase heat to high. Add water and soy sauce. Cover and steam quickly until cabbage is wilted. Serve immediately.

Italian Green Beans with Mushrooms

Makes 6 servings

2 slices bacon, cut in half
2 cups sliced fresh mushrooms
1/2 cup chopped onions
1 small garlic clove, minced
1/2-1 tsp. dried basil, according to your taste preference
10¾-oz. can condensed tomato soup, or 8-oz. can pureed tomatoes, or 1 cup fresh tomatoes, chopped
1/4 cup water
1-lb. pkg. frozen Italian green beans, cooked and drained
1/2 cup grated cheddar cheese

1. Fry bacon until crisp. Remove bacon, but reserve drippings.
2. In drippings, saute mushrooms, onions, garlic, and basil until mushrooms are brown and onions are tender.
3. Combine tomatoes and water. Add to pan. Stir in cooked beans. Heat, stirring often, until heated through.
4. Just before serving, garnish with cheese and top with crumbled bacon.

107

Zucchini Provencal

Nancy Perkins

Makes 2-3 servings

1 Tbsp. olive oil
2 cups sliced zucchini
1/2 tsp. minced garlic
1/2 cup sliced onions
1 Tbsp. chopped fresh basil

1. Heat oil in heavy skillet. Add zucchini, garlic, and onions. Cook until just soft.
2. Stir in basil. Cook for one minute; then serve.

Stuffed Zucchini

Makes 4 servings

4 large zucchini
1/2 lb. fresh mushrooms, sliced
1/4 cup (1/2 stick) butter
1/4 cup sour cream
salt to taste
pepper to taste
4 Tbsp. chopped parsley
4 Tbsp. firm dry bread crumbs
2 Tbsp. melted butter
Parmesan cheese

1. Cut zucchini into 2"-3" pieces. Cut each of those pieces in half lengthwise. Steam for 5 minutes. Scoop out centers, leaving each piece with a 1/4"-thick shell. Set aside.
2. Saute mushrooms in 1/4 cup butter. Stir in sour cream. Season with salt and pepper. Spoon into centers of squash pieces.

3. Combine parsley, bread crumbs, and 2 Tbsp. butter. Sprinkle over squash.
4. Bake at 350° for 20 minutes.
5. Sprinkle with Parmesan cheese.

Yellow Squash and Onions

Makes 4 servings

3-4 medium yellow squash
salt to taste
pepper to taste
1-2 medium onions, sliced thin
2-3 Tbsp. bacon drippings or butter

1. Cut squash into slices 1/4-inch thick. Sprinkle with salt and pepper.
2. Place 1/4-inch of water in heavy skillet. Bring to boil.
3. Add squash. Lay onion slices on top. Cover and steam over medium heat until water has evaporated, being careful not to burn the squash.
4. Add bacon drippings, stirring so that squash is well coated.
5. Cook, uncovered, over low heat for 30 minutes, or until tender, stirring occasionally.

Asparagus Frittata

Makes 4 servings

12 asparagus spears, cooked
8 eggs
2 Tbsp. grated onion
salt to taste
pepper to taste
1/2 tsp. Tabasco sauce
1 cup shredded Swiss cheese, divided
3 Tbsp. butter

1. Cut asparagus into 1 1/2" pieces.
2. Beat together eggs, onion, salt, pepper, and Tabasco until well blended.
3. Stir in asparagus and 3 Tbsp. grated cheese.
4. Melt butter over medium heat in 10" skillet. Pour in asparagus-egg mixture. Cook gently until eggs start to set, about 5 minutes.
5. Sprinkle with remaining cheese. Place under preheated medium broiler, about 6" from the flame, for about 1 1/2 minutes, until eggs are set and top is lightly browned.
6. Loosen edges of frittata with spatula. Slide onto plate.

> The person who strays away from the source is unrooted and is like dust blown about by the wind.
> — Molefikete Asante

Stir-Fried Asparagus with Snow Peas

Rev. Walter Price

Makes 4-5 servings

1 Tbsp. peanut oil
1 lb. fresh asparagus, cut diagonally in 1"-long pieces
1/2 lb. snow peas, ends and strings removed
3 Tbsp. rich chicken broth
1 Tbsp. soy sauce
2 Tbsp. lemon juice
1 tsp. sesame oil

1. Heat peanut oil in pan over high heat. Drop in asparagus and snow peas and stir-fry for several minutes, just until vegetables are well coated and shiny.
2. Combine broth, soy sauce, and lemon juice. Pour over vegetables in pan. Cover.
3. Cook on high, stirring occasionally for 4 minutes, or until liquid is gone.
4. Put vegetables in serving dish. Sprinkle with sesame oil. Serve hot.

Asparagus with Parmesan Cheese

Rev. Walter Price

Makes 6 servings

2 lbs. fresh asparagus
2/3 cup Parmesan cheese
5 Tbsp. butter, melted

1. Cook asparagus in salted water for 1-2 minutes. Plunge in cold water until chilled. Spread in bottom of cake pan.
2. Top with cheese and butter.
3. Bake at 350° for 10 minutes.

Creamed Asparagus

Willie Jean Murray

Makes 6-8 servings

2 lbs. fresh asparagus, trimmed and
** cooked until crisp-tender**
4 Tbsp. (1/2 stick) butter
4 Tbsp. flour
1 tsp. salt
2 cups milk
1 cup grated cheese
1 oz. chopped pimento
4 slices buttered bread, cut into cubes

1. Place asparagus in baking dish.
2. Melt butter in saucepan. Add flour and salt and blend until smooth. Gradually stir in cold milk. Cook, stirring constantly, until sauce boils and becomes thick and smooth. Add cheese and pimiento. When fully blended, pour over asparagus.
3. Top with buttered bread cubes. Bake at 350° until golden brown, about 15 minutes.

Asparagus Casserole

Rebecca Carter

Makes 6 servings

103/4-oz. can cream of mushroom soup
1 lb. fresh asparagus
1/4-1/2 lb. butter crackers
1 Tbsp. onion, grated
1/2 cup grated cheese
1/2 cup cracker crumbs

1. Cut asparagus into 2-inch lengths and cook until just tender. Reserve cooking liquid. Set asparagus aside.
2. Place soup in saucepan. Drain liquid from asparagus into soup. Heat slowly.
3. Place layer of crackers in buttered 2-quart baking dish. Add one-third of asparagus. Sprinkle with one-third grated onion. Repeat process for 2 more layers.
4. Pour soup over ingredients in casserole.
5. Spread cheese and cracker crumbs over top.
6. Bake at 375° for 15 minutes, or until soup bubbles and top turns slightly brown.

Creamed Vegetable Dish

Willie Jean Murray

Makes 8-10 servings

2 carrots, sliced
2 stalks celery, sliced
3 small onions, cut in bite-sized pieces
half a head of cabbage, cut in bite-sized
    pieces
1/2 tsp. salt
1/4 tsp. pepper
1/2 cup chopped ham
2 Tbsp. butter
2 Tbsp. flour
1/2 tsp. salt
1 cup milk
fresh parsley

1. Place carrots, celery, and onions in small amount of boiling water. Simmer until almost done.

2. Add cabbage. Continue to cook until all vegetables are soft. Drain. Place in serving dish and keep warm.

3. Sprinkle with salt, pepper, and ham, and stir through.

4. While vegetables are cooking, melt butter in saucepan. Add flour and salt and blend until smooth. Gradually stir in cold milk. Cook, stirring constantly, until sauce boils and becomes thick and smooth. Pour over vegetables.

5. Garnish with fresh parsley.

Vegetables Au Gratin

Christel Wayne

Makes 6-8 servings

2 Tbsp. butter
2 Tbsp. flour
1/2 tsp. salt
1 cup milk
1 cup shredded cheddar cheese
4 cups lightly cooked vegetables of your
    choice, drained
1/2 cup fine, soft bread crumbs
1 Tbsp. butter, melted

1. Melt 2 Tbsp. butter in saucepan. Add flour and salt and blend until smooth. Gradually stir in cold milk. Cook, stirring constantly, until sauce boils and becomes thick and smooth.

2. Stir in cheese until smooth. Add vegetables. Pour into greased 1 1/2-quart casserole dish.

3. Toss crumbs with 1 Tbsp. butter. Sprinkle over top of casserole.

4. Bake at 350° for 20-25 minutes, or until browned.

There is time enough, but none to spare.

— Frederick Douglass

Cauliflower Cheese Casserole

Rebecca Carter

Makes 4 servings

medium-sized head of cauliflower
1/4 cup (1/2 stick) butter or margarine
1/2 cup flour
1/2 tsp. dill weed
1/2 tsp. salt
1/8 tsp. pepper
2 cups milk
1 cup grated cheddar cheese
1 Tbsp. butter
1/2 cup bread cubes
fresh dill weed
black pepper

1. Trim leaves and stalk from cauliflower and separate into florets. Cook in boiling, salted water until just tender (about 10 minutes). Drain and place pieces in a greased 2-quart baking dish.
2. Melt 1/4 cup butter in saucepan. Stir in flour, 1/2 tsp. dill weed, salt, and pepper. Gradually blend in milk. Cook, stirring constantly, until sauce thickens.
3. Add grated cheese and stir until melted. Pour over cauliflower.
4. Melt remaining 1 Tbsp. butter. Blend with bread cubes. Scatter buttered bread crumbs over top of casserole.
5. Bake at 350° for 30 minutes.
6. Garnish with a few sprigs of fresh dill weed and freshly ground pepper just before serving.

Browned Brussels Sprouts

Makes 4 servings

2 pts. fresh brussels sprouts
  (or 2 10-oz. pkgs.)
3 Tbsp. butter or margarine
2 Tbsp. lemon juice, or the juice from
  1 lemon
2 tsp. caraway seeds
salt to taste
pepper to taste

1. Cook brussels sprouts in a bit of water until just tender, about 15 minutes for fresh sprouts. Drain.
2. Heat butter until lightly browned. Add sprouts, lemon juice, caraway seeds, and seasonings. Heat for 2 minutes, stirring sprouts to coat.

Tomato Bake

Cregg Carter

Makes 8-10 servings

2 large cans whole or stewed tomatoes
salt to taste
8 whole cloves
8 whole peppercorns
1 bay leaf
half a yellow onion, chopped
3/4 cup brown sugar
3-4 slices bread, torn into dime-sized
    pieces
2 Tbsp. butter or margarine

1. Pour tomatoes into saucepan. Season with salt.
2. Place cloves, peppercorns, and bay leaf into cheesecloth bag. Add to pan.
3. Cook over medium heat for 30 minutes, stirring occasionally. Remove spice bag.
4. Add onion, sugar, bread, and butter or margarine. Pour into greased baking dish.
5. Bake at 400° for 60 minutes.

I had it often impressed upon my mind that I should one day enjoy my freedom; for slavery is a bitter pill . . .
— Rev. Richard Allen

Beets with Onions and Tomatoes

Makes 4-6 servings

2 15-oz. cans whole beets
2 to 4 Tbsp. vegetable oil
1 tsp. whole cumin seeds
1 clove garlic, minced
1 large onion, coarsley chopped
1 Tbsp. flour
1/4-1/2 tsp. cayenne pepper, according to
    your preference
2-4 whole tomatoes, chopped
1/2 tsp. salt, or to taste
1 cup beet liquid

1. Drain beets, reserving liquid. Cut beets into quarters.
2. Sizzle cumin seeds in hot oil for 5 seconds. Add garlic and stir-fry until golden brown.
3. Add onion and stir-fry 2 minutes.
4. Stir in flour and cayenne pepper. Stir-fry 1 minute.
5. Add remaining ingredients. Cook, uncovered, for 5 minutes, or until sauce is slightly thickened.

Go Down, Moses

When Israel was in Egypt's land;
Let my people go;
Oppressed so hard they could not stand;
Let my people go.

Go down Moses, 'Way down in Egypt's land.
Tell old Pharaoh, Let my people go!

Thus saith the Lord, bold Moses said,
Let my people go;
If not, I'll smite your firstborn dead,
Let my people go.

Go down Moses, 'Way down in Egypt's land.
Tell old Pharaoh, Let my people go!

No more shall they in bondage toil;
Let my people go;
Let them come out with Egypt's spoil,
Let my people go.

Go down Moses, 'Way down in Egypt's land.
Tell old Pharaoh, Let my people go!

This was a call to let enslaved Africans know that an escape was planned. "Egypt's land" refers to the plantation. "Israel" refers to the enslaved Africans. The number of verses sung indicated the number of passengers.

Salads

*M*ost enslaved Africans did not have the opportunity to eat fresh vegetables, even though they were agricultural giants, using their knowledge to grow and cultivate the finest farms on the plantations where they were confined. The orchards grew the sweetest and plumpest of fruits. But if an African was caught eating a piece of fruit from the Massa's orchards, he or she was whipped.

Avocado salad was a summer favorite in our home. I loved shrimp and scallops, and my mother would make a seafood salad for me.

I never knew how she could afford it, nor did I ever question her. Somehow God always made a way for her to treat her children special.

— Phoebe Bailey

Salads — Traditional

Potato Salad

Anna Gantt

Makes 8-10 servings

6 medium-sized potatoes, cooked,
    peeled, cubed
2 large ribs celery, diced
1 medium-sized onion, diced
3 hard-boiled eggs, diced
1/2 tsp. salt
1 cup mayonnaise, or salad dressing

1. Combine potatoes, celery, onions,
and eggs.
2. Sprinkle with salt.
3. Stir in mayonnaise.
4. Chill and serve.

*Note: For additional flavor, add 1 tsp. dry
mustard and a scant 1/4 tsp. black pepper to
Step 2. Add a dusting of paprika in Step 4,
just before serving.*

Potato Salad

Ann Beardan and Dana Beardan Frierson

Makes 8 servings

1 1/2 cups light mayonnaise or salad
    dressing
1 Tbsp. vinegar
1-2 Tbsp. sugar, according to your
    preference
1 Tbsp. prepared mustard
1 tsp. salt
1/4 tsp. pepper
2 lbs. potatoes, cooked, peeled, cubed
2 medium ribs celery, chopped
1/4 cup chopped onions
1/3 cup pickle relish
3 hard boiled-eggs, chopped

1. Combine mayonnaise, vinegar,
sugar, mustard, salt, and pepper.
2. In large separate bowl, gently stir
together potatoes, celery, onions, and
pickle relish. Fold in dressing.
3. Add eggs. Chill.

*Note: Add half a green pepper, seeded and
chopped, to Step 2, if you wish.*

Potato Salad for a Crowd

Brothers and Sisters Cafe

Makes 30 servings

10 lbs. potatoes, cooked, peeled, cubed
1 cup chopped onions
12 hard-boiled eggs, cut up
1 cup celery
1 qt. mayonnaise
1 cup sweet relish
¼ cup prepared mustard
¼ cup sugar
paprika to taste
soul seasoning
salt to taste

1. Gently combine first 4 ingredients in large bowl.
2. Combine next 7 ingredients in a separate bowl. When thoroughly mixed, fold into potato mixture.
3. Refrigerate, and serve when well chilled.

Then the fire must be kindled in the cabin, the corn ground in the small hand-mill, and supper and dinner for the next day in the field prepared. All that is allowed them is corn and bacon, which is given out at the corncrib and smokehouse every Sunday morning.

Each one receives, as his weekly allowance, three and a half pounds of bacon, and corn enough to make a peck of meal. That is all—no tea, coffee, sugar, and, with the exception of a very scanty sprinkling now and then, no salt.

When the corn is ground and the fire is made, the bacon is taken down from the nail on which it hangs, a slice cut off and thrown upon the coals to broil.

The majority of the slaves have no knife, much less a fork. They cut their bacon with the axe at the woodpile. The cornmeal is mixed with a little water, placed in the fire, and baked. When it is "done brown," the ashes are scraped off and, being placed upon a chip which answers for a table, the tenant of the slave house is ready to sit down upon the ground to supper. By this time it is usually midnight.

— Solomon Northup,
Twelve Years a Slave.
Buffalo: Miller, Orton & Mulligan,
1854.

Salads — Other Favorites

Dill Potato Salad

Makes 8-10 servings

12 new, red bliss potatoes, cooked
3 scallions, chopped fine
1/2 bunch fresh dill, or 3 tbsp. dried dill,
  chopped fine
1 1/2 tsp. salt
1/4 cup wine vinegar
1/2 tsp. black pepper
1/2 cup olive oil, or salad oil

1. Peel and dice potatoes.
2. Add scallions and dill. Mix well.
3. Add remaining ingredients. Mix well.
Refrigerate, chilling well before serving.

My mother used to make potato salad. We had used all the salad dressing for sandwiches, so she had to use vinegar in the jar and cook the potatoes almost like mashed potatoes and use that. But it was still delicious.
— Reutilla Smith,
a member of Bethel AMEC,
Lancaster, PA

Dijon Potato Salad

Makes 4-5 servings

1 cup mayonnaise
2 Tbsp. Dijon mustard
2 Tbsp. chopped fresh dill, or 1 1/2 tsp.
  dried dill weed
1 tsp. salt
1/4 tsp. pepper
1 1/2 lbs. small red potatoes, cooked and
  quartered
1 cup sliced radishes
1/2 cup chopped green onions

1. Combine mayonnaise, mustard, dill, salt, and pepper.
2. In separate bowl, mix together remaining ingredients.
3. Pour dressing over vegetables and fold together. Chill.

Red-Skin Potato Salad

Makes 8 servings

2-3 lbs. red potatoes, unpeeled
1 large onion, chopped
2/3 cup sweet relish, or sweet mixed
    pickles, chopped
3 hard-boiled eggs
1 Tbsp. sugar
1 dash dry mustard
1 1/2 cups diced celery,
    or 1 1/2 tsp. celery seed
1-2 cups mayonnaise, or salad dressing
chopped parsley

1. Cook potatoes until tender. Do not peel. Cube to desired size.
2. Lightly combine all ingredients except parsley. Pour into serving dish.
3. Garnish with parsley just before serving.
4. Use with lettuce or other fresh greens for a salad.

Southwestern Potato Salad

Makes 6 servings

2 lbs. new potatoes, quartered
1 cup chopped peeled jicama
1/2 cup sliced pitted ripe olives
1/4 cup sliced green onions
18 cherry tomatoes, halved
1 large avocado, chopped
8-oz. bottle ranch salad dressing
2 small fresh jalapeno peppers, finely
    chopped and seeds removed
2 Tbsp. chopped cilantro or parsley
1 tsp. lime zest
1/4 tsp. salt
1/4 tsp. pepper
lime juice

1. Cook potatoes in lightly salted boiling water for 10-15 minutes, until just tender. Drain. Cool.
2. Add jicama, olives, onions, tomatoes, and avocado to potatoes. Toss lightly.
3. Stir together salad dressing, chili peppers, cilantro, lime zest, salt, and pepper. Pour over potato mixture and mix lightly. Refrigerate for at least 8 hours before serving.
4. Squeeze lime juice over salad before serving to brighten flavors.

Macaroni Salad

Makes 5 servings

8-oz. pkg. dry elbow macaronis
1 Tbsp. salt
3 qts. water
1/2 cup chopped celery
1/4 cup diced green pepper
2 Tbsp., or more, thinly sliced radishes
3/4 cup mayonnaise, or salad dressing
2 Tbsp. prepared mustard
1/4 tsp. onion salt

    1. Cook macaronis in 3-qts. salted boiling water for 11 minutes. Rinse with cold water. Drain.
    2. Combine all ingredients. Toss lightly. Chill for several hours.

Green Goddess Salad Dressing

Mary Alice Bailey

Makes 8 servings

1 cup mayonnaise
2/3 cup sour cream
1/2 cup fresh parsley, chopped, or
   3 Tbsp. dried
2 Tbsp. chives, chopped, or 2 tsp. dried
1 Tbsp. fresh tarragon, or 1 tsp. dried
2 tsp. lemon juice
2 tsp. anchovy paste
salt to taste
pepper to taste

    1. Combine all ingredients in food processor. Pulse until well blended.
    2. Pour over any fresh green salad.

Low-Fat Chicken Salad

Makes 4 servings

3 cups diced, cooked chicken
1 cup chopped celery
1 small apple, chopped
2 Tbsp. chopped onions
1/2 cup low-fat cottage cheese
1 tsp. milk
pepper to taste
lettuce leaves, bread, or sandwich rolls

    1. Combine chicken, celery, apple, and onions.
    2. In blender, mix cottage cheese and milk. Whip for 2 minutes. Add to chicken mixture.
    3. Season with pepper. Mix well.
    4. Serve over lettuce leaves or as sandwich filling.

Turkey Salad

Makes 12-14 sandwiches on rolls

6 cups cooked turkey breast, cubed
1 small onion, chopped fine
1 1/2 -2 cups coarsely chopped celery
8-oz. can crushed pineapple, undrained
1 Tbsp. sugar
1 dash dry mustard
1/2 tsp. celery seed
1 cup mayonnaise, or salad dressing

    1. Combine all ingredients except mayonnaise. Chill.
    2. Add mayonnaise just before serving.

Tuna Salad

Makes 6-8 servings

6-oz. can tuna
1 1/2 cups diced celery
3 hard-boiled eggs, diced
2 Tbsp. minced onions
1/4 tsp. salt
1/4 tsp. pepper
1/2 cup mayonnaise, or salad dressing
lettuce leaves, bread, or sandwich rolls

1. Combine all ingredients, except lettuce or bread, mixing lightly.
2. Chill. Serve as a salad, or as sandwich filling.

Macaroni & Tuna Pasta Salad

Makes 9-12 servings

1 lb. dry elbow macaronis, cooked
half a red pepper, diced
half a green pepper, diced
half a yellow pepper, diced
3/4 cup chopped black olives
1 small red onion, diced
2 ribs celery, diced
4 hard-boiled eggs, chopped
3 6-oz. cans tuna
1 cup shredded carrots
1 Tbsp. salt
1/4-1/2 tsp. black pepper, according to your preference
3 cups, or more, mayonnaise

1. Combine all ingredients except mayonnaise.
2. Stir in 3 cups mayonnaise. Add more if needed, so that salad coheres, but isn't runny.

Grapefruit Tuna Salad

Nancy Perkins

Makes 3-4 lunch-size servings

1 1/2 cups grapefruit sections, drained and cut up
7-oz. can tuna, drained and flaked
1 cup diced celery
2 Tbsp. chopped pimento
lettuce
tart French dressing

1. Combine grapefruit, tuna, celery, and pimento. Chill about 30 minutes.
2. Serve on lettuce with dressing.

Shrimp Salad

Makes 6 servings

2 cups cooked shrimp
1 1/2 cups chopped green bell pepper
1 1/2 cups chopped celery
1/4 cup sliced pimentos
1 cup mayonnaise
1 1/2 Tbsp. lemon juice
1 tsp. salt
1/4 tsp. lemon pepper, or celery seed
lettuce leaves

1. Combine shrimp, green pepper, celery, and pimentos.
2. Combine remaining ingredients in separate bowl. Pour over shrimp mixture. Toss lightly. Chill.
3. Serve on lettuce.

Note: To add more color to the salad, use a mixture of green, red, and yellow bell peppers, instead of just green.

Shrimp and Rice Salad

Makes 10-12 servings

1½ cups cooked rice
1½ cups cooked shrimp, cut into pieces
1 rib celery, chopped
1 carrot, shredded
3-4 Tbsp. mayonnaise, or salad dressing
1 Tbsp. lemon juice
1 cup sliced radishes
½ cup chopped green onions
½ lb. fresh, or 10-oz. pkg. frozen,
   asparagus
pimento strips
tomato wedges
hard-boiled eggs, sliced

1. Combine rice, shrimp, celery, carrot, mayonnaise, lemon juice, radishes, and onions.
2. Cook asparagus until just tender. Cut into 2-inch lengths. Add to rice mixture and toss lightly. Chill.
3. Garnish with pimento, tomato, and hard-boiled eggs.

> We have a formidable history, replete with the voice of God, the ancestors, and the prophets.
> — Molefikete Asante

Seafood Salad

Makes 2 quarts salad

½ lb. box dry elbow macaronis, cooked
   and drained
½ lb. cooked shrimp, cut up
½ lb. imitation crabmeat, cut up
1 cup mayonnaise
1 tsp. prepared mustard
1 Tbsp. ketchup
1 Tbsp. sugar
½ cup celery, chopped fine
¼ cup green pepper, chopped fine
salt to taste
pepper to taste
seasoning salt to taste
garlic powder to taste
paprika

1. Combine all ingredients except paprika. Mix well. Pour into serving bowl.
2. Sprinkle with paprika. Chill.

Crab Salad

Makes 4 servings

1 pt. lump crabmeat
2 ribs celery, finely diced
5 Tbsp. mayonnaise
1 Tbsp. French dressing
1 tsp. salt
ground red pepper to taste
lettuce
hard-boiled eggs, sliced

1. Combine all ingredients except lettuce and eggs. Chill salad ingredients.
2. Serve on lettuce. Garnish with eggs.

Note: If you're budget-conscious, substitute imitation crabmeat for the lump crabmeat.

Cold Crab Salad

Makes 1 serving

1 cup freshly shredded cabbage
3 ozs. cooked crabmeat
one-quarter of an apple, unpeeled and
    diced
half a small celery rib, finely chopped
salt to taste
pepper to taste
1/2 Tbsp. melted margarine
lettuce, or whole, cored tomato

1. Toss together cabbage, crabmeat, apple, celery, seasonings, and margarine. Chill.
2. Serve over lettuce or stuffed in tomato.

Cranberry Salad

Makes 6 servings

6-oz. pkg. orange-flavored gelatin
1 cup boiling water
1/2 cup cold water
1 Tbsp. lemon juice
14-oz. jar cranberry-orange relish
2 Tbsp. crystallized ginger
5-oz. can water chestnuts, drained and
    chopped
1/2 tsp. celery seed
lettuce leaves

1. Dissolve gelatin in boiling water. Add cold water and lemon juice. Chill until slightly thickened.
2. Fold in relish, ginger, water chestnuts, and celery seed.
3. Pour into mold. Chill until firm.
4. Unmold on lettuce-lined salad plates.

Fruity Gelatin Salad

Michael Flack

Makes 12-15 servings

6-oz. pkg. raspberry gelatin
1 cup hot water
16-oz. can whole cranberry sauce
20-oz. can crushed pineapples, undrained
2.25-oz. pkg. chopped walnuts
lettuce leaves, optional

1. Dissolve gelatin in water.
2. When partially set, stir in remaining ingredients.
3. Pour into mold or serving bowl and chill until completely set.
4. To serve, unmold on lettuce-lined plate, or pass in serving bowl.

Fruit Salad

Makes 4-6 servings

2½ cups pineapple chunks, drained
11-oz. can mandarin oranges
1 cup seedless grapes
1 cup small marshmallows
3½-oz. can flaked coconut
2 cups dairy sour cream, or frozen
    whipped topping, thawed

1. Combine pineapple, mandarin oranges, grapes, marshmallows, and coconut.
2. If using sour cream, whip until stiff peaks form. Fold into fruit mixture. Cool 8 hours before serving.
   If using whipped topping, fold gently into fruit and serve immediately.

Cranberry Jewel Salad

Makes 6 servings

3-oz. pkg. raspberry-flavored gelatin
½ cup hot water
½ cup cold water
1-lb. can jellied cranberry sauce
1 orange
lettuce leaves, optional

1. Dissolve gelatin in hot water. Add cold water. Chill until mixture begins to gel.
2. Beat cranberry sauce until saucy. Fold into gelatin. Chill until mixture is partially gelled.
3. Quarter orange. Remove seeds. Chop rind and pulp in food processor. Fold into gelatin.
4. Pour into mold or serving dish. Chill until firm.
5. Unmold on lettuce-lined salad plates, or pass in serving dish.

Frosted Fruit Salad

Makes 15-18 servings

2 3-oz. pkgs. strawberry gelatin
2 cups hot water
24-oz. pkg. frozen strawberries, thawed
2 large ripe bananas
20-oz. can crushed pineapples, undrained
8-oz. container sour cream
2.25-oz. pkg broken nuts
lettuce leaves

1. Dissolve gelatin in hot water.
2. Stir in thawed strawberries.
3. Mash bananas in separate bowl. Stir pineapples into bananas. Fold into gelatin mixture.
4. Pour into rectangular dish. Refrigerate for 8 hours.
5. Half an hour before serving, spread top of fruit salad with sour cream. Sprinkle with nuts. Cut into squares and serve on lettuce-lined salad plates.

Pickled Beets

Makes 4 pints

4 lbs. fresh beets
1 clove garlic, sliced
a few thin slices of onion
1 1/2-1 3/4 cups sugar, according to your preference
1 Tbsp. pickling spices
3/4 cup water
1 1/4 cups cider vinegar

1. Steam beets in small amount of water for 30-40 minutes, or until crispy tender. Do not overcook. Drain. Rinse with cold water. Peel and slice.
2. Place beets in four sterilized pint jars. Add garlic and onion slices.
3. Combine sugar, pickling spices, water, and vinegar in saucepan. Bring to boil. Pour over beets, filling jars to within 1 inch of tops. Seal tightly.

Note: If you don't have time to start from scratch with fresh beets, use canned beets. Slice them into jars, and continue with Step 2.

Pickled Eggs and Beets

Dorothy Vancheri

Makes 20-30 servings of beets, 24 servings of eggs

2 cups water
2 cups white vinegar
1 1/2 cups sugar
6 bay leaves
20 whole cloves
5 1-lb. cans sliced red beets, undrained
2 large onions, sliced into rings
2 dozen, hard-boiled eggs, peeled

1. Combine water, vinegar, and sugar in large kettle. Boil and stir until sugar is dissolved.
2. Stir in bay and cloves. Add beets. Chill for 8 hours.
3. Add onions and eggs. Refrigerate for 2-3 days before eating to allow spices to permeate eggs.
4. Serve beets and eggs together when chilled.

Thousands of my ancestors had waited, as I had done, for nightfall to cover their steps, had leaned on one true friend to help them, had felt, as I did, the very teeth of the dogs at the heels. It was simple. I had to be worthy of them.

— Angela Davis

Golden Eggs

Makes 8-10 servings

3 Tbsp. prepared mustard
2/3 cup sugar
1/2 cup vinegar
1 cup water
1/8 tsp. salt
8-10 hard-boiled eggs, quartered

1. In saucepan, combine mustard, sugar, vinegar, water, and salt. Bring to boil. Allow to cool to room temperature.
2. Place eggs in container with lid. Cover with sauce. Refrigerate for 24 hours.
3. Serve cold or at room temperature.

Green Tomato Chow Chow

Inez B. William

Makes 12 pints, approximately

2 gallons green tomatoes, ground
6 green peppers, ground
6 onions, ground
2 Tbsp. cinnamon
5 cups vinegar
2 cups brown sugar
1 tsp. salt
2 Tbsp. cloves

1. Combine all ingredients in large kettle. Boil for 2 hours.
2. Transfer ingredients to glass jars. Seal while hot.

Bread and Butter Pickles

Emma Turney

Makes 10-12 pints

4 qts. thinly sliced cucumbers
6 medium onions, thinly sliced
2 green peppers, chopped
3 cloves garlic, chopped
1/3 cup salt
2 bags ice
5 cups sugar
3 cups vinegar
1 1/2 tsp. turmeric
1 1/2 tsp. celery seed
2 Tbsp. mustard seed
netting
large rubber band or sturdy string

1. Combine cucumbers, onions, green peppers, and garlic in very large bowl. Stir in salt.

2. Cover with ice. Place netting over bowl. Secure with large rubber band or string. Place another bag of ice on top of netting. Let stand 3 hours. Drain.

3. Place cucumber mixture in large kettle.

4. Add sugar, vinegar, turmeric, celery seed, and mustard seed. Bring to rolling boil. Cook until cucumbers turn green. Remove sliced cucumbers, but keep cooking syrup hot in kettle.

5. Spoon cucumbers and other vegetables into sterilized glass canning jars. Cover with boiling syrup, close with lids, and seal.

14-Day Sweet Pickles

Makes 8 pints

1 gallon sliced cucumbers
1 cup salt
1 Tbsp. alum
4 cups boiling vinegar
4 cups sugar, divided
1 tsp. celery seed
1 tsp. ground cinnamon
1 Tbsp. pickling spices
1 tsp. whole allspice

1. Place cucumbers in large kettle. Add salt. Cover with boiling water. Let stand 6 days.

2. On Day 7, drain. Cover with fresh boiling water mixed with alum. Let stand 24 hours.

3. Drain. Cover with boiling water. Let stand 24 hours. Repeat and let stand for 24 hours.

4. Drain. Combine boiling vinegar, 1 cup sugar, celery seed, cinnamon, pickling spices, and allspice. Pour over cucumbers. Let stand 24 hours.

5. Each day for the next 3 days, drain liquid and reserve it. Bring to boil. Add additional cup of sugar. Pour back over cucumbers.

6. On Day 14, drain syrup into a saucepan and bring to a boil. Spoon sliced pickles into sterilized jars. Cover with boiling syrup, close with lids, and seal.

Let Us Break Bread Together

Let us break bread together on our knees,
Let us break bread together on our knees.
When I fall on my knees, With my face to the rising sun,
O Lord, have mercy on me.

Let us drink wine together on our knees,
Let us drink wine together on our knees.
When I fall on my knees, With my face to the rising sun,
O Lord, have mercy on me.

Let us praise God together on our knees,
Let us praise God together on our knees.
When I fall on my knees, With my face to the rising sun,
O Lord, have mercy on me.

This song gives location, time, and day. The breaking of the bread and drinking of wine refers to Holy Communion, which is taken at a church (location). Most people met for worship on Sundays (day of week). The time to meet— "with my face to the rising sun"—was sunrise.

Breads

*T*ill this day, I don't know anyone who makes yeast rolls like my mother. The holidays were always special because I knew there would be an abundance of freshly made yeast rolls on the table.

My mother's table was a work of art. Her finest china, sterling silverware, long-stemmed glasses, beautiful centerpieces . . . and serving dishes filled with the finest of "Mrs. Bailey's cuisine."

In Africa grain was an essential and pleasant staple in the diet. Here in America, the most common grain allowed was cornmeal, often served in the form of mush, given to the Africans to keep them healthy enough to work harder and longer. Frederick Douglass recalls that mush was placed in a trough, in the center of the room, and all of the enslaved children on the farm were to eat from it. Hopefully, you were big enough and strong enough to get your share.

— Phoebe Bailey

Breads — Traditional

Buttermilk Cornbread

Makes 4-6 servings

1 cup cornmeal
2 tsp. baking powder
1/2 tsp. salt
1 rounded tsp. sugar
1/8 tsp. baking soda
1 cup buttermilk
1 egg
2-4 Tbsp. bacon drippings

1. Combine cornmeal, baking powder, salt, and sugar in mixing bowl.
2. In separate bowl stir baking soda into buttermilk. Add egg. Mix well. Add to dry ingredients.
3. Pour bacon drippings into iron skillet. Heat in 450° oven.
4. Pour cornbread batter into skillet. Bake for 20 minutes.

> I sincerely regret the absence of statistics that would enable me to furnish you with many events, that would assist you in describing the operations of the Underground Railroad. I never kept record of those persons passing through my hands, nor did I ever anticipate that the history of that perilous period would ever be written.
> — William Whipper

Old-Fashioned Cornbread

Makes 9-12 servings

3 Tbsp. shortening
3/4 cup sifted flour
1 Tbsp. baking powder
1 tsp. salt
3 Tbsp. sugar
3/4 cup cornmeal
2 eggs
1/2 cup evaporated milk
1/4 cup water

1. Melt shortening in 8" square baking pan in 400° oven.
2. Meanwhile, sift together flour, baking powder, salt, and sugar. Stir in cornmeal.
3. In separate bowl, slightly beat eggs. Stir in evaporated milk and water.
4. Remove baking pan from oven. Tilt pan in order to coat inside of pan with shortening, including the sides. Pour excess shortening into egg mixture and stir.
5. Add egg mixture to cornmeal mixture. Stir until dry ingredients are moistened. Pour into pan.
6. Bake for 15 minutes, until lightly browned.

Cracklin Cornbread

Makes 9-12 servings

1 cup cornmeal
1/2 cup flour
1/4 cup sugar
2 tsp. baking powder
1/4-1/2 tsp. salt
3/4 cup milk
1 egg
1/2 cup cracklins
1/4 cup shortening, melted

1. Combine cornmeal, flour, sugar, baking powder, and salt.
2. Stir in milk and egg. Gradually stir in cracklins and shortening.
3. Pour batter into greased 8" square baking pan, cornstalk pan, or muffin tin.
4. Bake at 400° for 25-30 minutes.

Note: Render sliced salt pork or bacon to make cracklins. To render, put salt pork in frying pan and cook until crisp. The cracklins are the crispy part that remains after the fat is cooked off.

Biscuits

Makes 18 biscuits

5 or more cups flour
1/2 cup sugar
4 tsp. baking powder
2 tsp. salt
1 1/4 cups milk
1/2 cup solid shortening
4 large eggs

1. Combine flour, sugar, baking powder, and salt until well blended.
2. Pour milk, shortening, and eggs into well in center of dry mixture. Mix with hands until eggs and milk are blended. (There will be some lumps of shortening.) Slowly work with fingertips until smooth. The finished dough should be soft but not sticky. Add additional flour if needed.
3. Turn dough onto lightly floured surface. Roll out to 1/2" thick. Cut into 3 1/2" rounds. Place biscuits, slightly touching on greased 11" x 17" baking pan. Let stand in warm place 10-15 minutes.
4. Bake at 400° for 20 minutes, until deep golden brown and light to touch when you pick them up. Break apart and serve.

Buttermilk Biscuits

Mrs. Margaret Bailey

Makes 2½-3 dozen biscuits

6 cups flour
2 tsp. baking powder
1½ tsp. baking soda
1¼ tsp. salt
1½ cups shortening, at room
   temperature
2 cups buttermilk

1. Sift together flour, baking powder, baking soda, and salt.
2. Cut in shortening.
3. Make well in center. Add 2 cups buttermilk. Stir until just moist.
4. Knead 7-8 times.
5. Roll to ½" thick. Cut with floured biscuit cutter. Place biscuits on greased cookie sheet.
6. Bake at 450° for 12-15 minutes, or until biscuits are lightly browned.

> My mother made delicious potato rolls. As soon as they came out of the oven we were ready to eat them. They were made out of fresh potatoes.
>
> — Anna Gantt,
> a member of Bethel AMEC,
> Lancaster, PA

Buttermilk Rolls

Makes approximately 24 rolls

1¾ cups buttermilk
¼ cup sugar
2 tsp. salt
¾ cup oil
½ tsp. baking soda
1 pkg. dry yeast
¾ cup lukewarm water
4½-5½ cups sifted flour
melted butter

1. Scald buttermilk. Stir in sugar, salt, oil, and baking soda. Cool to lukewarm.
2. Dissolve yeast in water. Add to buttermilk mixture.
3. Stir in enough flour to make soft dough. Knead until smooth.
4. Shape into rolls.
5. Place in greased pans or on baking sheet. Brush tops with melted butter. Cover.
6. Let rise in warm place until double in size.
7. Bake at 425° for 15-20 minutes.

Tasty White Bread

Minnie Wilson

Makes 2 loaves

2 eggs
4 Tbsp. sugar
1 Tbsp. salt
2 pkgs. dry yeast
7 cups sifted flour
2 cups boiling water
4 Tbsp. shortening, melted

1. Beat together eggs, sugar, salt, and yeast. Let stand for 10 minutes.
2. Stir in remaining ingredients. Set mixture in warm place and let rise until nearly double in size.
3. Shape into 2 loaves and place in greased bread pans.
4. Bake at 400° for 12-15 minutes.

Whole Wheat Bread

Tamika Williams

Makes 2 loaves

2 pkgs. dry yeast
1/4 cup molasses or honey
1 cup lukewarm water
1 Tbsp. salt
1/4 cup melted butter or oil
2 cups milk
6-8 cups whole wheat flour

1. In large mixing bowl, dissolve yeast and molasses in water. Allow to sit until bubbly.
2. Add remaining ingredients, saving approximately 1 cup flour to knead into bread.

3. Knead until dough stops sticking and looks smooth and shiny, about 15 minutes.
4. Place in greased bowl. Cover and let rise in warm place until double in size.
5. Punch down. Form into 2 loaves. Place in greased pans. Allow to rise until double in size.
6. Bake at 425° for 10 minutes. Reduce heat to 375° and bake for 30 minutes. Bread is done when a tap on the crust sounds hollow.

Whole Wheat Rolls or Bread

Makes 9-12 servings

2 eggs, slightly beaten
1 cup milk
4 Tbsp. shortening, melted
2 Tbsp. brown sugar or honey
1 tsp. salt
2 1/2 tsp. baking powder
1 1/2 cups whole wheat flour

1. Mix together eggs, milk, shortening, and brown sugar or honey.
2. In separate bowl combine salt, baking powder, and flour. Add to liquid mixture. Stir only enough to dampen dry ingredients. Let stand for a few minutes.
3. Drop mixture by spoonfuls into greased muffin tin, or pour into greased 8" x 8" baking pan.
4. Bake at 425° for 20 minutes.

Homemade Rolls

Makes about 40 rolls

2 pkgs. dry yeast
1/2 cup lukewarm water
1 cup milk
7 Tbsp. solid shortening
6 Tbsp. sugar
1/4 tsp. salt
2 eggs
1 small cooked potato, mashed
5 cups flour

1. Dissolve yeast in water. Cover. Set aside.
2. Combine milk, shortening, sugar, and salt in saucepan. Scald. Cool to warm.
3. In large mixing bowl, beat together eggs, mashed potato, and yeast mixture. Stir in milk mixture. Mix well.
4. Stir in 1 cup flour. Continue adding flour until it can be turned onto floured board and kneaded. Place in large greased bowl. Cover. Allow to rise until double in size, about 60 minutes.
5. Form into small rolls. Let rise another 60 minutes.
6. Bake at 350° for 10-15 minutes.

Raisin Bread

Hester Prince

Makes 3 loaves

1 cup raisins
1 1/2 cups boiling water
3/4 cup butter (1 1/2 sticks), at room temperature
3/4 cup sugar
3 eggs
1 tsp. cinnamon
4 cups flour
3 tsp. baking powder
dash of salt
dash of nutmeg
1 1/2 cups evaporated milk
1 1/2 tsp. lemon extract
grated rind from 1 orange or 1 lemon

1. Soak raisins in boiling water overnight. Drain.
2. Cream together butter, sugar, and eggs.
3. Sift together cinnamon, flour, baking powder, salt, and nutmeg. Add to creamed mixture.
4. Add remaining ingredients, including the raisins. Mix well.
5. Pour into 3 greased and floured loaf pans.
6. Bake at 350° for 45-60 minutes.

Hush Puppies

Makes about 12 pieces

cooking oil
2½ cups cornmeal
1 tsp. salt
2 Tbsp. baking powder
½ cup-1 cup chopped onions,
   according to your preference
1¼ cups milk, approximately
½ cup water, approximately

1. Pour cooking oil into deep skillet or deep fryer to a depth of ½ inch and heat to 360°.
2. While oil is heating, combine cornmeal, salt, and baking powder.
3. Add onions. Mix well.
4. Blend in milk and water until dough is stiff enough to handle.
5. Shape dough into oblong, thumb-sized cakes. Drop into hot oil. Turn occasionally, until browned.

Hush Puppies

Rina Mckee

Makes about 16 pieces

oil for frying
1 egg, slightly beaten
1 cup milk
2 Tbsp. green onions, minced
1 cup white cornmeal
½ cup flour
¾ tsp. baking powder
¼ tsp. baking soda
¼ tsp. salt

1. Heat oil to 375°.
2. Combine egg, milk, and onions.
3. In separate bowl, combine cornmeal, flour, baking powder, baking soda, and salt. Stir into egg mixture.
4. Drop by 1½ Tbsp. into hot oil. Cook for 3 minutes, or until brown. Drain on paper towels. Serve warm.

Old South Hush Puppies

Makes approximately 3 dozen pieces

½ lb. onions, ground or finely
   chopped
¼ cup ketchup
1 cup canned tomatoes
1 small egg
½ cup buttermilk
1¼ cups yellow or white cornmeal
2 cups flour
3 tsp. baking powder
1 tsp. salt
½ tsp. black pepper
oil
honey

1. Combine onions, ketchup, tomatoes, egg, and buttermilk.
2. In separate bowl, mix together cornmeal, flour, baking powder, salt, and pepper. Stir into liquid mixture.
3. Drop by tablepoonsful into deep oil. Fry until golden brown.
4. Serve with honey.

Note: These hush puppies are also good dipped in salsa, ranch dressing, or prepared mustard.

Breads — Other Favorites

Cornbread

Makes 6-8 servings

1 1/2 cups self-rising cornmeal
1/2 cup self-rising flour
1 tsp. sugar
1/4 cup shortening
3/4 cup milk
1 egg

1. Combine cornmeal, flour, and sugar. Cut in shortening until mixture is crumbly.
2. In separate bowl, combine milk and egg. Pour wet ingredients into dry and stir until well mixed.
3. Pour into greased iron skillet or square baking pan.
4. Bake at 425° for 25 minutes.

Southern Style Cornbread

Makes 5-6 servings

2 Tbsp. bacon drippings
1 1/4 cups cornmeal
7 1/2-oz. pkg. corn muffin mix
2 tsp. baking powder
1 tsp. salt
1 1/2 cups buttermilk
2 eggs, beaten

1. Pour bacon drippings into 8-inch square baking pan. Place in 400° oven.
2. Combine dry ingredients. Stir in buttermilk and eggs. Mix until dry ingredients are just moistened.

3. Pour into hot pan.
4. Bake at 400° for 25-30 minutes, or until golden brown.

Braided Easter Bread

Mary Alice Bailey

Makes 8-10 servings

2 1/2 cups flour, divided
1/4 cup white sugar
1 tsp. salt
1 pkg. dry yeast
2/3 cup milk
2 Tbsp. butter
2 eggs
1/4 cup raisins
5 hard-boiled eggs in their shells,
   dyed if desired
2 Tbsp. butter, melted

Glaze:
1 egg yolk
2 Tbsp. milk

1. In large bowl, combine 1 cup flour, sugar, salt, and yeast. Mix well.
2. Combine milk and butter in small saucepan. Heat until milk is warm and butter is softened but not melted. Gradually add the milk and butter to the flour mixture, stirring constantly.
3. Add eggs and 1/2 cup more flour. Beat well.
4. Add remaining flour, 1/2 cup at a time, stirring well after each addition.

5. Turn bread onto lightly floured surface. Knead for 8 minutes, until smooth and elastic. Place in lightly oiled bowl. Turn to coat with oil. Cover with damp cloth and let rise in warm place until double in size, about 1 hour.

6. Punch down dough. Knead in raisins. Turn onto lightly floured surface. Divide dough in half. Cover and let rest for 10 minutes.

7. Roll each round into a long roll, about 36" x 1½". Twisting the two rolls of dough together, form a loosely braided ring. Seal the ends of the ring together and use your fingers to slide the eggs between the braided strands of dough.

8. Place loaf on buttered baking sheet and cover loosely with a damp towel. Place in warm place. Let rise until double in size, about 45 minutes.

9. Combine glaze ingredients and brush over risen ring.

10. Bake at 325° for 50-55 minutes, or until golden brown.

> In coming to a fixed determination to run away, we did more than Patrick Henry when he resolved upon liberty or death. With us it was a doubtful liberty at most, and almost certain death if we failed. For my part, I should prefer death to hopeless bondage.
> — Frederick Douglass

Mother's Bread

Makes 4 loaves

2 cups dry oatmeal
¼ cup brown sugar
½ cup molasses
2 Tbsp. margarine, melted
2 Tbsp. oil
1½ tsp. salt
1 cup wheat germ
5 cups boiling water
2 pkgs. yeast
1 tsp. sugar
¼ cup warm water
4 cups whole wheat flour
5½-6 cups flour

1. Combine oatmeal, brown sugar, molasses, margarine, oil, salt, and wheat germ. Stir in boiling water and allow to soften for 15-20 minutes.

2. Dissolve yeast and sugar in warm water. Add to oatmeal mixture.

3. Stir in whole wheat flour. Mix well.

4. Stir in flour. Mix well. Knead 5-7 minutes.

5. Place in covered bowl. Let rise until double in size.

6. Knead and shape into 4 loaves. Place in greased loaf pans. Let rise again until double in size.

7. Bake at 375° for 45 minutes. (If bread begins to brown too much, reduce heat to 350°.) Remove from pans and grease tops with butter. Allow to cool before slicing.

Country Cinnamon Rolls

Minnie Wilson

Makes 1 dozen rolls

1 pkg. dry yeast
1/2 cup warm water (105°-115°)
1 egg, slightly beaten
2 Tbsp. milk
1 Tbsp. sugar
3 cups buttermilk baking mix
2 Tbsp. butter or margarine, softened
1 Tbsp. sugar
1 tsp. cinnamon
1/2 cup raisins

Icing
1 cup powdered sugar
1 1/2 Tbsp. water
3/4 tsp. almond extract

1. Dissolve yeast in warm water in large mixing bowl.
2. Stir in egg, milk, sugar, and baking mix. Beat well.
3. Turn onto well-floured board. Knead about 50 times.
4. Roll dough into 12" x 10" rectangle. Spread with butter.
5. Combine sugar and cinnamon. Sprinkle over rectangle.
6. Sprinkle on raisins.
7. Roll up tightly, beginning at 12" side. Seal by pinching edges of dough into roll.
8. Cut into 1" slices. Place slices, cut sides down, in well greased muffin cups.
9. Cover. Let rise for 30 minutes.
10. Bake at 375° for 12-15 minutes. Immediately remove from pan. Let stand 5 minutes.
11. Combine powdered sugar, water, and almond extract. Spread over rolls. Serve warm.

Sunday Brunch Cherry Nut Rolls

Minnie Wilson

Makes 12 muffins

1/3 cup butter or margarine, softened
1/2 cup brown sugar, packed
1/4 cup chopped almonds
12 candied cherries
1 pkg. dry yeast
2/3 cup warm water (105°-115°)
2 1/2 cups buttermilk baking mix
2 Tbsp. butter or margarine, softened
1/4 cup brown sugar, packed
1/4 cup cut-up candied cherries

1. Combine 1/3 cup butter, 1/2 cup brown sugar, and almonds. Place about 1 Tbsp. mixture in each of 12 medium muffin cups. Place cherry in each muffin cup.
2. Dissolve yeast in warm water.
3. Stir in baking mix. Beat well. Form into ball. Knead on floured surface until smooth, about 20 times.
4. Roll dough into 16" x 9" rectangle. Spread with butter. Sprinkle with 1/4 cup brown sugar and 1/4 cup cut-up cherries.
5. Roll up, beginning at 16" side. Pinch edges to seal. Cut into 12 1 1/4" slices. Place slices, cut sides up, in muffin cups.
6. Cover. Let rise in warm place until double, about 60 minutes.
7. Bake at 400° for 15 minutes. Immediately invert onto baking sheet. Leave pan over rolls for a minute. Serve warm.

Yankee Doughnuts

Minnie Wilson

Makes about 16 doughnuts

oil
2 cups buttermilk baking mix
2 Tbsp. sugar
1 tsp. vanilla
1 egg
1/4 cup milk
1/4 tsp. cinnamon
1/4 tsp. nutmeg

Chocolate Glaze:
2 ozs. semisweet chocolate
3 Tbsp. butter or margarine
1 cup powdered sugar
3/4 tsp. vanilla
1-3 tsp. hot water

1. Heat 3-4" oil in deep fryer or in kettle to 375°.
2. Combine baking mix, sugar, vanilla, egg, milk, cinnamon, and nutmeg until smooth. Form into ball. Knead 8-10 times on floured board.
3. Roll dough 1/4" thick. Cut with floured doughnut cutter. Drop rings into hot oil. Fry about 30 seconds on each side, or until golden brown. Drain.
4. Melt chocolate and butter over low heat. Remove from heat. Stir in sugar and vanilla. Add hot water, 1 tsp. at a time, until glaze is of spreading consistency. Spread over doughnuts.

Party Crescents

Minnie Wilson

Makes 16 biscuits

2 cups buttermilk baking mix
1/2 cup cold water
butter or margarine, melted
celery seeds or sesame seeds

1. Combine baking mix and water. Form into ball. Knead 5 times on floured surface.
2. Roll dough into 12" circle. Brush with butter.
3. Cut into 16 wedges. Roll up each wedge, beginning at rounded edge. Place biscuits with points underneath on ungreased baking sheet. Curve ends of each biscuit to form crescents.
4. Brush tops with butter. Sprinkle with seeds.
5. Bake at 425° for 10-12 minutes.

April 1825 — On my return I stopped at Lancaster; the Church (Bethel African Methodist Episcopal Church) was opened, and I preached to large congregations, and with powerful success; the dead were brought to life by the preaching of the cross of Christ. From there I left for Philadelphia.

— Jarena Lee,
first woman AME preacher

Jam Dandies

Minnie Wilson

Makes 8 servings

2 cups buttermilk baking mix
2 Tbsp. sugar
1/2 cup cold water
1/2 cup jam or jelly
1/4 cup finely chopped walnuts
2 Tbsp. sugar

1. Combine baking mix, 2 Tbsp. sugar, and water to make soft dough. Form dough into ball. Knead 5 times on floured surface. Divide in half. Pat or roll each half into 8″ circle.
2. Place one circle in ungreased round layer pan. Spread with jam. Top with remaining circle.
3. Combine walnuts and 2 Tbsp. sugar. Sprinkle over top of dough.
4. Bake at 400° for 15-18 minutes. If the top begins to brown too much before the Dandies are done in the middle, tent with tin foil.
5. Allow to cool for 10 minutes, then cut into 8 wedges and serve.

Herby Biscuits

Mrs. Margaret Bailey

Makes 3–4 dozen biscuits

6 1/2 cups flour
4 tsp. baking powder
2 tsp. salt
1 1/2 cups (3 sticks) butter, cold
1 1/2 cups milk
3 eggs
2-3 Tbsp. dried herbs — basil, thyme, oregano, parsley, etc.

1. In large mixing bowl sift together flour, baking powder, and salt.
2. Cut in butter. Form well in center.
3. In separate bowl combine milk, eggs, and herbs. Pour into well in dry ingredients. Mix together.
4. Drop biscuits onto a greased sheet by tablespoonfuls. Bake at 450° for 12-15 minutes, until biscuits are lightly browned.

Yogurt and Onion Biscuit Squares

Minnie Wilson

Makes 9-12 squares

2 cups sliced onions
1/2 tsp. salt
dash of pepper
2 Tbsp. shortening
2 cups buttermilk baking mix
1/2 cup cold water
1 egg
1/2 cup plain yogurt
1/4 tsp. salt

1. In skillet, saute onions, 1/2 tsp. salt, and pepper in shortening until onions are tender and golden. Set aside.

2. Combine baking mix and water. Form into ball.

3. Gently roll dough into 11" square. Pat firmly in bottom and up sides of greased 9" x 9" pan.

4. Spread onions over top.

5. Combine egg, yogurt, and 1/4 tsp. salt. Spread evenly over onions.

6. Bake at 425° for 20 minutes, or until light brown. Cut into squares. Serve warm.

Yogurt and Chives Biscuits

Minnie Wilson

Makes 10-12 biscuits

2 cups buttermilk baking mix
1/3 cup cold water
1/3 cup plain yogurt
1 Tbsp. snipped chives, or
** 1 1/2 tsp. dried chives**

1. Combine all ingredients. Form into ball.

2. Gently press dough out onto board into 1/2"-3/4" thick circle. Cut with floured 2" round cutter. Place biscuits in greased round cake pan.

3. Bake at 425° for 8-11 minutes, depending on the biscuits' thickness.

Blueberry Muffins

Makes 1 dozen muffins

2 cups flour
1/3 cup sugar
2 tsp. baking powder
1/2 tsp. salt
1 egg, slightly beaten
3/4 cup milk
1/2 cup (1 stick) butter or margarine,
** melted**
1 cup blueberries

1. Combine dry ingredients.

2. Combine egg, milk, and butter. Add to dry ingredients. Mix until just moistened.

3. Fold in blueberries.

4. Spoon into greased and floured medium-sized muffin tin, filling each cup 2/3 full.

5. Bake at 400° for 15-20 minutes, or until golden brown.

> Lord, I remember when I worked from "can't see in the mornin'" to "can't see at night" — I remember the pain in my back from bending over so long. But, through it all, Lord, you kept me.
> — *Living the Experience*

Whole Wheat Muffins

Makes 1 dozen muffins

1 cup whole wheat flour
3/4 cup flour
1 Tbsp. baking powder
1 cup sugar
1 tsp. salt
3/4 cup milk
1/4 cup honey
3 Tbsp. oil
1 egg

1. Combine all dry ingredients.
2. In separate bowl mix together milk, honey, oil, and egg. Stir into dry ingredients until they are just moistened.
3. Spoon into greased and floured medium-sized muffin tin, filling each cup 2/3 full.
4. Bake at 325° for 20-25 minutes.

Yummy Healthy Muffins

Minnie Wilson

Makes 12 muffins

2 cups buttermilk baking mix
1 cup whole-bran cereal
3 Tbsp. wheat germ
2 Tbsp. sugar
1 egg
2/3 cup milk
2 Tbsp. molasses

1. Combine all ingredients. Mix well.
2. Grease bottoms of 12 muffin cups. Fill each cup 2/3 full.
3. Bake at 400° for 15-17 minutes. Serve warm.

Granola Muffins

Minnie Wilson

Makes 1 dozen muffins

2 cups buttermilk baking mix
1 cup granola
2 Tbsp. honey
1 egg
2/3 cup milk
1/3 cup raisins

1. Combine all ingredients until well mixed.
2. Grease bottom of 12 muffin cups. Fill each cup 2/3 full.
3. Bake at 400° for 15 minutes. Serve warm with butter and honey.

Cheesy Muffins

Minnie Wilson

Makes 12 muffins

2 cups buttermilk baking mix
2 Tbsp. sugar
1 cup shredded cheddar cheese
1 egg
2/3 cup water or milk

1. Combine all ingredients. Mix well.
2. Grease bottoms of 12 muffin cups. Fill each cup 2/3 full.
3. Bake at 400° for 15 minutes. Serve warm.

Gift Muffs

Minnie Wilson

Makes 1½ dozen muffins

2 cups buttermilk baking mix
2 Tbsp. sugar
1 egg
⅓ cup orange juice
½ cup orange marmalade
½ cup chopped pecans

Topping:
¼ cup sugar
1 Tbsp. flour
½ tsp. cinnamon
¼ tsp. nutmeg
1 Tbsp. butter or margarine, softened

1. Combine baking mix, 2 Tbsp. sugar, egg, orange juice, marmalade, and pecans. Mix well.
2. Grease bottoms of 18 muffin cups. Fill each half-full.
3. Combine topping ingredients. Sprinkle over batter.
4. Bake at 350° for 15-20 minutes. Serve warm.

Supermuffs

Minnie Wilson

Makes 12 muffins

2 cups buttermilk baking mix
2 Tbsp. sugar
1 egg
⅔ cup water or milk
1½ cups Total cereal

1. Combine all ingredients except cereal. Mix well.
2. Fold in cereal.
3. Grease 12 muffin cups thoroughly. Fill each cup ⅔ full.
4. Bake at 400° for 15 minutes. Serve warm.

Ham, Cheese, & Raisin Sticks

Minnie Wilson

Makes 2 dozen bread sticks

½ cup (1 stick) butter or margarine
2 cups buttermilk baking mix
½-1 tsp. dry mustard
⅔ cup raisins
½ cup finely chopped cooked ham
½ cup shredded cheddar cheese
½ cup cold water

1. Melt butter in 9″ x 13″ baking pan.
2. Combine remaining ingredients. Form into ball. Knead 5 times on floured board.
3. Roll dough into 10″ x 6″ rectangle. Cut in half lengthwise. Cut each half into 12 sticks, each about ¾ inch wide. Roll each stick in butter in pan.
4. Grease a second baking pan. After all the sticks have been buttered, divide the sticks between the two baking pans and bake at 425° for 15 minutes. Serve hot.

Hobo Bread

Makes 3 loaves

4 tsp. baking soda
2 cups dark raisins
2 cups boiling water
2 cups sugar
4 Tbsp. oil
1/2 tsp. salt
4 cups flour

1. Combine baking soda, raisins, and boiling water in large bowl. Let sit overnight.
2. Add sugar, oil, salt, and flour to raisin mixture.
3. Divide dough between 3 greased and floured 1-lb. coffee cans.
4. Bake at 350° for 30 minutes. Reduce heat to 325° and bake an additional 30 minutes.
5. Remove from oven. Place cans on their sides for 10 minutes. Roll can to other side. Bread should slide out easily.

I remember when I was little and at home, my grandfather got the name "Coffee Bread," cause if he would drink coffee, he would dip his bread in his coffee. That was a favorite thing he would do. Dip his bread in the coffee.

— Sandra Polite Simms,
a member of Bethel AMEC,
Lancaster, PA

Pumpkin Nut Bread

Makes 2 loaves

1 cup (2 sticks) butter or margarine,
   at room temperature
3 cups sugar
3 eggs
1 tsp. vanilla
16-oz. can solid packed pumpkin
3 cups sifted flour
1 1/2 tsp. salt
1 tsp. baking soda
1 tsp. baking powder
1 1/2 tsp. cinnamon
1 tsp. cloves
1/2 tsp. nutmeg
1 cup chopped walnuts
1 cup dark or golden raisins

1. Cream together butter and sugar.
2. Beat in eggs and vanilla. Add pumpkin. Mix well.
3. Sift together flour, salt, baking soda, baking powder, cinnamon, cloves, and nutmeg. Blend into pumpkin mixture.
4. Stir in nuts and raisins.
5. Pour into 2 greased and floured 9" x 5" x 3" loaf pans.
6. Bake at 350° for 60-65 minutes. Let stand 10 minutes. Remove from pan. Cool on rack before slicing.

Nutty Pumpkin Bread

Hester Prince

Makes 3 loaves

6 eggs
3¾ cups sugar
1½ cups oil
¾ cup water
3 cups cooked pumpkin
3½ cups flour plus 2 Tbsp. flour
¾ tsp. baking powder
3 tsp. baking soda
1½ tsp. salt
2 tsp. cinnamon
1½ tsp. ground cloves
2 cups chopped nuts
1 cup raisins

1. Combine eggs and sugar until thoroughly blended. Stir in oil and water and mix well. Stir in pumpkin until smooth.
2. In separate bowl, mix together flour, baking powder, baking soda, salt, cinnamon, and cloves. Stir into pumpkin mixture until well combined.
3. Stir in nuts and raisins.
4. Pour into 3 greased and floured 9″ x 5″ x 3″ loaf pans.
5. Bake at 350° for 45-60 minutes.

Bake Sale Pineapple Bread

Minnie Wilson

Makes 1 loaf

2½ cups buttermilk baking mix
⅓ cup sugar
¼ cup (½ stick) butter or margarine, softened
2 eggs
8¾-oz. can crushed pineapple, well drained (reserve 3 Tbsp. syrup and mix into batter)
½ cup chopped nuts

1. Combine all ingredients in electric mixing bowl. Beat 2 minutes at medium speed.
2. Pour into greased and floured 9″ x 5″ x 3″ loaf pan.
3. Bake at 350° for 55 minutes. Cool 10 minutes. Remove from pan. Cool thoroughly before slicing.

Banana Bread

Sharee Denson

Makes 1 loaf

2 1/2 cups flour
1/2 cup sugar
1/2 cup brown sugar
1 tsp. salt
3 1/2 tsp. baking powder
3 Tbsp. vegetable oil
2 eggs
3/4 cup milk
1 cup mashed ripe bananas
1 tsp. vanilla extract

1. Combine dry ingredients in electric mixer bowl. In separate bowl mix together oil, eggs, and milk.
2. Mix wet ingredients into dry. Fold in bananas and vanilla.
3. Beat at medium speed for 3 minutes.
4. Pour into 9" x 5" x 3" greased and floured loaf pan.
5. Bake at 350° for 55-65 minutes. Remove from pan. Cool before slicing.

> Surely, God had put his curse not alone upon the slave, but upon the stealer of men! . . . The weed had been cut down, but its root remained, deeply imbedded in the soil, to spring up and trouble a new generation.
> — Frederick Douglass

Sunshine Loaf

Minnie Wilson

Makes 1 loaf

3 cups buttermilk baking mix
1/2 cup sugar
3 eggs
1 Tbsp. grated orange peel
1/2 cup orange juice
1 package pitted dates, cut up
2 large bananas, mashed

1. Combine first 5 ingredients in large electric mixer bowl.
2. Stir in dates and bananas. Mix at medium speed for 2 minutes.
3. Pour into greased and floured 9" x 5" x 3" loaf pan.
4. Bake at 350° for 60-70 minutes. Cool 10 minutes. Remove from pan. Cool thoroughly before slicing.

Carrot Bread

Mrs. Margaret Bailey

Makes 2 loaves

3 eggs, beaten
1/2 cup oil
2/3 cup honey
8-oz. can crushed pineapples, undrained
2 cups shredded carrots
1/2 cup chopped pecans, optional
1 1/2 cups whole wheat flour
1 cup flour
1 tsp. baking powder
1 tsp. baking soda
1 1/2 tsp. ground cinnamon
1/4 tsp. salt

1. In large mixing bowl beat eggs with whisk. Add oil and honey. Whisk well.

2. Add pineapple, carrots, and pecans.

3. In a separate bowl stir together flours, baking powder, baking soda, cinnamon, and salt. Stir into wet ingredients. Mix well.

4. Pour batter into 2 greased 8½" x 4½" loaf pans. Smooth and level tops.

5. Bake at 350° for 45 minutes. Remove from pan. Cool. Store a day before slicing.

Note: This bread is good spread with cream cheese.

Applesauce Bread

Minnie Wilson

Makes 1 loaf

2½ cups buttermilk baking mix
⅓ cup sugar
¼ cup (½ stick) butter or margarine, softened
2 eggs
1 cup applesauce
1 tsp. cinnamon
½ tsp. ground nutmeg
¼ tsp. ground cloves
1 cup raisins

1. Combine all ingredients except raisins in large electric mixer bowl. Mix on low for 30 seconds. Beat at medium speed for 2 minutes.

2. Fold in raisins.

3. Pour batter into greased and floured 9" x 5" x 3" loaf pan.

4. Bake at 350° for 55 minutes. Remove from pan and cool before slicing.

Zucchini Nut Bread

Makes 2 loaves

3 eggs
1 cup cooking oil
2 cups sugar
1 tsp. vanilla
2 cups raw, peeled and grated zucchini, drained
1 tsp. baking soda
½ tsp. baking powder
3 cups flour
1 tsp. salt
3½ tsp. cinnamon
1 cup chopped nuts

1. Beat eggs until foamy. Add oil, sugar, and vanilla. Mix well.

2. Stir in zucchini.

3. Sift together dry ingredients. Add to egg mixture. Mix well.

4. Fold in nuts.

5. Pour mixture into two 9" x 5" greased bread pans.

6. Bake at 350° for 55 minutes.

Hobby-Bakers Coffee-Breakers

Minnie Wilson

Makes 12 rolls

1/4 cup (1/2 stick) butter or margarine
1/3 cup brown sugar, packed
1 tsp. light corn syrup
1/3 cup chopped pecans
1 pkg. dry yeast
2/3 cup warm water (105°-115°)
2 1/2 cups buttermilk baking mix
2 Tbsp. butter or margarine, softened
1/4 cup brown sugar
1 tsp. cinnamon

1. Melt 1/4 cup butter in small saucepan. Stir in brown sugar and corn syrup. Heat to boiling. Spread immediately in 15 1/2" x 10 1/2" jelly-roll pan. Sprinkle with pecans.
2. Dissolve yeast in warm water. Stir in baking mix. Beat well.
3. Form into ball. Knead 10 times on floured board.
4. Roll dough into 12" square. Brush with 2 Tbsp. butter.
5. Combine sugar and cinnamon. Sprinkle half of the mixture down center of dough.
6. Fold a third of dough over sugar/cinnamon mixture. Sprinkle with remaining sugar/cinnamon mixture. Fold over the remaining third of dough.
7. Cut into 4" x 1" strips. Twist two ends of each strip in opposite directions. Seal ends securely.
8. Place 1 1/2" apart in jelly-roll pan. Cover. Let rise in warm place for 60 minutes.
9. Bake at 400° for 15 minutes. Immediately invert onto heatproof tray. Leave pan over rolls for 1 minute. Serve warm.

Frontier Nut Bread

Minnie Wilson

Makes 1 loaf

3 cups buttermilk baking mix
1/2 cup sugar
3 eggs
3/4 cup milk
3/4 tsp. anise extract
3/4 cup coarsely chopped walnuts or
    pecans
1/2 cup mixed candied fruit

1. Combine baking mix, sugar, eggs, and milk in large electric mixer bowl. Mix on low for 30 seconds. Beat for 3 minutes at medium speed.
2. Stir in remaining ingredients.
3. Pour into greased and floured 9" x 5" x 3" loaf pan.
4. Bake at 350° for 50-60 minutes. Cool 10 minutes. Remove from pan. Cool before slicing.

Monkey Bread

Carletha Akins

Makes 10 servings

¾ cup granulated sugar
1 tsp. ground cinnamon
1 cup chopped walnuts or pecans
3 cans refrigerated biscuits (8-10 in each
   can)

Topping:
¼ lb. (1 stick) butter
1 cup brown sugar
1 tsp. vanilla

1. Pour sugar, cinnamon, and nuts in paper or plastic bag. Shake to mix.
2. Cut each biscuit into quarters. Add a few biscuit pieces to bag. Shake until dough is well coated. Repeat until all biscuits are coated.
3. Pour coated biscuit quarters into a buttered tube or bundt pan. Arrange neatly.
4. Melt butter in saucepan. Stir sugar and vanilla into melted butter. Crumble over top of dough mixture.
5. Bake at 350° for 25-35 minutes.

French Toast

Rina McKee

Makes 3 servings of 2 slices each

2 eggs, lightly beaten
1¼ cups milk
1 Tbsp. sugar
½ tsp. vanilla
4 Tbsp. (½ stick) butter
6 pieces bread, thickly sliced
warm syrup
powdered sugar

1. Whisk together eggs, milk, sugar, and vanilla.
2. Melt half the butter in heavy skillet.
3. Dip bread, a slice at a time, in egg mixture. Brown both sides of each slice in skillet, adding butter when needed.
4. Serve topped with warm syrup and powdered sugar.

You made mush by putting meal in water, stirring it up, and cooking it awhile. Then you put it in your bowl and poured milk over it. Some people knew how to make it good! When you were poor, you just used meal, salt, and water.

When my oldest brothers, Lawrence and Moses, went to school, the kids would say, "What did you have for breakfast?" They stretched it a little and said, "We had chicken and rice and all sort of stuff!" Then the kids asked my sisters Mary and Martha what they had for breakfast and they said, "We had mush and milk."

Lawrence and Moses just went overboard! Now who eats all that for breakfast?!

— Frances Morant,
Bothers & Sisters Cafe

Follow the Drinking Gourd

When the sun come back,
When the firs' quail call,
Then the time is come,
Follow the drinking gourd.

Chorus:
Follow the drinking gourd,
Follow the drinking gourd,
For the ole man say,
"Follow the drinking gourd."

The rivers bank am a very good road,
The dead trees show the way,
Left foot, peg foot going on,
Follow the drinking gourd.

The river ends between two hills,
Follow the drinking gourd.
Another River on the other side
Follows the drinking gourd.

Wait the Little River
Meet the great big one,
The old man waits —
Follow the drinking gourd.

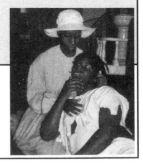

This traditional spiritual was a map for escaping Africans, telling them to follow the Big Dipper and the North Star.

Soups

*D*addy made the greatest soups. The memory of a bowl of Daddy's chicken and vegetable soup still warms my spirit.

In the slave quarters, where enslaved Africans lived in overcrowded conditions, too hot in the summer and freezing in the winter, the kettle pot sat in or over a small fire. In it was every piece of edible vegetable, and sometimes meat scraps, cooking. The pot was put on early in the morning, providing a source of nourishment, and sometimes comfort, for those who ate from it.

— Phoebe Bailey

Soups — Traditional

Homemade Tomato Soup

Mrs. Margaret Bailey

Makes 4-6 servings

2 Tbsp. oil
1 large onion, chopped
1 clove garlic, crushed
28-oz. can crushed tomatoes
2 cups chicken broth
2 potatoes, peeled and grated
salt to taste
pepper to taste
1 cup shredded cheese for garnish

1. Saute onion and garlic in oil for 5 minutes.
2. Stir in tomatoes, chicken broth, potatoes, salt, and pepper. Cook 20 minutes or until potatoes are tender.
3. Ladle into bowls. Sprinkle with cheese just before serving.

Turkey Soup

Makes 6-8 servings

3 cups cut-up turkey
1 cup water
2 cups diced turnips, optional
2 cups chopped celery
1 cup chopped onions
2 cups stewed tomatoes
2 cups diced potatoes
1 tsp. salt
1 tsp. pepper

1. Combine all ingredients in large kettle.
2. Cover and simmer for 1 1/2-2 hours, or until vegetables are tender. Add more water as soup simmers if it seems too dry.

I don't know how we got a hold of it but we had an old abandoned refrigerator in our house, and it was full of Cheerios. We never ran out of cereal. We had Cheerios galore.
— Barbara McFadden Enty, a member of Bethel AMEC, Lancaster, PA

Chicken and Rice Soup

Makes 4-5 servings

2-2½-lb. chicken
salt to taste
pepper to taste
5 cups water
1 cup uncooked rice

   1. Cut chicken into small pieces. Season with salt and pepper. Put in large kettle. Add water. Cover. Cook on medium heat until chicken is tender, about an hour.

   2. Remove chicken from broth. Debone and skim excess fat from top.

   3. Add chicken and rice to broth. Season to taste. Cover. Simmer approximately 20 minutes, or until rice is tender.

Note: Add 1 cup chopped celery when stirring in uncooked rice for additional flavoring.

Pig's Feet Soup

Makes 4-6 servings

1½ lbs. pig's feet
water to cover pig's feet
1 Tbsp. vinegar
2 tsp. salt
¼ tsp. red pepper
2 tomatoes, chopped
1 cup cooked lima beans
1 cup cooked corn

   1. Combine water, vinegar, pig's feet, salt, and pepper in large stockpot. Cover, bring to boil, and simmer for 1½ hours, until meat is tender.

   2. Stir in tomatoes, lima beans, and corn. Bring to boil. Remove pig's feet and debone.

   3. Reduce heat. Stir meat back into soup. Cover and simmer for 15 minutes.

Soups — Other Favorites

Washington Chowder

Makes 8-10 servings

4 strips bacon, diced
1 medium onion, diced
2 ribs celery, diced
1 Tbsp. flour
4 cups chicken broth
2 medium-sized potatoes, diced
2½ cups corn
⅛ tsp. savory
¼ tsp. dried thyme
1½ cups diced tomatoes
2 cups milk
salt to taste
pepper to taste

1. Brown bacon in heavy soup pot. Remove bacon and reserve drippings.
2. Add onions and celery. Cook until soft in drippings.
3. Sprinkle in flour. Cook, stirring for 3 minutes.
4. Whisk in broth. Slowly bring to a boil.
5. Add potatoes, corn, savory, thyme, and tomatoes. Simmer until potatoes are soft, about 25 minutes.
6. Stir in milk. Season with salt and pepper. Simmer 20 minutes.

Tomato and Rice Soup

Makes 4 servings

1 lb. beef stewing cubes
1 Tbsp. shortening
2 cups water
2 cups stewed tomatoes
1½ tsp. pepper
½ tsp. salt
1 lb. cut-up okra
¾ cup uncooked rice

1. Brown beef in shortening. Drain off drippings.
2. Add water, tomatoes, pepper, and salt. Bring to brisk boil.
3. Add okra and rice. Bring back to boil.
4. Cover and reduce heat. Simmer 40 minutes.

We were so poor, Mother cut up her dresses to make dresses for my sister and me. Mother said that when she married she had 12 dresses with shoes and hats to match. After we children came, that was the end of her getting more fine clothing.
— Elizabeth McGill,
a member of Bethel AMEC,
Lancaster, PA

Beef Barley Minestrone

Mrs. Margaret Bailey

Makes 4 servings

1-2 meaty soup bones
6 cups water
2 onions, chopped
1 carrot, sliced
1 rib celery plus leaves, chopped
6-oz. can tomato paste
3 Tbsp. regular barley, uncooked
garlic salt to taste
pepper to taste
dried oregano to taste
dried basil to taste
2 cups shredded cabbage

1. In stockpot simmer bones in water for an hour. Remove from heat and chill until melted fat hardens on surface and can be lifted off. Discard fat. Trim meat off bones and reserve.
2. Combine all ingredients in stockpot except cabbage and reserved meat. Heat to boiling. Mix well. Cover and simmer for 40 minutes.
3. Add cabbage and meat. Simmer 15-20 minutes more.

Minestrone Soup

Makes 6-8 servings

1 1/2 lbs. round steak, cut in 1" cubes
2 Tbsp. oil
6 cups water
15-oz. can herby tomato sauce
1 onion, chopped
1 clove garlic, chopped
1 cup chopped celery
2 Tbsp. chopped parsley
1 Tbsp. salt
1/2 tsp. dried oregano
1/4 tsp. pepper
1 cup broken, uncooked spaghetti
1 1/2 cups sliced zucchini
10-oz. pkg. frozen peas, partially thawed
Parmesan cheese

1. Brown beef in oil in heavy kettle.
2. Add water, tomato sauce, onions, garlic, celery, parsley, and seasonings. Cover and simmer 2 hours.
3. Add spaghetti. Simmer 15 minutes.
4. Add vegetables. Simmer 5 minutes.
5. Ladle into individual soup bowls and sprinkle each with cheese.

Minestrone with Tortellini

Carol Grassie

Makes 10-12 servings

1/3 cup olive oil
1 large yellow onion, cut into thin rings
4 large carrots, peeled and thickly sliced
2 large potatoes, peeled and diced
1 green bell pepper, cored, seeded, and cut
    into 1/2" squares
3 medium-sized zucchini, diced
1 1/2 cups green beans, sliced diagonally
5 cups (or 3 14 1/2-oz. cans) beef stock
5 cups water
28-oz. can Italian plum tomatoes
2 Tbsp. dried oregano
1 Tbsp. dried basil
salt to taste
freshly ground pepper to taste
outer rind of a 2" chunk of Parmesan or
    Romano cheese
19-oz. can white kidney (or cannellini)
    beans, drained
1 lb. uncooked cheese tortellini
grated Parmesan or Romano cheese

    1. Saute onion in oil for 10-15 minutes.

    2. Stir in carrots. Saute 2-3 minutes, tossing occasionally.

    3. One-by-one, add potatoes, green pepper, zucchini, and green beans, sauteing each vegetable 2-3 minutes before adding the next.

    4. Add stock, water, tomatoes with juice, oregano, basil, salt, and pepper.

    5. Bury cheese rind in the middle of the soup. Heat to boiling. Reduce heat. Cover and simmer for 2 1/2-3 hours. The soup will be very thick.

    6. Fifteen minutes before serving, stir in cannellini beans and tortellini. Increase heat to cook tortellini, stirring occasionally to keep pasta and vegetables from sticking to bottom of pot.

    7. Remove cheese rind. Ladle soup into individual bowls. Top with grated Parmesan or Romano cheeses.

Three-Bean Soup

Mrs. Margaret Bailey

Makes 6 servings

2 Tbsp. olive oil
1 large onion, diced
2 garlic cloves, minced
2 (14-oz.) cans beef bouillon
1/4 cup dry rice
15-oz. can chickpeas, drained
15-oz. can red kidney beans, drained
15-oz. can white kidney (cannellini) beans,
    drained
2 Tbsp. red wine vinegar
salt to taste
freshly ground black pepper to taste

    1. In stockpot saute onion and garlic over medium high heat in oil for 5 minutes.

    2. Stir in bouillon, rice, chickpeas, and beans. Simmer 20 minutes, or until rice is tender.

    3. Remove half of soup and puree in blender. Return to pot.

    4. Stir in vinegar. Season with salt and pepper.

> Race prejudice is the devil unchained.
>
> — Charles W. Chesnutt

Bean Soup

Wanda Davis

5½ quarts soup

½ cup dry Great Northern beans
½ cup dry kidney beans
½ cup dry navy beans
½ cup dry lima beans
½ cup dry butter beans
½ cup dry pinto beans
½ cup dry lentils
ham hock or beef soup bone
2 chicken bouillon cubes
28-oz. can diced tomatoes and juice
1 very large onion, chopped
4 ribs celery, chopped
2 garlic cloves, minced
3 bay leaves
2 Tbsp. parsley
1 tsp. dry thyme
1 tsp. ground mustard
½ tsp. cayenne pepper, optional
2 carrots, grated

1. Pour beans (but not lentils) into large stockpot and cover with water. Bring water to boil and allow to boil for 2 minutes. Cover, remove pot from heat, and soak 60 minutes.
2. While beans are soaking, place soup bones in another kettle and cover with water. Simmer meat for 30 minutes.
3. Add meat and its broth, and all remaining ingredients except carrots, to beans in large stockpot. Add more water if needed so that water is 2" above ingredients. Cook on low for 2-3 hours or until beans are tender.
4. Discard meat bone and bay leaves. Add carrots and additional water if needed. Cook 15 minutes.

Mushroom Soup

Mrs. Margaret Bailey

Makes 4 to 6 servings

1½ lbs. fresh mushrooms
5 Tbsp. butter
1 medium onion, chopped
⅓ cup flour
4 cups chicken stock
1 Tbsp. butter
1 tsp. salt
¼ tsp. ground nutmeg
white pepper to taste
1 cup heavy cream
whipped cream, lightly salted, for garnish

1. Wash mushrooms. Finely chop half of mushroom caps and all of the stems. Slice remaining mushroom caps.
2. Saute onion in 5 Tbsp. butter until translucent.
3. Add chopped (not sliced) mushroom caps and stems. Saute 3 minutes.
4. Stir in flour. Add chicken stock. Bring to boil, stirring constantly. Lower heat and simmer 15 minutes.
5. In a separate saucepan saute sliced mushrooms in 1 Tbsp. butter until they have given up their moisture but are not yet browned. Add to soup.
6. Season to taste with salt, nutmeg, and white pepper.
7. Stir in heavy cream. Heat.
8. Serve with a teaspoon of salted whipped cream floated on top of each bowlful.

Broccoli Soup

Carol Grassie

Makes 6 servings

4 Tbsp. (1/2 stick) butter
1 small onion, finely chopped
1 rib celery, finely chopped
2 cups chicken stock
salt to taste
pepper to taste
1 small potato, finely chopped
3-4 cups finely chopped broccoli
1-2 cups half-and-half
salt, if needed
pepper, if needed

1. Saute onion and celery in butter until tender.
2. Stir in chicken stock, salt and pepper to taste, potato, and broccoli. Cook until vegetables are tender.
3. Remove a few pieces of broccoli. Pour remaining cooked vegetables and 1/2 cup broth into blender or food processor. Puree. Return to saucepan.
4. Stir in half-and-half. Add reserved broccoli. Heat well, but do not boil.
5. Season with salt and pepper if needed.

Zucchini Soup

Mrs. Margaret Bailey

Makes 4 servings

1 onion, chopped
10 ozs. condensed chicken broth
2 cups boiling water
4 fresh zucchini, sliced
1 clove garlic, minced
4 Tbsp. chopped fresh parsley
1 Tbsp. chopped fresh basil, or
   1 tsp. dried
4 tsp. grated Parmesan cheese
1 cup grated sharp cheddar cheese

1. Simmer onion in chicken broth for 5 minutes.
2. Stir in remaining ingredients, except cheeses. Simmer uncovered for 3-4 minutes.
3. Spoon into soup bowls. Sprinkle with Parmesan and cheddar cheeses.

Variation: For Creamy Zucchini Soup follow the recipe above, but reduce water to 1 cup. Simmer ingredients an extra 5 minutes until zucchini is very tender. Pour hot soup mixture into blender or food processor. Add 1/2 cup ricotta cheese to soup mixture and puree until smooth. Serve immediately.

Vegetable Broth

Rina Mckee

1 gallon water
2 ribs celery, coarsely chopped
2 large onions, coarsely chopped
3 carrots, coarsely chopped
1 cup diced tomatoes
1/2 cup chopped cabbage
1 tsp. minced garlic
8 stems parsley
1 turnip, coarsley chopped
salt to taste
pepper to taste

1. Combine all ingredients in large kettle. Slowly bring to boil.
2. Reduce heat and simmer for 2 1/2 hours.
3. Strain through colander, or puree in blender. Use as soup base.

Chicken Soup

Makes 4-6 servings

2 chicken legs
6 cups water
1 scallion, sliced
1 sm. piece ginger, peeled
1 Tbsp. sherry
6 Chinese mushrooms
1/2 cup warm water
1 small bamboo shoot, sliced, or 1 small
    can bamboo shoots, drained
1 1/2 tsp. salt
1/2 tsp. monosodium glutamate, optional

1. Wash chicken in running hot water.
2. Boil chicken in water until tender. Debone and return meat to broth. Add scallion, ginger, and sherry. Bring water to boil, skimming off foam.
3. Meanwhile, soak mushrooms in mixing bowl in warm water for 10 minutes. Remove stems. Slice mushrooms.
4. Add mushroom and bamboo shoot slices to soup. Reduce heat. Simmer for 30 minutes. Remove ginger.
5. Season with salt and monosodium glutamate, if desired, and serve.

We used Arm and Hammer for toothpaste.
— Hattie McFadden,
a member of Bethel AMEC,
Lancaster, PA

159

Stracciatella

Mrs. Margaret Bailey

Makes 4 servings

4 cups chicken stock
2 eggs
1/4 cup grated Parmesan cheese
2 Tbsp. chopped fresh Italian parsley

1. In stockpot bring chicken stock to full boil.
2. Beat together eggs, cheese, and parsley. Stirring constantly, pour the egg mixture slowly into the boiling stock. Cook 60 seconds or until the egg mixture is set.

Crab Soup

Makes 12 servings

1 lb. crabmeat
1 Tbsp. prepared mustard
salt to taste
2 Tbsp. Old Bay Seasoning
28-oz. can diced tomatoes
6 potatoes, diced
2 cups whole-kernel corn
2 carrots diced
1 cup lima beans
1 cup green beans
2 ribs celery, diced
1/2 cup chopped parsley

1. Cover crabmeat with water.
2. Combine mustard, salt, and seasoning. Add to crabmeat. Simmer 30 minutes.
3. Stir in remaining ingredients. Simmer until vegetables are tender. Add additional Old Bay Seasoning if desired.

Shrimp and Vegetable Gumbo

Mrs. Margaret Bailey

Makes 8-10 servings

2 Tbsp. oil
1 cup chopped onions
1 cup chopped green peppers
1/2 cup chopped celery
1 clove garlic, pressed
1 bay leaf
1/2 tsp. salt
1/4 tsp. pepper
1-lb. 12-oz. can tomatoes, undrained
13 3/4-oz. can chicken broth
10-oz. pkg. frozen okra, thawed
1/2-1 lb. large shrimp in shells
3-4 cups fluffy cooked rice
chopped parsley

1. Saute onions, green peppers, celery, and garlic in oil in 6-quart Dutch oven. Stir over medium heat until celery is tender.
2. Add bay leaf, salt, pepper, tomatoes, and chicken broth. Mash tomatoes with fork. Bring to boil, stirring frequently. Cover and simmer for 30 minutes.
3. Add okra to tomato mixture. Cover and simmer 15 minutes.
4. Shell and devein shrimp. Cut in half lengthwise. Add to tomato mixture. Cover and cook for 3 minutes or until tender.
5. Spoon gumbo over 1/4 cup cooked rice in each warm serving bowl. Sprinkle with parsley.

Shrimp Gumbo with Rice

Rina Mckee

Makes 4-6 servings

4 Tbsp. (½ stick) butter
¼ cup flour
4 cups chicken broth
1 medium onion, diced
half a red bell pepper, diced
half a yellow bell pepper, diced
2 tsp. garlic, minced
6 ozs. okra, sliced
1 lb. raw shrimp, peeled and deveined
dash Tabasco sauce

1. Melt butter in heavy stockpot. Whisk in flour. Cook over medium heat, stirring frequently until well mixed.
2. Add chicken broth. Bring to simmer, whisking until broth is smooth and thickened.
3. Stir in vegetables. Simmer for 45-60 minutes or until vegetables are just soft.
4. Add shrimp and Tabasco. Simmer for 10 more minutes.
5. Serve over rice.

I loved Ketchup sandwiches.
— Barbara McFadden Enty,
a member of Bethel AMEC,
Lancaster, PA

Seafood Bisque

Makes 12-15 servings

2 Tbsp. oil
2 onions, diced
4 ribs celery, diced
12 shrimp, peeled and deveined
6 ozs. fresh halibut
6 ozs. fresh cod
6 ozs. fresh red snapper
6 ozs. fresh perch
2 qts. water
14½-oz. can tomato sauce
2 14½-oz. cans tomatoes
2 cans shrimp bisque
Old Bay Seasoning to taste
1 qt. whole milk

1. In large kettle, saute onions and celery in oil.
2. Add seafood and water. Bring to boil.
3. Add tomato sauce, tomatoes, bisque, and Seasoning. Simmer for 20 minutes.
4. Stir in milk. Bring soup to simmer but do not boil. Serve immediately.

Note: If you're budget-conscious, you may substitute any white fish for the halibut, cod, and perch.

Seafood Soup

Makes 8-10 servings

3 10½-oz. cans beef broth
14½-oz. can whole tomatoes
6 cups water
¼ cup chopped onions
2-2½ Tbsp. Old Bay Seasoning
5 cups diced potatoes
2 10-oz. boxes frozen mixed vegetables
10-16 ozs. fresh fish, crab, or shrimp

1. Combine broth, tomatoes, water, and onion in large pot. Bring to boil.
2. Add Seasoning, potatoes, and vegetables. Simmer 1½-2 hours.
3. Stir in meat. Simmer 15-20 minutes.

Sins, like chickens, come home to roost.

— Charles W. Chesnutt

Salmon Corn Chowder

Mrs. Margaret Bailey

Makes 6 servings

15-oz. can salmon
2 Tbsp. butter
1 large onion, chopped
1 cup chopped celery
2 cups milk
2 cups chicken broth
10-oz. pkg. frozen chopped spinach,
    defrosted and squeezed dry
17-oz. can creamed corn
1 tsp. dried thyme

1. Drain salmon. Remove skin and bones. Flake. Set aside.
2. In stockpot saute onion and celery in butter for 5 minutes.
3. Stir in milk, chicken broth, spinach, corn, and thyme. Simmer 15 minutes.
4. Stir in salmon. Bring back to simmer and continue cooking until heated through.

Harvest Salmon Chowder

Mrs. Margaret Bailey

Makes 4 to 6 servings

7¾-oz. can salmon
1 clove garlic, minced
½ cup chopped onion
½ cup chopped celery
2 Tbsp. margarine
1 cup diced potatoes
1 cup diced carrots
2 cups chicken broth
1 tsp. salt
¼ tsp. pepper
¼ tsp. dried thyme
½ cup chopped broccoli
17-oz. can creamed corn
8½-oz. can evaporated milk
minced parsley

1. Drain and flake salmon, reserving liquid. Set salmon aside.
2. Saute garlic, onion, and celery in margarine.
3. Add potatoes, carrots, liquid from salmon, chicken broth, and seasonings. Cover and simmer for 20 minutes, or until vegetables are nearly tender.
4. Add broccoli. Cook for 5 minutes.
5. Add salmon, corn, and evaporated milk. Heat well.
6. Sprinkle with parsley.

1825 — I took stage and went on to Lancaster; but prospect not so good there; they had a new Church (Bethel African Methodist Church) but not paid for; the proprietor took the key in possession and deprived them of worshipping God in it. But I spoke in a dwelling house, and I felt a great zeal for the cause of God to soften that man's heart, or kill him out of the way; one had better die than many. Brother Israel Williams, a few days, called to converse with him on the subject, and he gave him the key; he was then on his deathbed, and died in a short time afterwards, and we must leave him in the hands of God, for he can open and no man can shut.

— Jarena Lee,
first woman AME preacher

Bethel AME's Annual Cookout

Historic Bethel African Methodist Episcopal Church in Lancaster, Pennsylvania, holds an annual cookout, and it always includes food, fellowship, and fun — the primary ingredients for a great summer get-together! On a warm Sunday afternoon, after a spiritually uplifting combined service, we venture out to the church yard, paying respect to the gravesites of the members of the past, those who served as pastors, those who served as conductors on the Underground Railroad, and those who served in the Civil War to fight for the Africans' freedom. We rally around for a word of prayer and thanksgiving, before we start competing for the first place in line for some of the pastor's famous ribs!

Menu:
Rev. Bailey's Famous Ribs
Fried Turkey
Fried Chicken
Hot Dogs
Hamburgers
Garden Salad
Potato Salad
Three-Bean Salad
Macaroni Salad with Hard-boiled Eggs
Pasta Salad with Seafood
Pickled Red Beet Eggs
Baked Bean Casserole
Cakes
Watermelon
Fruit Salad
Plenty to Drink

Bethel AME Church's Vision —
To serve as Christ-centered, African-centered leadership
for holistic community-building within ChurchTowne of the
Seventh Ward, Lancaster, Pennsylvania.

Sweets

When my twin brothers went away to college in Connecticut, it was the first time they had been away from our mother. Every month Mama sent them a care package of her homemade cookies: chocolate chip, oatmeal, butter, and what she called her Fun Cookies, made with extra love.

My job was to protect the twins' cookies from everyone else in the family before Mama got them packed off. Naturally, I was rewarded for my hard work, in cookies, of course. My brothers turned out to be very enterprising. They started a "Mama's Cookies" business.

The women before my mother, who worked in the Big House, prepared the finest desserts and pastries for the plantation owner's family and guests. African women expressed their creativity on trays of sweet cakes, butter cakes, pies, and shortbreads. The sweetest thing the enslaved African desired, of course, was freedom!

— Phoebe Bailey

Sweets — Traditional

Sweet Potato Pudding

Carrie Alford

Makes 10 servings

5 eggs, beaten
1 cup sugar
2 Tbsp. butter or margarine, melted
3 cups grated raw sweet potatoes
2 cups milk
1/2 cup dark molasses
1/2 tsp. salt
1/2 tsp. ground cinnamon
1/2 tsp. ground allspice
1/2 tsp. ground nutmeg

1. Combine eggs, sugar, and butter. Mix well.
2. Stir in remaining ingredients.
3. Pour into 10" cast-iron skillet.
4. Bake uncovered at 375° for 35 minutes, or until top is browned. Stir top crust under.
5. Bake an additional 25 minutes, or until knife inserted in center comes out clean.
6. Serve warm topped with whipped cream, whipped topping, or vanilla ice cream.

Sweet Potato Pie

Makes 6-8 servings

4-6 medium-sized sweet potatoes
1/2 lb. (2 sticks) butter, softened
1 1/2 cups sugar
4-6 eggs
2 Tbsp. flour
1/2 cup milk
ground nutmeg to taste
9" unbaked pie crust

1. Boil potatoes until soft. Peel, then mash to smooth consistency.
2. Add butter, sugar, eggs, and flour. Mix well.
3. Add milk and nutmeg. Mix well.
4. Pour into pie shell.
5. Bake at 350° for 1 3/4-2 hours, until lightly browned and set. Cool before slicing.

Pecan Pie

Brothers and Sisters Cafe

Makes 1 9" pie

1/2 cup brown sugar
1/2 cup sugar
4 Tbsp. flour
1 cup corn syrup
3 eggs
1 tsp. vanilla
1 Tbsp. butter, softened
2 cups pecans
9" pie crust, unbaked

1. Combine sugars and flour.
2. Stir in remaining ingredients. Mix well. Pour into pie crust.
3. Bake at 350° until firm, 55-60 minutes. If edge of crust begins to brown too much, cover it with a rim of tin foil, while center of pie bakes sufficiently.

Pecan Pie

Makes 1 9" pie

3/4 cup light corn syrup
1/4 cup light molasses
1 cup light brown sugar
1 Tbsp. butter, at room temperature
1/4 tsp. salt
1 tsp. vanilla
3 eggs, slightly beaten
1 cup coarsely chopped pecans
9" unbaked pie crust

1. Combine syrup, molasses, brown sugar, and butter. Blend well, but do not overmix.
2. Add salt, vanilla, and eggs.
3. Fold in pecans.
4. Pour into pie crust.
5. Bake at 350° for 45-50 minutes, or until knife inserted in center comes out clean.

One of my fondest memories of cooking with my mother (Margaret Bailey) is the first time she taught me to make pudding, the kind you had to stir and stir. I wasn't tall enough, so she pulled a chair up to the stove for me to stand on. I felt like a giant!
— Phoebe Bailey

Pumpkin Pie

Makes 1 9" pie

1 1/2-2 cups mashed, cooked pumpkin
1/2 tsp. salt
1/2 tsp. ground nutmeg
2 eggs, beaten
12-oz. can evaporated milk
2/3 cup brown sugar
1/2 tsp. cinnamon
3 Tbsp. molasses
9" unbaked pie crust
whipped cream
cinnamon

1. Combine pumpkin, salt, nutmeg, eggs, evaporated milk, brown sugar, cinnamon, and molasses. Mix until smooth.
2. Pour into pie crust.
3. Bake at 500° for 8 minutes. Reduce heat to 325°. Bake for 50-60 minutes.
4. Cool to room temperature. Top with whipped cream before serving. Sprinkle with cinnamon.

Peach Cobbler

Makes 12-15 servings

1/2 cup (1 stick) butter, melted
1/2 cup milk
1/2 cup sugar
scant 1 cup flour
1 1/2 tsp. baking powder
1/2 tsp. salt
3/4 cup sugar
1/2 tsp. ground nutmeg
1/2 tsp. cinnamon
3 15-oz. cans sliced peaches, drained

1. Pour butter into 9" x 13" pan.
2. Combine milk, 1/2 cup sugar, flour, baking powder, and salt until a paste is formed. Pour over butter. Do not stir together.
3. Sprinkle 3/4 cup sugar, nutmeg, and cinnamon over peaches. Spoon on top of batter. Do not stir together.
4. Bake at 350° for 40 minutes or longer, until brown.
5. Serve warm with milk or ice cream.

Sweets — Other Favorites

Baked Honey Pears

Makes 4 servings

4 firm pears
2 Tbsp. brandy or pear liqueur
2 Tbsp. honey
3 Tbsp. butter, melted
3 Tbsp. half-and-half

1. Place pears in small baking dish.
2. Combine brandy and honey. Brush over pears.
3. Bake at 325° for 45-60 minutes, until tender, brushing pears with brandy/honey mixture every 15 minutes.
4. Place pears on serving dish.
5. Combine butter and half-and-half. Briefly cook over medium heat. Pour over pears. Serve warm.

Poached Pears

Rina Mckee

Makes 2 servings

2 firm medium-sized pears, peeled
1 1/2 cups red wine
1/4 cup sugar
1/8 tsp cinnamon
1 Tbsp. brandy, optional

1. Combine all ingredients in small saucepan. Simmer about 15 minutes, until pears are just soft.

2. Remove pears to bowl. Cool to room temperature.
3. Raise flame to medium heat. Reduce sauce by half, simmering uncovered about 10 minutes. Cool. Pour over pears.
4. Cover and refrigerate for at least 2 hours before serving.

Baked Pears

Mrs. Margaret Bailey

Makes 4 servings

4 small ripe pears, halved and cored
1/2 cup water
1/2 tsp. vanilla
sprinkle of ground cinnamon

1. Arrange pears in shallow baking pan.
2. Combine water and vanilla. Pour over pears.
3. Sprinkle with cinnamon.
4. Bake at 350° for 40-45 minutes or until tender.

Note: For a sweeter dessert, sprinkle pears lightly with sugar before baking.

Pear Au Chocolate

Makes 8 servings

2-lb. can pear halves, chilled and drained
1 can chocolate frosting, or your favorite
   homemade frosting
whipped cream
cherries

1. Spread 1 Tbsp. frosting in each pear cavity. Top with another pear. Stand upright in serving dish. Keep pears cool while melting frosting.
2. Melt remaining chocolate frosting in top of double boiler. Pour over pears.
3. Garnish each with whipped cream and a cherry and serve immediately.

Glazed Apple Rings

Makes 6-8 servings

¼ cup margarine or butter
4 apples, cored, peeled or unpeeled
½ cup dry white wine or apple juice
1 Tbsp. lemon juice
¼ tsp. ginger
¼ tsp. cinnamon
½ cup sugar, or less, according to your
   taste preference
whipped cream, whipped topping, or
   vanilla ice cream

1. Melt margarine in 10″ skillet over medium heat.
2. Slice apples in ½″-thick rings. Fry apple slices, a few at a time, in margarine until golden brown, adding more margarine if necessary.
3. When all slices have been browned, return all apples to skillet.

4. Combine wine, lemon juice, ginger, and cinnamon. Pour over apples. Sprinkle with sugar.
5. Cover and cook over medium heat, turning once, until apples are tender and glazed, about 5 minutes.
6. Serve warm, drizzled with remaining syrup, and with topping of your choice.

Fried Apples

Makes 4 servings

4 apples, preferably still green
2 Tbsp. butter
⅓ cup brown sugar
2 Tbsp. water

1. Core apples. Cut into circles or slices.
2. Saute in butter, turning often until soft, but still holding their shape.
3. Stir in brown sugar and water. Continue cooking until apples are coated wtih syrup.

Note: You may choose to peel—or not to peel—the apples.
   If you like more syrup, double the amount of water.

> My mother used to make cherry dumplings, and I helped her make them, too. You'd put them in cloth napkins and dip them in hot water and that's the way you cooked them. We didn't make them in the oven.
>
> — Nelson Polite, Sr.,
> a member of Bethel AMEC,
> Lancaster, PA

Fluffy Cream Sauce over Fruit

Makes 4-5 servings

²/₃ cup whipping cream, unwhipped
¹/₃ cup dairy sour cream
2-3 cups assorted fresh fruit (strawberries,
   sliced peaches, pineapple, or
   raspberries)
nutmeg or sugar

1. Whip cream, then gently fold into sour cream. Cover and refrigerate until ready to serve.
2. Prepare fruit in individual serving dishes, dollop with cream sauce, and sprinkle with nutmeg or sugar.

Chocolate Covered Strawberries

Makes 8-10 servings

1 qt. fresh strawberries with stems
8 ozs. sweet chocolate
1¹/₂ Tbsp. Grand Marnier, optional

1. Melt chocolate in double boiler. Whisk in Grand Marnier.
2. Hold each strawberry by its stem and dip its lower half, or more, into chocolate. Place on sheet of waxed paper. Cool.

Fruit Pizza Cookies

Makes as many servings as you have cookies

sugar cookies
frozen whipped topping, thawed
fruit, such as apples, kiwi, strawberries,
   blueberries, mangoes, peaches, grapes,
   bananas

1. Spread cookies with whipped topping.
2. Cut fruit into bite-sized pieces.
3. Arrange fruit on top of frosted cookies and serve.

Fresh Strawberry Mousse

Makes 8-10 servings

1 pt. fresh strawberries
2 3-oz. pkgs. strawberry gelatin
¹/₄ cup sugar
1 pt. whipping cream

1. Crush strawberries. Drain, reserving juice.
2. Add enough water to juice to make 1¹/₂ cups. Bring to boil.
3. Add gelatin. Stir until dissolved. Cool.
4. Fold in crushed strawberries and sugar.
5. Whip cream until it stands in soft peaks. Fold into strawberry mixture.
6. Pour into 1¹/₂-qt. soufflé dish with 2" collar and serve immediately.

Deluxe Strawberry Pie

Makes 6-8 servings

1 qt. fresh whole strawberries, stemmed
9″ baked pie crust
3-oz. pkg. cream cheese, softened
8-oz. container frozen whipped topping, thawed

1. Stand whole strawberries upright in pie crust.
2. Combine cream cheese and whipped topping. Spread over strawberries.
3. Chill until serving time.

Baked Cherries and Custard

Makes 8 servings

2 cups pitted dark sweet cherries
3 eggs
1 cup milk
1/2 cup flour
1/4 cup sugar
1 tsp. vanilla
powdered sugar

1. Spread cherries in lightly greased 6″ x 10″ or 8″ x 8″ baking dish.
2. Beat together eggs, milk, flour, sugar, and vanilla until smooth. Pour over cherries.
3. Bake at 350° for 45-60 minutes.
4. Sprinkle with powdered sugar. Serve warm.

Cherries and Cream Roll

Makes 12 servings

3 eggs
3/4 cup sugar
1 Tbsp. frozen orange juice concentrate, thawed
2 Tbsp. water
1 cup cake flour
1 tsp. baking powder
1/4 tsp. salt
powdered sugar
21-oz. can red cherry pie filling
2 cups heavy whipping cream
1/2 cup powdered sugar
1/2 tsp. almond extract
fresh mint, optional

1. Beat eggs until thickened. Beat in sugar, 1 Tbsp. at a time. Continue to beat until mixture is very thick and creamy.
2. Slowly add orange juice concentrate and water.
3. Sift together flour, baking powder, and salt. Gradually add to batter. Beat until smooth.
4. Grease 15″ x 10″ jelly-roll pan. Line bottom with waxed paper. Grease paper.
5. Pour batter into prepared pan, spreading gently to corners.
6. Bake at 375° for 12 minutes.
7. Dust clean towel with powdered sugar. Loosen cake around edges with paring knife. Invert onto towel. Trim 1/4″ from all sides for easier rolling. Roll up cake and towel together. Cool completely on wire rack.
8. Drain cherry filling. Reserve cherries.
9. Beat cream until stiff. Fold in powdered sugar and almond extract.
10. Unroll cake. Spread with half of cream. Spoon 3/4 of cherries over cream. Roll up cake. Place roll seam down on plate.

Spread with remaining cream. Garnish with cherries and mint.

11. Slice and serve.

Note: Substitute blueberries or sliced peaches for cherries, if you wish.

Pumpkin Cheese Roll

Makes 10-12 servings

2/3 cup chopped nuts
3 eggs
1 cup sugar
2/3 cup cooked pumpkin
3/4 cup flour
1 tsp. baking soda
2 heaping tsp. cinnamon

Filling:
8-oz. pkg. cream cheese, at room
   temperature
1 cup powdered sugar
4 Tbsp. (1/2 stick) butter, softened
2 tsp. vanilla

1. Sprinkle greased jelly-roll pan with nuts.
2. Combine eggs, sugar, pumpkin, flour, baking soda, and cinnamon. Spread over nuts.
3. Bake at 375° for 15 minutes.
4. Loosen sides with knife and turn upside down on 2 sections of paper towels. Roll up. Cool for 1 hour. Unroll. Remove towels.
5. Combine cream cheese, powdered sugar, butter, and vanilla. Beat well. Spread over cake. Roll up.
6. Refrigerate until ready to slice and serve.

Strawberry Roll

Makes 12 servings

4 eggs, separated
1/2 cup granulated sugar
1 Tbsp. lemon juice
1 Tbsp. water
3/4 cup cake flour
1/4 tsp. salt
3/4 tsp. baking powder
1 tsp. vanilla
1/4 cup granulated sugar
powdered sugar
1 cup heavy whipped cream
2 cups fresh sliced strawberries
several whole strawberries

1. Beat eggs yolks until thick and lemon-colored. Beat in 1/2 cup granulated sugar, lemon juice, and water until well mixed.
2. Sift together flour, salt, and baking powder. Mix into egg-sugar mixture. Stir in vanilla.
3. In separate bowl beat egg whites until soft peaks form. Gradually add 1/4 cup granulated sugar, beating until stiff peaks form. Fold egg whites into batter.
4. Pour onto jelly-roll pan which has been lined with greased and floured waxed paper.
5. While cake is baking, spread out towel and sprinkle with powdered sugar.
6. Bake cake at 350° for 15 minutes, or until cake springs back when touched in center.
7. Immediately loosen cake from baking pan and turn onto towel. Cut rough edges off cake. Roll cake up in towel. Cool for at least an hour.
8. Unroll cake and remove towel. Spread cake with whipped cream. Sprinkle with sliced strawberries. Roll up again (without towel).
9. Refrigerate until ready to slice and serve. Place slices on individual plates and garnish each with whole strawberries.

Prune Tarts in Egg Pastry

Wanda Davis

Makes 6-8 servings

3 cups flour
1 tsp. salt, optional
1 cup shortening
1 egg, beaten
1 Tbsp. cold water
1 tsp. vinegar
flour
16-oz. pkg. dried prunes
sugar to taste
evaporated milk or whipping cream

1. Combine flour and salt.
2. Cut in shortening until mixture crumbles coarsely.
3. Add egg, cold water, and vinegar until mixture forms a ball of dough.
4. Sprinkle flat surface with flour. Pat down pastry. Sprinkle flour on top of dough. Roll to ¼" thick. Cut into 6-8 rounds with cookie cutter or large glass. Shape into tarts and place on greased cookie sheet.
5. Bake at 350° until browned. Remove from oven and cool.
6. Cook prunes and sugar in saucepan until thick and syrupy. Remove from heat and cool.
7. Cut up fruit.
8. Spoon fruit into tart pastries. Drizzle with evaporated milk or garnish with whipping cream.

Apple Dumplings

Makes 8 servings

2 cups flour
1 tsp. salt
2 tsp. baking powder
½ cup shortening
½ cup milk
8 small apples
¼ cup brown sugar
¼ tsp. ground nutmeg
2 Tbsp. butter

1. Sift together flour, salt, and baking powder.
2. Cut in shortening. Add milk to make soft dough.
3. Roll out fairly thin. Cut into 4" squares.
4. Peel and core apples, but keep them whole. Place an apple on each square.
5. Combine sugar and nutmeg. Divide sugar mixture and butter evenly into centers of apples.
6. Pull corners of dough squares up over apples. Seal.
7. Bake at 375° for 40 minutes. Serve hot or cold.

Baked Apple Pudding

Minnie Wilson

Makes 8-10 servings

1/3 cup margarine, softened
1 cup sugar
1 egg
1 cup unsifted flour
1 tsp. baking soda
1/4 tsp. salt
1/4 tsp. ground nutmeg
1/4 tsp. cinnamon
1 tsp. vanilla
2 cups grated unpared apples
1/2 cup chopped walnuts

1. Combine margarine, sugar, and egg. Beat until light and syrupy.
2. Mix together flour, baking soda, salt, nutmeg, and cinnamon in a separate bowl.
3. Gradually blend dry ingredients into wet ones.
4. Stir in vanilla, apples, and walnuts.
5. Pour into ungreased 8" x 8" baking pan.
6. Bake at 350° for 35 minutes. Serve warm or cold, topped with whipped cream or ice cream.

Baked Apple Pudding

Colleen Porter

Makes 9 servings

1/2 cup shortening
1 cup sugar
1 egg
1 cup flour
1/2 tsp. cinnamon
1/2 tsp. allspice
1/2 cup buttermilk
1/2 tsp. baking soda
1 1/4 cups pared, diced apples
1/2 cup broken nuts

1. Cream together shortening and sugar. Add egg. Beat well until creamy.
2. Sift together flour, cinnamon, and allspice.
3. Combine milk and baking soda. Alternately add dry mixture and wet mixture to creamed mixture.
4. Fold in apples and nuts.
5. Pour into 8" or 9" square baking pan.
6. Bake at 300° for 45-50 minutes, until a tester inserted in the center comes out clean.

Oh my, my mom made some slamming apple dumplings! I tried to learn how to make the crust and I could never do it and I watched her every time.

— Betty Cunningham,
a member of Bethel AMEC,
Lancaster, PA

Fresh Apple Squares

Makes 20 servings

1¾ cups sugar
3 eggs
1 cup oil
2 cups flour
1 tsp. baking soda
1 tsp. cinnamon
¼ tsp. salt
1 cup chopped nuts
2 cups pared, chopped apples
powdered sugar

1. Combine sugar, eggs, and oil. Mix well.
2. Stir together flour, baking soda, cinnamon, and salt. Mix into wet ingredients.
3. Fold in apples and nuts.
4. Spread into greased 9" x 13" pan.
5. Bake at 350° for 60 minutes. Cool.
6. Dust with powdered sugar.

Blueberry Delight

Makes 15-18 servings

20-oz. can crushed pineapples, drained
1 can blueberry pie filling
1 box deluxe yellow cake mix
¼ lb. (1 stick) butter, melted

1. Layer ingredients in greased 9" x 13" baking dish in order given.
2. Bake at 325° for 45--55 minutes, until lightly browned.

Orange Pineapple Delight

Makes 16 servings

3-oz. pkg. orange gelatin
1 cup hot water
1-oz. pkg. dry whipped topping
3-oz. pkg. instant vanilla pudding
1 cup milk
20-oz. can crushed pineapples, well drained

1. Dissolve gelatin in hot water. Cool until room temperature.
2. In a separate bowl, prepare whipped topping according to package directions.
3. In a large bowl, combine pudding and 1 cup milk. Mix well.
4. Fold gelatin and whipped topping into pudding. Mix well.
5. Fold in pineapples.
6. Refrigerate until firm.

Banana Split Delight

Makes 15-18 servings

2 cups graham cracker crumbs
5 Tbsp. butter, melted
2 cups powdered sugar
2 eggs, beaten
¼ lb. (1 stick) butter, softened
5 bananas
20-oz. can crushed pineapples, drained
16-oz. container frozen whipped topping, thawed
½ cup chopped nuts
¼ cup maraschino cherries, halved or quartered

1. Combine crumbs and 5 Tbsp. butter. Press firmly in bottom of 9" x 13" pan.

2. Bake at 350° for 8 minutes. Cool.

3. Combine powdered sugar, eggs, and ¼ lb. butter. Beat well. Spread over crumbs.

4. Slice bananas lengthwise. Arrange over creamed mixture.

5. Top with pineapples. Spread with whipped topping.

6. Sprinkle with nuts and cherries.

7. Refrigerate 8 hours before cutting and serving.

Favorite Flavors in Layers

Makes 12-18 servings

2 cups graham cracker crumbs
5 Tbsp. butter, melted
8-oz. pkg. cream cheese, at room
    temperature
⅓ cup peanut butter
1 cup powdered sugar
1 cup frozen whipped topping, thawed
1 small box vanilla instant pudding
1 small box chocolate instant pudding
2½ cups milk
frozen whipped topping, thawed

1. Combine crumbs and butter. Press firmly in bottom of 9" x 13" pan.

2. Bake at 350° for 8 minutes. Cool.

3. Combine cream cheese and peanut butter, mixing until well combined. Stir in powdered sugar. Fold in 1 cup whipped topping. Spread over crust.

4. Combine puddings and milk. Beat until thickened. Spread over cream cheese mixture.

5. Spread top with additional whipped topping. Refrigerate until ready to cut and serve.

Butterscotch Delight

Makes 12-18 servings

¼ lb. (1 stick) margarine, softened
1 cup flour
½ cup chopped walnuts or pecans
8-oz. pkg. cream cheese, softened
1 cup powdered sugar
1 cup frozen whipped topping, thawed
2 small boxes butterscotch pudding
9-oz. container frozen whipped topping,
    thawed
½ cup chopped nuts

1. Combine margarine, flour, and ½ cup nuts. Press into bottom of 9" x 13" pan.

2. Bake at 350° for 15 minutes. Cool.

3. Beat together cream cheese and sugar. Fold in 1 cup whipped topping. Spread over baked crust.

4. Prepare pudding as directed on box. Spread over cream cheese layer.

5. Spread 9-oz. container whipped topping over pudding. Sprinkle with nuts. Chill until ready to serve.

Selfishness is the most constant of human motives. Patriotism, humanity, or the love of God may lead to sporadic outbursts which sweep away the heaped-up wrongs of centuries; but they languish at times, while the love of self works on ceaselessly, unwearyingly, burrowing always at the very roots of life, and heaping up fresh wrongs for other centuries to sweep away.

— Frederick Douglass

Holiday Squares

Makes 28 pieces

1½ cups sugar
1 cup (2 sticks) butter or margarine, at
    room temperature
4 eggs
2 cups flour
1 Tbsp. lemon juice or vanilla
1 can pie filling, flavor of your choice
powdered sugar

1. Cream together sugar and butter until
fluffy.
2. Add eggs, one at a time, beating well.
3. Add flour and lemon juice. Beat well.
4. Pour into greased jelly-roll pan.
5. Lightly mark off 2" squares. Place 1
Tbsp. pie filling in center of each square.
6. Bake at 350° for 35 minutes.
7. Sift powdered sugar over warm cake.
Cool. Cut in squares.

Today, slaves are too often
portrayed as passive victims waiting to
be led out of slavery. But long before
the invisible Underground Railroad was
organized, slaves in Colonial America
had frequently escaped alone or with
others from their owners to seek
freedom.
— Charles Blockson, *Hippogreen
Guide to the Underground Railroad*

Lemon Squares

Makes 20 pieces

½ cup (1 stick) butter or margarine,
    softened
1 cup flour
½ cup finely chopped salted cashews
1 cup powdered sugar
8-oz. pkg. cream cheese, softened
½ cup chilled whipping cream,
    unwhipped, or frozen whipped topping,
    thawed
2 small pkgs. instant lemon pudding
3 cups milk
1 Tbsp. lemon zest
¼ cup whipping cream
lemon-peel curls

1. Combine butter, flour, and cashews.
Press into 9" x 13" pan.
2. Bake at 375° for 15 minutes. Cool.
3. Beat ½ cup powdered sugar and cream
cheese together until fluffy.
4. Beat ½ cup whipping cream. Fold into
creamed mixture. Spread over crust.
Refrigerate.
5. Combine pudding, milk, and lemon
zest. When thickened, spread over cream
cheese mixture.
6. Whip ¼ cup whipping cream. Drop
over tops of squares and garnish with lemon-
peel curls.

Chocolatey Coconut Squares

Rebecca Carter

Makes 25 squares

1/4 cup (1/2 stick) melted butter
1 cup graham cracker crumbs
1 cup flaked coconut
1 cup chocolate chips
12-oz. can evaporated milk
1 cup chopped nuts

1. Combine butter and graham cracker crumbs. Press into 8" x 8" or 9" x 9" baking pan.
2. Combine coconut, chocolate chips, milk, and nuts. Pour over cracker-crumb crust.
3. Bake at 350° for 30 minutes. Cut into squares. Cool.

Cheesecake Cookies

Makes 25 bars

1/3 cup brown sugar
1 cup flour
1/2 cup chopped black walnuts
1/3 cup (5 1/3 Tbsp.) butter
8-oz. pkg. cream cheese, at room temperature
1/4 cup sugar
1 egg
1 Tbsp. lemon juice
2 Tbsp. cream
1 tsp. vanilla

1. Combine brown sugar, flour, and nuts. Cut in butter until mixture is crumbly. Reserve 1 cup mixture for topping. Place remaining crumbs in 8" x 8" pan. Press firmly.
2. Bake at 350° for 12-15 minutes.
3. Cream together cream cheese and sugar. Beat in egg, lemon juice, cream, and vanilla. Pour over baked crust. Top with remaining crumbs.
4. Bake at 350° for 20-25 minutes, until lightly browned. Cool.
5. Cut into squares. Refrigerate.

Czechoslovakian Cookies

Makes 4-5 dozen bars

1/2 lb. (2 sticks) butter, at room
   temperature
1 cup sugar
2 egg yolks
2 cups flour
1 cup chopped walnuts
1 1/2 cups strawberry jam

   1. Cream together butter and sugar. Add egg yolks. Mix well.
   2. Gradually add flour. Mix well.
   3. Fold in nuts.
   4. Spread half of batter into pan. Press gently. Spread with jam. Spoon remaining batter over jam.
   5. Bake at 350° for 40-50 minutes, or until lightly browned.
   6. Before bars cool, cut into squares.

Sweet Potato Pone

Makes 4-5 servings

1/2 cup sugar
1/2 cup (1 stick) butter, softened
2 cups grated uncooked sweet potatoes
1/2 cup milk
1/2 tsp. salt
1 tsp. ground ginger
1/4 tsp. cinnamon
1/4 tsp. nutmeg
grated rind of one orange

   1. Combine sugar and butter.
   2. Stir in sweet potatoes and milk. Mix well.
   3. Add remaining ingredients.
   4. Pour into shallow buttered baking pan.
   5. Bake at 325° for 60 minutes. Serve slightly warm.

Sweet Potato Soufflé

Makes 8-10 servings

1 large can sweet potatoes, drained
2 eggs
½ cup (1 stick) butter, melted
½-¾ cup sugar, according to your taste
    preference
1 tsp. vanilla
⅓ cup evaporated milk

Topping:
¾ cup light brown sugar
½ cup flour
⅓ cup (5⅓ Tbsp.) melted butter
¾ cup crushed pecans or walnuts
1 tsp. cinnamon

1. Combine sweet potatoes, eggs, butter, sugar, vanilla, and milk. Mash together until smooth.
2. Pour into greased casserole dish.
3. Combine topping ingredients until crumbly. Sprinkle over casserole.
4. Bake at 350° for 20-30 minutes.

Bread Pudding

Makes 4-6 servings

2 cups bread cubes
2 cups milk
3 Tbsp. butter, at room temperature or
    melted
¼ cup sugar
2 eggs, slightly beaten
½ tsp. vanilla
dash of salt

1. Place bread cubes in buttered 1-quart baking dish.
2. Scald milk. Stir in butter and sugar.
3. Stir in eggs, vanilla, and salt. Pour over bread cubes.
4. Set baking dish in larger baking pan. Fill outer pan with water up to the level of the pudding.
5. Bake at 350° for 60-65 minutes, or until knife inserted in middle of pudding comes out clean.

> I remember my mother used to make rice pudding, and most people who make rice pudding nowadays don't bake it, but she used to always bake it with custard on top. None of us were able to make rice pudding like that. That's one thing I really miss.
> — Doris Johnson,
> a member of Bethel AMEC,
> Lancaster, PA

Crepeselle

Rina Mckee

Makes 4-6 servings

2 eggs, lightly beaten
1 cup flour
1 cup milk
2 tablespoons butter, melted
1/4 tsp. salt

1. Whisk flour into eggs.
2. Whisk in milk and butter. Add salt. Refrigerate for 30 minutes.
3. Oil or butter small skillet. Heat, then pour in batter, a scant 1/4 cup at a time. Swirl immediately. Cook for 45 seconds. Turn and cook other side for 45 seconds, or until lightly browned.
4. Serve topped with syrup, jam, or cut-up fruit.

Pecan Pie

Mrs. Margaret Bailey

Makes 1 10" pie

1/4 cup (1/2 stick) butter, softened
1/2 cup sugar
1 cup light corn syrup
1/4 tsp. salt
3 eggs, beaten
2 cups broken pecans
10" unbaked pie crust

1. Cream butter. Add sugar. Cream until well mixed.
2. Add syrup, salt, and eggs. Mix until smooth and blended.
3. Stir in pecans. Pour into pie crust.
4. Bake at 350° for 55-60 minutes.

Nectarine Pie

Mrs. Margaret Bailey

Makes 2 10" pies

6 cups sliced nectarines, peeled
1 tsp. lemon juice
1/2 cup sugar
1/4 cup flour
1/4 cup water, or nectarine or orange juice
1/4 tsp. nutmeg or mace
1/8 tsp. powdered ginger, or 1/2 tsp. grated
  fresh ginger
2 10" unbaked pie crusts
1 1/2 Tbsp. butter

1. Combine all ingredients except pie crusts and butter. Mix gently but well.
2. Pour into pie crusts. Dot with butter. Top with pastry cut-outs, lattice crust, or a crumb topping.
3. Bake at 450° for 30 minutes, or until bubbly.

Your power is in your faith. Keep it and pass it on to other bloods.
— Molefikete Asante

Moist 'n Chewy Brownies

Marvin Murray

Makes 40 brownies

1 cup (6 ozs.) semisweet chocolate chips
1/4 cup (1/2 stick) butter or margarine
2 cups buttermilk baking mix
14-oz. can sweetened condensed milk
1 egg, beaten
1 cup chopped walnuts

1. Place chocolate chips and butter in greased saucepan. Stir over low heat until melted. Remove from heat.
2. Stir in baking mix, milk, and egg. Mix well.
3. Fold in nuts.
4. Pour into greased 9" x 13" baking pan.
5. Bake at 350° for 20-25 minutes. Cool before cutting into bars.

Sugar Cookies

Makes 7 dozen cookies

1 3/4 cups sugar
1 cup (2 sticks) margarine or butter, at
    room temperature
3 eggs
1 tsp. baking soda
1 cup buttermilk or sour milk
1 tsp. vanilla or coconut extract
4 1/2 cups flour
2 tsp. baking powder

1. Cream together sugar, butter, and eggs. Mix well.
2. Combine baking soda, milk, and vanilla. Add to creamed mixture. Mix well.

3. Sift together flour and baking powder. Add to creamed mixture. Mix well.
4. Drop by teaspoonfuls onto greased cookie sheet.
5. Bake at 400° for 8-10 minutes.

Sugar Cookies

Minnie Wilson

Makes approximately 6 1/2 dozen cookies

2 cups (1 lb. or 4 sticks) butter or
    margarine, softened
2 cups sugar
4 eggs
1/4 cup milk
5 cups sifted flour
1 tsp. baking powder
1 tsp. salt
3 tsp. vanilla
colored sugar, optional

1. Cream together butter and sugar. Blend in eggs. Add milk and mix well.
2. In separate bowl, stir together dry ingredients, except colored sugar.
3. Stir dry ingredients into creamed ones. Mix in vanilla.
4. Drop batter by teaspoonfuls onto greased cookie sheet. Sprinkle each with colored sugar, if desired.
5. Bake at 350° for 12-15 minutes.

English Semis

Makes 3-4 dozen cookies

2½ cups flour
pinch of salt
1 tsp. baking soda
2 tsp. baking powder
½ cup (1 stick) butter, at room
    temperature
4 Tbsp. sugar
2 eggs
1 cup sour milk
raisins

1. Mix together flour, salt, baking soda, and baking powder.
2. In separate bowl, cream together butter and sugar. Blend in eggs, and then milk.
3. Mix dry ingredients into creamed ingredients.
4. Roll out dough and cut with cookie cutter, or drop by teaspoonfuls onto greased cookie sheet. Place a raisin in the center of each cookie.
5. Bake at 350° for 12-15 minutes.

Molasses Crumbles

Minnie Wilson

Makes about 3 dozen cookies

¾ cup shortening
1 cup brown sugar
1 egg, beaten
¼ cup dark baking molasses
2¼ cups flour
⅛ tsp. salt
1 tsp. baking soda
½ tsp. ground cloves
1 tsp. cinnamon
½ tsp. ground ginger
sugar

1. Cream together shortening, brown sugar, egg, and molasses.
2. Sift together flour, salt, baking soda, cloves, cinnamon, and ginger. Add to creamed mixture. Mix well.
3. Refrigerate for 60 minutes.
4. Shape into balls the size of walnuts. Roll in sugar. Place on greased cookie sheet. Do not flatten cookies.
5. Bake at 350° for 8-9 minutes.

Toll House Cookies

Makes 5-6 dozen cookies

1 cup shortening
3/4 cup sugar
3/4 cup brown sugar
1 tsp. vanilla
1 Tbsp. hot water
2 eggs
3 cups flour
1 tsp. baking soda
1 tsp. salt
12 ozs. (2 cups) chocolate chips

1. Cream together shortening and sugars. Add vanilla, water, and eggs. Mix well.
2. Sift together flour, baking soda, and salt. Add to creamed mixture. Mix well.
3. Stir in chocolate chips.
4. Drop by teaspoonfuls onto greased cookie sheets.
5. Bake at 350° for 10-12 minutes, being careful not to overbake.

Monster Cookies

Makes about 11 dozen 2-inch cookies

2 cups brown sugar
1/2 Tbsp. corn syrup
1 cup (2 sticks) margarine, at room temperature
1 1/2 lbs. peanut butter
6 eggs
1/2 Tbsp. vanilla
4 tsp. baking soda
2 cups flour
5 cups quick oats
1/2 lb. chocolate chips
1/2 lb. M&M's

1. Cream together brown sugar, corn syrup, margarine, and peanut butter. Add eggs and vanilla. Mix well.
2. Mix together baking soda, flour, and oats. Add to creamed mixture. Mix well.
3. Stir in chocolate chips and candy. Mix thoroughly.
4. Drop by tablespoonfuls onto greased cookie sheet.
5. Bake at 350° for 10 minutes.

I remember my mother preparing the food to make jelly preserve. She had this bag she would put the fruit inside of and squeeze and squeeze, and we'd help her do that. She always made all types of preserves. We never ran out.

— Anna Gantt,
a member of Bethel AMEC,
Lancaster, PA

Lassers Cookies

Minnie Wilson

Makes 2 dozen cookies

1/2 cup corn syrup
2/3 cup sugar
1/2 cup (1 stick) margarine or butter
1 cup flour
1 cup chopped nuts or flaked coconut

1. Bring corn syrup, sugar, and margarine to boil in double boiler. Remove from heat.
2. Stir in remaining ingredients.
3. Drop by teaspoonfuls onto greased cookie sheet.
4. Bake at 325° for 12-15 minutes. Cool completely before lifting from cookie sheet. Use a metal spatula and work carefully to remove.

Sand Tarts

Makes 2 1/2 dozen cookies

1/2 cup (1 stick) butter, softened
1 cup sugar
2 eggs, separated
1 Tbsp. milk
1/2 tsp. vanilla extract
1 1/2 cups flour
1/2 tsp. salt
1 tsp. baking powder
1/4 tsp. cinnamon
1 Tbsp. sugar
15 unblanched almonds, split

1. Cream together butter and 1 cup sugar. Add egg yolks, milk, and vanilla. Beat until light and fluffy.

2. Sift together flour, salt, and baking powder. Add to creamed mixture. Mix well. Chill for at least 3 hours.
3. Roll out dough very thinly. Cut with 3" cookie cutters. Place on greased cookie sheet.
4. Brush tops of cookies with reserved egg whites. Combine cinnamon and 1 Tbsp. sugar. Decorate cookies with almonds and sprinkle with cinnamon/sugar mixture.
5. Bake at 375° for 8 minutes.

Rum Balls

Makes about 28 pieces

1 cup finely crushed vanilla wafers
1 cup powdered sugar
1 cup chopped nuts
2 Tbsp. cocoa powder
2 Tbsp. light corn syrup
3-4 Tbsp. rum
1/2 cup fine granulated sugar
1/2 cup finely chopped nuts
6-oz. jar marschino cherries, with cherries
    cut into halves
corn syrup

1. Combine crushed wafers, sugar, nuts, and cocoa powder.
2. Stir in 2 Tbsp. syrup and rum. Mix well.
3. Shape into 1" balls.
4. Roll half the balls in sugar and the other half in nuts.
5. Spread cut sides of cherry halves with corn syrup. Press one cherry half on each ball.

French Cremes

Makes about 4 dozen cookies

1½ cups (3 sticks) butter, at room
   temperature
1 cup powdered sugar
⅓ cup orange juice
2 Tbsp. whiskey
1 tsp. baking powder
2¾ cups flour
powdered sugar

1. Cream together butter and 1 cup sugar.
2. Add orange juice. Mix well.
3. Add whiskey. Mix well.
4. Stir together baking powder and flour. Mix into batter.
5. Drop by half-teaspoonfuls onto greased cookie sheet, or form into small balls and flatten on greased cookie sheet.
6. Bake at 325° for 10-12 minutes, or until light brown. Cool.
7. Sift powdered sugar over cooled cookies.

Danish Cookies

Makes about 2 dozen cookies

2 cups flour
¾ cup (1½ sticks) margarine or butter,
   softened
⅓ cup sugar
½ tsp. salt
2 eggs
⅓ cup jam

Vanilla frosting:
1 cup powdered sugar
1 Tbsp. margarine or butter
1 Tbsp. plus 1 tsp. milk
¼ tsp. vanilla

1. Combine flour, ¾ cup margarine, ⅓ cup sugar, salt, and eggs.
2. Roll dough ⅛″ thick on lightly floured board. Cut into 2″ circles. Place on greased cookie sheet.
3. Bake at 375° for 8-10 minutes. Cool.
4. Cream together powdered sugar, margarine, milk, and vanilla until smooth.
5. Spread jam between two cookies to form sandwich. Spread tops of each sandwich with frosting.

Italian Sweets

Makes 4 dozen sweets

2½ cups flour
1 cup sugar
2 tsp. baking powder
½ tsp. salt
¼ cup (½ stick) margarine or butter,
    softened
1 egg, separated
1 tsp. almond extract
½ cup whipping cream, unwhipped
1¾ cups powdered sugar
½ tsp. almond extract
½ cup chopped almonds
¼ cup cut-up red candied cherries
¼ cup cut-up green candied cherries

1. Combine flour, 1 cup sugar, baking powder, salt, margarine, egg yolk, 1 tsp. extract, and whipping cream. Mix well. Cover. Refrigerate for 60 minutes.
2. Divide dough in half. Roll each half into 8" x 6" rectangle on well floured board. Square off corners. Lift onto greased cookie sheet.
3. Beat egg white until foamy. Fold in powdered sugar and ½ tsp. extract. Beat until stiff and glossy. Spread over dough.
4. Arrange almonds and cherries over tops of two rectangles.
5. Bake at 375° for 10 minutes, until edges are light brown.
6. Cut into strips 2" x 1". Cool.

Scotch Shortbread

Lora C. Wayne

Makes 2½ dozen cookies

1 cup (2 sticks) butter (no substitutions),
    at room temperature
½ cup brown sugar
2½ cups sifted flour

1. Cream together butter and sugar. Stir in flour. Mix well with hands. Chill.
2. Shape into 1" balls. Place on ungreased cookie sheet. Press crisscross design on top of each cookie with floured fork.
3. Bake at 300° for 20-25 minutes.

The songs of the slave represent the sorrows of his heart; and he is relieved by them, only as an aching heart is relieved by its tears.
— Frederick Douglass

Honey Ice Cream

Mrs. Margaret Bailey

Makes 1 quart ice cream

2 + cups milk
1 vanilla bean, split open lengthwise
¼ cup honey
6 egg yolks
generous ⅔ cup granulated sugar
1 + cup heavy cream

1. Place milk, vanilla bean, and honey in saucepan. Slowly bring to boil, stirring to dissolve the honey.
2. In a mixing bowl beat egg yolks and sugar until mixture whitens and forms a ribbon.
3. Pour a bit of the hot liquid into egg/sugar mixture, whisking constantly. Remove saucepan from heat. Pour egg/sugar mixture into milk mixture, stirring constantly.
4. Return saucepan to low heat and cook, stirring constantly until temperature on candy thermometer reaches 185° (5-10 minutes). Do not boil. Remove from heat. Continue stirring for 1-2 more minutes.
5. Remove vanilla bean.
6. Add heavy cream. Mix well.
7. Cool completely before pouring into ice cream freezer. Run the ice-cream maker according to manufacturer's directions.

Chocolate Fudge

Makes 5-6 dozen pieces

4½ cups sugar
12-oz. can evaporated milk
¼ cup (½ stick) butter
dash of salt
½ tsp. vanilla
1-lb. chocolate bar, grated
2 pkgs. chocolate chips
2 squares unsweetened chocolate
1 pt. marshmallow cream
2 cups chopped walnuts

1. Combine sugar, milk, butter, and salt in saucepan. Boil 10 minutes.
2. Stir in vanilla.
3. Combine remaining ingredients. Pour hot ingredients over chocolate-marshmallow-nut mixture. Beat until completely melted together.
4. Pour onto lightly greased jelly-roll pan. Chill.
5. Cut and store in covered tins.

Chocolate Peanut Butter Fudge

Makes about 2 dozen pieces

½ lb. (2 sticks) butter
4 Tbsp. peanut butter
1 tsp. vanilla
1 lb. powdered sugar, sifted
3 Tbsp. cocoa powder

1. Melt butter. Stir in peanut butter and vanilla.
2. Add powdered sugar and cocoa powder. Mix well.
3. Pour into 9" x 13" pan. Refrigerate.
4. When well chilled, cut into pieces.

Cream Cheese Fudge

Minnie Wilson

Makes 20-25 pieces

3-oz. pkg. cream cheese, softened to room temperature
2½ cups sifted powdered sugar
2 Tbsp. peanut butter
¼ tsp. vanilla
dash of salt
¼ cup chopped salted peanuts, optional

1. Beat cream cheese until soft and smooth.
2. Slowly fold in sugar.
3. Stir in peanut butter. Mix well.
4. Add vanilla, salt, and nuts. Mix until just blended.
5. Press into well greased 8" x 8" pan. Refrigerate for 15 minutes. Cut into squares.

Big Batch No-Cook Fudge

Makes about 4 dozen pieces

7 cups (about 2 1-lb. boxes) powdered sugar
½ cup cocoa powder
3⅓ sticks margarine, melted
2 Tbsp. vanilla
12-oz. jar peanut butter, crunchy or smooth

1. Combine sugar and cocoa powder.
2. Stir in margarine, vanilla, and peanut butter. Mix well.
3. Press into 9" x 13" greased pan.
4. Cool in refrigerator before cutting and serving.

Opera Fudge

Makes about 5½ dozen pieces

2 lbs. powdered sugar
8-oz. pkg. cream cheese, softened
¼ lb. (1 stick) butter, softened
1 tsp. vanilla
4 squares unsweetened chocolate
⅓ of a ¼-lb. bar paraffin

1. Combine powdered sugar, cream cheese, butter, and vanilla.
2. Roll into small balls. Refrigerate 8 hours.
3. Heat chocolate and paraffin over low heat until melted.
4. Dip candy into chocolate. Place on waxed paper to cool.

Peanut Butter Easter Eggs

Makes about 4 dozen eggs

18-oz. jar peanut butter
1/4 lb. (1 stick) butter or margarine, at
    room temperature
3 lbs. powdered sugar
pinch of salt
1 Tbsp. vanilla
1/2 cup evaporated milk, approximately
2 1/4 cups semi-sweet chocolate chips
2/3 of a 1/4-lb. bar paraffin wax
chopped peanuts, coconut flakes, or candy
    sprinkles, optional

    1. In large bowl, knead together peanut butter, butter, sugar, salt, and vanilla. Add milk to soften dough to pliable texture, but firm enough to take egg-shape. Form into eggs, each about 2 Tbsp. in size.

    2. Melt chocolate chips and paraffin together in top of double boiler.

    3. Spear eggs, one at a time, and quickly dip into chocolate to coat. Let cool, then dip a second time. Let cool, and dip a third time, so the coating is not too thin.

    4. Before final chocolate coating sets, sprinkle each egg with chopped peanuts, coconut flakes, or candy sprinkles, if you wish.

Peanut Brittle

Makes 2 large sheets

2 cups sugar
1 cup light corn syrup
1/2 cup water
1/2 tsp. salt
1 tsp. butter
3 cups raw Spanish peanuts, or whole
    peanuts
2 tsp. baking soda

    1. In large saucepan, boil sugar, corn syrup, water, and salt together until mixture reaches 236° and forms a thread.

    2. Stir in butter and peanuts. Cook, stirring constantly, until mixture reaches 290° and becomes golden brown.

    3. Remove from heat. Stir in baking soda. Mix well until candy thickens.

    4. Pour onto greased baking sheets. As mixture cools, spread as thinly as possible. Cool.

    5. Break into pieces. Store in airtight container.

> I remember the special luncheons my mother gave for her church friends. She would put out her finest china. She would fill the platters with wonderful delights, such as crepes filled with a fruit puree, topped with fresh fruit and homemade whipped cream. My favorite was her upside-down pineapple cake and watermelon boats.
>
> — Cornelia Bynum

A Newly Freed Man's Prayer

Dear Father, I come before you today with thanks in my heart for everything you have done for me. Thank you for allowing me to live as a free man just one more day. Thank you for all the things you have done for me in my life. I pray to you, Father, that I remain your humble servant and that I never think more of myself than I ought.

I pray, Father, that I will always remember that it was your grace and mercy which allowed me to reach the position I am currently in. I thank you, Father, for allowing Thomas Boude to set the price for my freedom at only 50 dollars. I thank you for giving me strength to work off my bondage in less than one year. I thank you for the gift of wisdom which enabled me to prosper in my first lumber business. I thank you for leading me to choose such an excellent wife as Harriet Lee.

Please, Father, keep fresh in my mind how it felt to be enslaved. If you do this, Father, I know I will continue with all of my strength and might to fight against this system for all of my people who are still being subjected to living as someone else's property. If you keep this fresh in my mind, Father, I will remember how it felt to work from "can't see in the morning" to "can't see in the night." This will remind me always to make sure I pay my workers a fair day's wage for a fair day's work.

Father, I thank you for not having to face this battle alone. I thank you, Father, for the countless number of fellow Christians who help to lift me up when I am down. Whose testimonies always inspire me to continue in this struggle, no matter how large or impossible it might seem to me that day. Father, I thank you for keeping it fresh in my mind that it is sin not skin, and that there are some whites who are willing to help us fight in the most holy war. I thank you, Father, for the gift of discernment which has allowed me to be able to recognize the evil one disguising himself as the truth.

Father, allow us to release all the pain, all the sorrow, we have endured during this life. We want to make sure these things are loosened here, because you said whatever is loosened on earth will be loosened in heaven, and what is bound on earth will be bound in heaven. Father, we ask you to bind up all our pain, all our misery, all our sorrow, all our fears, all our disappointments. We ask you, Father, to replace those things and let loose on this earth your love, your joy, your gentleness, your kindness, your peace, and your compassion. Once you have let loose these things, O heavenly Father, then please remind us daily that the world didn't give us these things, so the world can't take them away. Amen.

— by Stephen Smith in *Living the Experience*

"Prayer is the key that unlocked the door of our bondage."
— *Reverend Edward M. Bailey*

Cakes

I was an apron-string child, always staying very close to my mother as she worked in her kitchen. The benefit to me was that I got to see an incredible woman bake the finest cakes. She baked cakes for church, friends, and every one of her children's birthdays.

My oldest sister, Margaret, named after my mother, loved pineapple upside-down cake. Every birthday, that is what she got. Thankfully, she liked to share, so I always got a nice big piece.

Over time I began to realize that my mother made the majority of her recipes by memory. She measured when she needed to, but she was famous for a pinch of this or a sprinkle of that. What impresses me is that her dishes were often very complicated ones. All the information she needed was safely tucked away in her mind for future recall.

Our African ancestors, because of the perilous times, needed to memorize and retain every piece of information they heard or discovered, that would aid them in getting to freedom or preserving their lives on the plantation. Writing and reading were practices enslaved Africans could not display in mixed company. Exhibiting that knowledge would have cost them their lives. In fact, there were laws discouraging giving any African instructions in reading and writing. The intent was to hinder communication among Africans and to keep them in an ignorant, dependent state. Denmark Vessey, Frederick Douglass, and others understood differently—that if we as a people did not educate ourselves, the condition of slavery would never end.

— Phoebe Bailey

Cakes — Traditional

Pound Cake

Rebecca Carter

Makes 16 servings

1 cup (2 sticks) butter or margarine,
   softened
½ cup vegetable oil
3 cups sugar
pinch of salt
4 eggs
3 cups flour
1 cup whole milk
1 tsp. vanilla
1 tsp. lemon extract

1. Cream together butter, oil, sugar, and salt. Mix well.
2. Add eggs, one at a time, beating well after each addition.
3. Alternately add flour and milk. Mix well.
4. Stir in flavorings. Beat well.
5. Pour into greased and floured tube pan.
6. Bake at 300° for 90-95 minutes.
7. Invert pan and cool for 10 minutes before removing cake from pan. Serve pieces topped with fresh fruit or ice cream.

Pound Cake

Alice Mack

Makes 3 loaves

3½ cups sugar
1 lb. butter (4 sticks),
   at room temperature
10 eggs
4 cups flour
1½ tsp. nutmeg
2 cups nuts

1. Cream together sugar, butter, and eggs.
2. Add flour and nutmeg. Mix well.
3. Fold in nuts.
4. Pour into 3 greased and floured loaf pans.
5. Bake at 325° for 60 minutes.

Buttermilk Pound Cake

Shirley C. Owens

Makes 16-20 servings

1 cup (2 sticks) butter or margarine, at room temperature
2 cups sugar
4 eggs
2 tsp. vanilla
3 cups flour
½ tsp. baking soda
½ tsp. salt
1 cup buttermilk

Glaze:
1 cup sifted powdered sugar
1 or 2 Tbps. evaporated milk
½ tsp. vanilla

1. Cream together butter and sugar until light and fluffy.
2. Add eggs and vanilla. Mix well.
3. Combine flour, baking soda, and salt.
4. Alternately add dry ingredients and buttermilk to creamed mixture. Mix well.
5. Pour into greased and floured 10" tube pan.
6. Bake at 325° for 65 minutes.
7. Combine glaze ingredients. Pour over warm cake.

Shortbread

Makes 16 servings

2 cups flour
½ tsp. salt
½ cup brown sugar, packed
1 cup (2 sticks) butter, chilled

1. Sift together flour and salt.
2. Add brown sugar. Mix well.
3. Cut butter into dry mixture, until pea-sized lumps form. Use your fingertips to work the butter into the flour unitl the mixture is smooth.
4. Pat shortbread into 9" x 13" baking pan. Press down until dough is spread evenly.
5. With fork, prick shortbread all over.
6. Bake at 350° for 20 minutes, until shortbread turns brown and pulls away from the pan.
7. Cut in squares while still warm. Cool in pan.

> I always worked in the kitchen with my mother. I can remember mixing the cake up and licking the batter off the spoon!
> — Nelson Polite, Sr.,
> a member of Bethel AMEC,
> Lancaster, PA

Cakes — Other Favorites

Devil's Food Cake

Minnie Wilson

Makes 16-20 servings

2 cups sugar
½ cup vegetable oil
3 squares baking chocolate, melted
¾ cup sour milk or buttermilk
2 cups flour
1 tsp. salt
1⅓ tsp. baking soda
½ tsp. baking powder
½ cup buttermilk or sour milk
3 eggs
1 tsp. vanilla

1. Combine sugar, oil, chocolate, and ¾ cup milk. Mix well.
2. In separate bowl, mix together dry ingredients.
3. In a third bowl, mix together ½ cup milk, eggs, and vanilla.
4. Add dry ingredients to creamed chocolate mixture, alternately with egg mixture. Beat well after each addition until well blended.
5. Pour into greased and floured 9" x 13" pan.
6. Bake at 350° for 30-45 minutes.

Hershey's Chocolate Cake

Jean Townsend

Makes 9-12 servings

¼ cup (½ stick) butter, softened
¼ cup oil
2 cups sugar
1 tsp. vanilla
2 eggs
¾ tsp. baking soda
¾ cup unsweetened cocoa powder
1¾ cups flour
¾ tsp. baking powder
⅛ tsp. salt
1¾ cups milk

1. Cream together in electric mixing bowl the butter, oil, and sugar. Then blend in vanilla and eggs.
2. In separate bowl, stir together dry ingredients. Add alternately to creamed mixture with milk. Beat well after each addition until well combined.
3. Spread batter into greased 9-inch square baking dish.
4. Bake at 350° for 30-35 minutes, or until pick inserted into center of cake comes out clean.

Chocolate Chip Peanut Butter Cake

Makes 16-20 servings

2¼ cups flour
2 cups brown sugar
1 cup peanut butter
½ cup (1 stick) margarine, softened
1 tsp. baking powder
½ tsp. baking soda
1 cup milk
1 tsp. vanilla
3 eggs
1½ cups chocolate chips, divided

1. Combine flour, sugar, peanut butter, and margarine in electric mixing bowl. Blend at low speed until crumbly. Set aside 1 cup.
2. Add remaining ingredients, except chocolate chips, to crumb mixture. Mix well.
3. Stir in 1 cup chocolate chips.
4. Pour into greased 9″ x 13″ pan. Sprinkle with reserved crumbs and remaining chocolate chips.
5. Bake at 350° for 30 minutes.

Chocolate Texas Sheet Cake

Christel Wayne

Makes 24 servings

Cake:
1 cup (2 sticks) butter or margarine
7 Tbsp. unsweetened cocoa powder
1 cup water
2 cups sifted flour
2 cups sugar
2 eggs, slightly beaten
1 tsp. baking soda
½ cup buttermilk
1 tsp. vanilla extract

Frosting:
½ cup (1 stick) butter or margarine
4 Tbsp. unsweetened cocoa powder
6 Tbsp. milk
1-lb. box powdered sugar
1 tsp. vanilla
1 cup chopped pecans

1. In large saucepan, combine butter, cocoa powder, and water. Bring mixture to boil, stirring constantly.
2. Combine flour and sugar. Add to cocoa mixture. Mix well.
3. Beat eggs. Add baking soda, buttermilk, and vanilla. Add to cocoa mixture. Mix well.
4. Pour into greased and floured 10″ x 15″ jelly-roll pan.
5. Bake at 400° for 25 minutes.
6. Prepare frosting while cake is baking. Melt butter. Add cocoa powder and milk. Bring to boil, stirring constantly. Remove from heat.
7. Immediately add powdered sugar, vanilla, and pecans. Mix well.
8. Pour hot frosting over hot cake, spreading evenly. Cool.

Dieters' Chocolate Cheesecake

Mrs. Margaret Bailey

Makes 8 servings

¼ cup skim milk
1 pkg. unflavored gelatin
⅔ cup skim milk
2 egg yolks (reserve egg whites)
3 Tbsp. unsweetened cocoa powder
¼ cup sugar, or the equivalent of sugar
  substitute
1½ tsp. vanilla
1½ cups (12-oz. carton) creamed cottage
  cheese
2 egg whites
2 Tbsp. sugar
⅓ cup graham cracker crumbs
⅛ tsp. cinnamon
fresh or canned fruit, for garnish

1. Pour ¼ cup milk into blender. Add
gelatin. Allow to stand for 5 minutes.
2. Heat ⅔ cup milk to boiling point. Pour
into blender and process until gelatin
dissolves.
3. Add egg yolks, cocoa powder, ¼ cup
sugar, and vanilla. Process at medium speed
until well blended.
4. Add cottage cheese. Blend on high until
smooth.
5. Pour into bowl. Chill until mixture
mounds from a spoon.
6. Beat egg whites until frothy. Gradually
add 2 Tbsp. sugar. Beat until stiff peaks form.
Fold into chocolate mixture.
7. Combine graham cracker crumbs and
cinnamon. Sprinkle onto bottom of 8" round
springform pan.
8. Pour chocolate mixture into pan. Chill
several hours.
9. Arrange fruit on top just before serving.

Chocolate Swirl Coffee Cake

Minnie Wilson

Makes 9 servings

⅓ cup flaked coconut
¼ cup chopped nuts
¼ cup sugar
1 Tbsp. butter, softened
2 cups buttermilk baking mix
¼ cup sugar
2 Tbsp. butter or margarine, melted
1 egg
⅔ cup water or milk
⅓ cup semisweet chocolate pieces, melted

1. Mix coconut, nuts, ¼ cup sugar, and 1
Tbsp. butter. Set aside.
2. Combine baking mix, ¼ cup sugar, 2
Tbsp. butter, egg, and water or milk. Beat
well for 30 seconds. Spread in bottom of
greased 8" x 8" x 2" pan.
3. Spoon chocolate over batter. Lightly
swirl batter several times for marbled effect.
4. Sprinkle coconut mixture over top.
5. Bake at 400° for 20-25 minutes. Serve
warm.

One Bowl
Apple Nut Cake

Makes 16-20 servings

2 cups sugar
2 eggs, beaten slightly
1/4 cup oil
1/4 cup (1/2 stick) melted butter
1/2 tsp. vanilla or almond extract
1/2 tsp. lemon extract
2 1/4 cups flour
1 tsp. baking soda
1 tsp. baking powder
1/2 tsp. salt
4 cups diced apples
1 cup chopped nuts, of your choice

1. Combine all ingredients in the order listed. Mix well.
2. Spread into ungreased 9″ x 13″ pan.
3. Bake at 350° for 60 minutes, or until done in the center.

We used to grow whole fields of sugarcane. We would go out into the field and break pieces off. We would peel them and cut them into little pieces. Then we'd chew them until we got all the juice out and spit out the skin.

— Frances Morant,
Brothers & Sisters Cafe

Jewish
Apple Cake

Makes 16-20 servings

1 cup sifted flour
1/2 tsp. salt
1 1/2 tsp. baking powder
3 Tbsp. sugar
4 Tbsp. (1/2 stick) butter, at room
    temperature
1 egg
1/4 cup milk
4 cups peeled and sliced apples
1 tsp. cinnamon
6 Tbsp. sugar
1/4 lb. (1 stick) butter
1/2 cup currant jelly, optional

1. Sift together flour, salt, and baking powder. Add sugar. Work in 4 Tbsp. butter until mixture is crumbly.
2. Beat together egg and milk. Add to flour mixture. Mix to form dough.
3. Pat into buttered 8″ x 12″ pan.
4. Arrange apples in rows on dough. Sprinkle with cinnamon and sugar.
5. Melt butter and pour over cake.
6. Bake at 400° for 35-40 minutes. Brush with melted jelly while cake is hot.

Johnny Appleseed Coffee Cake

Minnie Wilson

Makes 8-10 servings

2 cups buttermilk baking mix
2 Tbsp. sugar
1 egg
2/3 cup water or milk
1 1/2 cups chopped apple

Topping:
1/4 cup sugar
2 Tbsp. buttermilk baking mix
2 tsp. cinnamon
2 Tbsp. firm butter or margarine

1. Combine baking mix, sugar, egg, and water or milk. Beat well.
2. Fold in apple. Batter will be stiff.
3. Spread batter in greased 9" round layer pan or 8" x 8" pan.
4. Make topping by combining sugar, baking mix, cinnamon, and butter until crumbly. Sprinkle over batter.
5. Bake at 400° for 20-25 minutes. Serve warm.

Old-Fashioned Applesauce Cake

Makes 16-20 servings

2 1/2 cups flour, sifted
1 1/2 cups sugar
1/4 tsp. baking powder
1 1/2 tsp. baking soda
1/2 tsp. salt
1 tsp. cinnamon
1/2 tsp. ground cloves
1/2 tsp. allspice
1/2 tsp. nutmeg
1/2 cup shortening, melted
15-oz. can applesauce
3 eggs
1 cup seedless raisins
1 cup chopped walnuts

1. Combine flour, sugar, baking powder, baking soda, salt, and spices.
2. Add shortening and applesauce. Mix well.
3. Add eggs. Mix well.
4. Stir in raisins and walnuts.
5. Pour into greased and floured 9" x 13" pan.
6. Bake at 350° for 45 minutes.

Applesauce Cake

Makes 20-24 servings

2/3 cup (10²/3 Tbsp.) butter, softened
2 cups sugar
4 egg yolks
3/4 cup unsweetened applesauce
1/2 cup milk
2 1/2 cups cake flour, or 2 1/4 cups regular
    flour
3 tsp. baking powder
4 egg whites, stiffly beaten

1. Cream together butter and sugar.
2. Add egg yolks and applesauce. Mix well.
3. Add milk. Mix well.
4. Sift together flour and baking powder. Add to wet mixture. Mix well.
5. Fold in egg whites.
6. Bake at 350° for 35-40 minutes.

Notes:

1. To add flavor, mix 1 tsp. cinnamon and 1/2 tsp. nutmeg with dry ingredients in Step 4.

2. If you use sweetened applesauce, reduce the sugar to 1 1/2 cups.

Cowboy Coffee Cake

Minnie Wilson

Makes 8-10 servings

12-oz. jar apricot, peach, strawberry, or
    seedless raspberry preserves
2 cups buttermilk baking mix
2 Tbsp. sugar
1 egg
2/3 cup water or milk

1. Spread preserves in greased 9″ round layer pan.
2. Combine remaining ingredients. Beat well. Spread over preserves to edge of pan.
3. Bake at 400° for 25-30 minutes.
4. Invert onto heatproof plate. Leave pan over cake a few minutes. Remove pan and serve warm.

Blueberry and Peach Shortcake

Makes 12 servings

6.5-oz. sponge cake mix
8-oz. pkg. cream cheese, softened
14-oz. can sweetened condensed milk
1/3 cup lemon juice
1 tsp. vanilla extract
2 Tbsp. sugar
2 tsp. cornstarch
1/4 cup water
1 Tbsp. lemon juice
1 cup blueberries
3 medium peaches, pecled, seeded, and
    sliced

1. Prepare and bake sponge cake according to directions on package.
2. Beat cream cheese until fluffy.
3. Gradually beat in milk until smooth.
4. Stir in 1/3 cup lemon juice and vanilla.
5. Spread on partially cooled cake. Chill.
6. In saucepan, combine sugar, cornstarch, water, and 1 Tbsp. lemon juice. Cook, stirring constantly, until thickened. Add blueberries. Cook until bubbly. Chill.
7. Top cake with peach slices and blueberry sauce. Refrigerate leftovers.

Surprisin' Carrot Cake

Makes 16-20 servings

3 eggs
1½ cups sugar
¾ cup mayonnaise
8-oz. can crushed pineapples, undrained
2 cups flour
2 tsp. baking soda
½ tsp. ground cinnamon
½ tsp. ground ginger
½ tsp. salt
2 cups coarsely shredded carrots
¾ cup chopped walnuts

1. Mix together eggs, sugar, mayonnaise, and pineapples.
2. Combine flour, baking soda, cinnamon, ginger, and salt. Add to pineapple mixture. Mix well.
3. Fold in carrots and walnuts. Pour into greased and floured 9" x 13" pan.
4. Bake at 350° for 35-40 minutes.
5. Cool and frost with Cream Cheese Icing.

Cream Cheese Icing

3-oz. pkg. cream cheese, softened
2 Tbsp. butter or margarine, softened
1 cup powdered sugar
1 tsp. vanilla

Combine ingredients. Beat in electric mixer on high until smooth.
Use on cakes, cinnamon rolls, and cookies.

Williamsburg Orange Cake

Makes 16-20 servings

Cake:
2½ cups flour
1½ cups sugar
1½ tsp. baking soda
¾ tsp. salt
1½ cups buttermilk
½ cup (1 stick) melted butter or margarine
¼ cup vegetable oil
3 eggs
1½ tsp. vanilla
1 cup raisins
½ cup chopped nuts
1 Tbsp. grated orange peel

1. Combine dry ingredients for cake in large mixing bowl. Mix well.
2. In separate bowl blend together milk, butter, oil, eggs, and vanilla. Stir into dry ingredients until thoroughly mixed. Stir in raisins, nuts, and orange peel.
3. Pour into greased and floured 9" x 13" pan, 2 9" round pans, or 3 8" round pans.
4. Bake 9" x 13" cake for 40-45 minutes at 350°. Bake either of the round pans for 30-35 minutes at 350°.
5. Cool and frost with Butter Frosting.

Butter Frosting

⅓ cup (5⅓ Tbsp.) melted butter or margarine
3 cups powdered sugar
3-4 Tbsp. orange juice
2 tsp. grated orange peel

Combine ingredients. Beat in electric mixer on high until smooth.

Use on cakes, cinnamon rolls, and cookies.

Cranberry Orange Butter Cake

Dianne Prince

Makes 15-20 servings

Cake:
1 pkg. butter cake mix
1/3 cup oil
2 Tbsp. frozen orange juice, thawed
3 eggs
16-oz. can whole cranberry sauce (reserve 3 Tbsp. for glaze)

Glaze:
1/4 cup firmly packed brown sugar
3 Tbsp. reserved cranberry sauce
3 Tbsp. frozen orange juice, thawed
3 Tbsp. butter or margarine

1. Mix together cake ingredients in electric mixing bowl. Beat well.
2. Pour into greased and floured tube pan.
3. Bake at 350° for 35-45 minutes.
4. Combine glaze ingredients in saucepan. Heat until well combined.
5. Using long tined fork, prick cake at 1/2-inch intervals. Pour half of glaze over cake.
6. Let stand 10 minutes. Invert onto serving plate. Prick cake again. Spoon remaining glaze over cake. Serve warm or cold.

Gold Rush Coffee Cake

Minnie Wilson

Makes 8-10 servings

2 cups buttermilk baking mix
2 Tbsp. sugar
1 egg
1 Tbsp. grated orange peel
2/3 cup orange juice
1 cup cut-up pitted prunes or cranberries

Orange Glaze:
1/2 cup powdered sugar
1 tsp. grated orange peel
2 tsp. orange juice

1. Combine baking mix, sugar, egg, orange peel, and orange juice. Beat well.
2. Fold in prunes or cranberries. Spread in greased 9" round layer pan.
3. Bake at 400° for 25-30 minutes.
4. To make glaze combine powdered sugar, orange peel, and orange juice. Drizzle over warm cake.

If something fell we picked it up, kissed it up to God, and ate it!
— Janet Gantz

Hester's Cake

Hester Prince

Makes 16-20 servings

5 eggs
2 cups sugar
1 cup (2 sticks) melted butter or
    margarine
3 cups graham cracker crumbs
15-oz. can crushed pineapples, undrained
1 cup lightly packed flaked coconut
1 cup chopped nuts
whipped cream

1. Combine all ingredients except whipped cream. Mix well.
2. Pour into greased and floured 9" x 13" cake pan.
3. Bake at 325° for 60 minutes, or until done in the center.
4. Serve topped with whipped cream.

Dump Cake

Makes 16-20 servings

21-oz. can cherry pie filling
20-oz. can crushed pineapples, undrained
1 box yellow or white cake mix
1 cup (2 sticks) butter, melted
3.5-oz. can flaked coconut
1 1/4 cups chopped pecans

1. Layer ingredients in order given in greased 9" x 13" pan.
2. Bake at 325° for 60 minutes.

Watergate Cake

Makes 16-20 servings

Cake:
1-lb. 2 1/4-oz. box white cake mix
3.4-oz. box instant pistachio pudding
1 cup vegetable oil, less 1 Tbsp.
3 eggs, slightly beaten
1 cup ginger ale
1/2 cup chopped nuts

Frosting:
2 envelopes Dream Whip
3.4-oz. box instant pistachio pudding
1 1/4 cups cold milk

grated coconut
maraschino cherries
chopped nuts

1. Combine all cake ingredients. Mix well.
2. Pour into greased and floured 9" x 13" pan.
3. Bake at 350° for 30-35 minutes. Cool.
4. Combine Dream Whip mix, pistachio pudding, and milk. Mix well. Spread on cake.
5. Garnish with coconut, cherries, and nuts.

> From my earliest recollection, I date the entertainment of a deep conviction that slavery would not always be able to hold me within its foul embrace.
> — Frederick Douglass

Tossed Butter Pecan Cake

Ann Beardan

Makes 8-12 servings

2 cups pecans, chopped
¼ cup (½ stick) butter
1 cup (2 sticks) butter, softened
2 cups sugar
4 unbeaten eggs
3 cups sifted flour
2 tsp. baking powder
½ tsp. salt
1 cup milk
2 tsp. vanilla

Frosting:
¼ cup (½ stick) butter, softened
1 lb. powdered sugar, sifted
1 tsp. vanilla
4-6 Tbsp. evaporated milk or cream

1. Toast pecans in ¼ cup butter in 350° oven for 20-25 minutes, stirring frequently.
2. Cream 1 cup butter. Gradually beat in sugar. Mix well.
3. Blend in eggs. Mix well.
4. Sift together flour, baking powder, and salt.
5. Alternately add dry mixture and milk to creamed mixture. Mix well.
6. Stir in vanilla and 1⅓ cups toasted pecans.
7. Grease and flour bottoms of three 8" or 9" round layer baking pans. Divide batter among the three pans.
8. Bake at 350° for 20-30 minutes. Cool.
9. Make frosting by creaming ¼ cup butter. Add powdered sugar and vanilla. Add milk until of spreading consistency. Sir in remaining pecans.
10. Spread between layers of cake and over top and sides.

Pecan Cake

Nancy C. Hill

Makes 16-20 servings

1 lb. butter, softened
2 cups sugar
6 eggs
1 Tbsp. lemon extract
4 cups flour
1½ tsp. baking powder
4 cups chopped pecans
6 cups white raisins

1. Cream together butter and sugar.
2. Add eggs, one at a time, beating well after each addition. Add lemon extract and mix well.
3. Sift flour and baking powder together three times.
4. Add pecans and raisins to flour.
5. Gradually add flour mixture to creamed mixture. Mix well.
6. Pour into greased and floured 10" tube pan.
7. Bake at 300° for 1½-2 hours. Cool 15 minutes in pan before removing.

Butter Cake

Rebecca Carter

Makes 16-20 servings

1 cup (2 sticks) butter, softened
2 cups sugar
4 eggs
1 cup buttermilk
2 tsp. vanilla
3 cups flour, sifted
1 tsp. baking powder
½ tsp. baking soda
1 tsp. salt

Sauce:
1 cup sugar
¼ cup water
½ cup (1 stick) butter
1 tsp. vanilla

1. Cream together butter and sugar.
2. Add eggs, one at a time. Mix well after adding each one.
3. Add buttermilk and vanilla. Mix thoroughly.
4. Sift together flour, baking powder, baking soda, and salt. Gradually add to creamed mixture. Mix well.
5. Pour into greased and floured 10" tube pan.
6. Bake at 325° for 60-65 minutes.
7. Meanwhile, in saucepan make sauce by combining sugar, water, and butter. Heat and stir until sugar is dissolved. Remove from heat. Add vanilla.
8. Poke holes in top of baked cake with a fork.
9. Pour glaze over hot cake. Cool. Remove cooled cake from pan.

Easy Two-Egg Cake

Linda Maison

Makes 12-18 servings

2 cups self-rising flour
1 cup sugar
1 cup milk
2 eggs
½ cup (1 stick) butter or margarine, melted
1 tsp. vanilla
butter or margarine
cinnamon sugar

1. Combine all ingredients except the last two. Beat until smooth.
2. Pour into greased and floured 8" x 10" pan.
3. Bake at 375° for 20-25 minutes.
4. Rub hot cake with butter or margarine and sprinkle with cinnamon sugar.
5. Cool on wire rack for 10 minutes before cutting to serve.

Cherry Zip Up

Makes 9 servings

21-oz. can cherry pie filling
2 cups white or yellow cake mix
½ cup (1 stick) melted butter
⅓ cup grated coconut
½ cup chopped nuts

1. Spread filling in bottom of 9" glass pie dish.
2. Sprinkle cake mix over pie filling. Pour butter over top. Do not mix together.
3. Bake at 350° for 40 minutes.
4. Sprinkle on coconut and nuts
5. Serve warm with ice cream.

Old-Fashioned Shortcake

Makes 18-24 servings

2 cups sugar
1/2 cup shortening
2 eggs
1 cup milk
2 1/2 cups flour
3 tsp. baking soda
1/8 tsp. nutmeg
1 tsp. vanilla

1. Cut shortening into sugar in mixing bowl until crumbly. Stir in eggs and milk.
2. Mix dry ingredients together in separate bowl. Stir into wet ingredients until well blended. Add vanilla and mix thoroughly.
3. Pour into greased 9" x 13" pan.
4. Bake at 350° for 35-40 minutes, or until toothpick tests clean in the middle of the cake.

Note: This is absolutely delicious topped with sliced fresh strawberries.

Human rights are mutual and reciprocal . . . If you take my liberty and life you forfeit your own.
— William Parker

Million Dollar Pound Cake

Rebecca Carter

Makes 16-20 servings

3 cups sugar
1 lb. butter, softened
6 eggs, at room temperature
4 cups flour
3/4 cup milk
1 tsp. almond extract
1 tsp. vanilla extract

1. Cream together sugar and butter until light and fluffy.
2. Add eggs, one at a time, beating well after each addition.
3. Add flour and milk alternately to creamed mixture, beating well after each addition.
4. Stir in flavorings. Mix well.
5. Pour batter into greased and floured 10" tube pan.
6. Bake at 300° for 1 hour and 40 minutes. Invert pan to cool.

Sour Cream Pound Cake

Rebecca Carter

Makes 16-20 servings

1 1/2 cups (3 sticks) butter, at room
   temperature
2 cups sugar
8 eggs
1 cup sour cream
4 cups self-rising flour

1. Cream together butter and sugar until light and fluffy.
2. Add eggs, one at a time, beating well after each addition.
3. Alternately add flour and sour cream.
4. Pour into greased and floured 10" tube pan.
5. Bake at 350° for 60 minutes. Invert and cool in pan 10 minutes. Remove from pan.
6. Serve with a topping of strawberries or blueberries.

Africans who were known to be great barterers and vendors continued to use their industrious talents in America. Many free Africans would vend, even at auction blocks. It is said that Harriet Tubman sold pies as a source of income.

Coconut Pound Cake

Makes 16-20 servings

2 1/2 cups sugar
1 cup (2 sticks) butter or margarine,
   softened
2/3 cup shortening
5 eggs
3 cups flour, sifted
1 tsp. baking powder
1/8 tsp. salt
1 cup milk
1 tsp. vanilla
1 tsp. coconut flavoring
1 tsp. butter flavoring
2 2/3 cups or 1 7-oz. can flaked coconut

1. Cream together sugar, butter, and shortening.
2. Add eggs, one at a time, beating after each addition.
3. Sift together flour, baking powder, and salt.
4. Alternately add dry mixture and milk to creamed mixture. Mix well.
5. Stir in flavorings and coconut.
6. Pour into greased and floured tube pan.
7. Bake at 325° for 90 minutes. Invert pan until cake cools.

Five-Flavor Pound Cake

Patricia Washington

Makes 16-20 servings

1 cup (2 sticks) butter or margarine,
   at room temperature
½ cup shortening
3 cups sugar
4 eggs, beaten
3 cups flour
½ tsp. baking powder
1 cup milk
1 tsp. coconut extract
1 tsp. lemon extract
1 tsp. rum flavoring
1 tsp. butter flavoring
1 tsp. vanilla

1. Cream together butter, shortening, and sugar until light and fluffy.
2. Add eggs one by one. Mix well after each addition.
3. Combine flour and baking powder.
4. Alternately add dry ingredients and milk to creamed mixture.
5. Stir in flavorings until well blended.
6. Pour into greased and floured tube pan.
7. Bake at 300° for 90 minutes. Invert pan and cool 10 minutes before removing cake from pan.

Best Yet Pound Cake

Patricia Washington

Makes 16 servings

8 ozs. cream cheese, at room temperature
1½ cups (3 sticks) butter, at room
   temperature
3 cups sugar
5 eggs
3 cups cake flour
1 Tbsp. butter flavoring

1. Cream together cream cheese and butter.
2. Add sugar. Beat well.
3. Add eggs, one at a time, beating well after each addition.
4. Gradually add flour. Mix well.
5. Stir in flavoring.
6. Pour into greased and floured tube pan.
7. Bake at 300° for 90-100 minutes, until cake tests done. Invert pan and cool for 10 minutes before removing from pan.
8. Cover slices with fruit topping before serving.

Note: You can substitute 1 tsp. vanilla extract for the butter flavoring.

— *Germaine W. Pickney*

Pineapple Pound Cake

Makes 16-20 servings

1/2 cup shortening
1 cup (2 sticks) butter, softened
2 3/4 cups sugar
6 large eggs
3 cups flour
1 tsp. baking powder
1/4 cup milk
3/4 cup crushed pineapples, *undrained*
1 tsp. vanilla

Topping:
1/4 cup (1/2 stick) butter, softened
1 1/2 cups powdered sugar
1 cup crushed pineapples, *drained*

1. In large bowl, cream together shortening, butter, and sugar.
2. Add eggs, one at a time, beating well after each addition.
3. In separate bowl, sift together flour and baking powder. Add alternately with milk to creamed mixture.
4. Stir in pineapples and vanilla. Mix well.
5. Pour into greased and floured 10" tube pan. Place in cold oven.
6. Turn oven to 325°. Bake for 1 1/2 hours, or until top springs back when lightly touched. Let stand for a few minutes before removing from pan.
7. Combine Topping ingredients: butter, powdered sugar, and pineapples. Pour over cake while cake is still hot.

7-Up Pound Cake

Shirley C. Owens

Makes 16-20 servings

1 cup (2 sticks) butter or margarine, softened
1/2 cup vegetable oil
3 cups sugar
5 eggs
3 cups flour
3/4 cup 7-Up
1 tsp. vanilla or lemon flavoring

1. Cream together butter, oil, and sugar.
2. Add eggs one at a time, beating well after each addition.
3. Alternately add flour and 7-Up. Mix well.
4. Stir in vanilla.
5. Pour into greased and floured tube pan.
6. Bake at 325° for 60-90 minutes, or until done. Invert pan to cool for 10 minutes before removing cake.
7. Serve slices topped with fruit sauce or ice cream.

Cool Whip Pound Cake

Rebecca Carter

Makes 16-20 servings

1 cup (2 sticks) butter or margarine,
    softened
3 cups sugar
6 eggs
3 cups flour
1½ tsp. vanilla
1 Tbsp. lemon extract
8-oz. container frozen whipped topping,
    thawed

1. Cream together butter and sugar.
2. Add eggs, one at a time. Beat well after each addition.
3. Gradually add flour. Mix well.
4. Fold in vanilla, lemon extract, and whipped topping until well blended.
5. Pour into greased and floured 10" tube pan.
6. Bake at 325° for 75 minutes. Invert pan to cool.

Spice Cake

Minnie Wilson

Makes 16-20 servings

2 cups brown sugar
½ cup (1 stick) butter, softened
3 eggs
2 cups flour
1 tsp. ginger
1 tsp. ground cloves
1 tsp. cinnamon
½ tsp. nutmeg
1 tsp. baking soda
1 cup sour milk
1 tsp. vanilla

1. Cream together brown sugar and butter in large mixing bowl.
2. Add eggs and beat until well mixed.
3. In separate bowl, stir together dry ingredients.
4. Add dry ingredients alternately with sour milk to creamed mixture, beating well after each addition. Stir in vanilla thoroughly.
5. Pour into greased and floured 9" x 13" pan.
6. Bake at 350° for 30-45 minutes.
7. When cooled, but still warm, frost with your favorite Cream Cheese Icing (see page 202).

Gingerbread

Hester Prince

Makes 16-20 servings

¾ cup honey
¾ cup vegetable oil
1¼ cups molasses
3 eggs
2 cups flour
1 cup whole wheat flour
½ tsp. salt
½ tsp. ground cloves
1 tsp. baking powder
1 tsp. ginger
1½ tsp. cinnamon
¾ cup scalded milk

1. In large bowl, combine honey, oil, molasses, and eggs.
2. Sift together flours, salt, cloves, baking powder, ginger, and cinnamon.
3. Add dry ingredients alternately with hot milk to creamed mixture.
4. When smooth, pour into greased 9" x 13" baking pan.
5. Bake at 350° 40-45 minutes.

Grand Champion Sponge Cake

Makes 16-20 servings

1¼ cups sifted flour
1 cup sugar
1½ tsp. baking powder
½ tsp. salt
6 egg yolks
¼ cup water
1 tsp. vanilla
6 egg whites
1 tsp. cream of tarter
½ cup sugar

1. Sift together flour, 1 cup sugar, baking powder, and salt.
2. In small electric mixer bowl, combine egg yolks, water, vanilla, and sifted dry ingredients. Beat at medium high speed for 4 minutes, or until mixture is light and fluffy.
3. In large electric mixer bowl, beat egg whites until frothy. Gently add cream of tartar.
4. Gradually beat in ½ cup sugar, one Tbsp. at a time. Beat until whites form stiff, not dry, peaks. Fold batter gently, but thoroughly, into the beaten egg whites.
5. Turn into an ungreased 10" tube pan. Bake at 350° for about 45 minutes. Invert pan to cool.

Note: For a change of flavor, substitute 1 tsp. lemon extract for 1 tsp. vanilla.

Jello Cake

Makes 16-20 servings

18½-oz. box yellow cake mix
3¼-oz. box gelatin
4 eggs, slightly beaten
⅔ cup oil
⅔ cup water
1 tsp. vanilla

1. Combine all ingredients. Mix well.
2. Pour into greased and floured 9″ x 13″ pan.
3. Bake at 325° for 45-60 minutes.

Wine Cake

Makes 16-20 servings

18½-oz. box yellow cake mix
3¼-oz. box instant vanilla pudding
4 eggs
1 cup oil
1 cup wine
1 tsp. nutmeg

1. Combine all ingredients. Mix well.
2. Pour into greased and floured 9″ x 13″ pan.
3. Bake at 325° for 45-50 minutes.

Rum Cake

Makes 12-15 servings

½ cup chopped pecans
18½-oz. box golden butter cake mix
3¼-oz. box instant vanilla pudding
½ cup water
½ cup vegetable oil
4 eggs, slightly beaten
½ cup light rum

Glaze:
¾ cup sugar
½ cup (1 stick) butter or margarine
¼ cup light rum
pinch of salt

1. Grease and flour bundt pan. Sprinkle nuts in bottom of pan.
2. Combine cake mix and dry pudding mix.
3. Add remaining cake ingredients. Mix well. Pour into bundt pan.
4. Bake at 325° for 60 minutes.
5. Combine glaze ingredients in saucepan. Boil for 2-3 minutes. Pour over hot cake. Let cake cool for 30 minutes, then remove from pan.

Harriet Tubman and those runaways that she assisted would often travel without eating until they reached their next station. There they were given food and shelter.

We Are Climbing Jacob's Ladder

We are climbing Jacob's ladder.
We are climbing Jacob's ladder.
We are climbing Jacob's ladder,
Soldiers of the cross.

Every round goes higher, higher.
Every round goes higher, higher.
Every round goes higher, higher,
Soldiers of the cross.

Sinner do you love my Jesus?
Sinner do you love my Jesus?
Sinner do you love my Jesus?
Soldiers of the cross.

If you love Him, why not serve Him?
If you love Him, why not serve Him?
If you love Him, why not serve Him?
Soldiers of the cross.

We are climbing higher higher.
We are climbing higher higher.
We are climbing higher higher,
Soldiers of the cross.

Through this spiritual, a conductor learned that an enslaved African was running and wanted to go North, as far as Canada.

Snacks and Appetizers

My mother's famous homemade eggnog was so rich and creamy. Our friends loved to come over to our house for food, because they never knew what special treat Mrs. Bailey was going to serve. My mother never refused anyone a meal; she welcomed everyone into our home, a tradition her children maintain in their homes today.

The enslaved Africans used the earth around them to make teas, to be shared with guests and used for medicinal purposes. First- and second-generation African immigrants were faced with unfamiliar plants—and new diseases—when they were brought to this country. Many adapted the foliages and tree barks they found in America to recipes they remembered and were taught by their grandmothers.

— Phoebe Bailey

Snacks and Appetizers — Other Favorites

Beggars Purses with Crabmeat

Rina Mckee

Makes 6 appetizer servings

½ lb. lump crabmeat
1 Tbsp. mayonnaise
1 tsp. lemon juice
1 tsp. Dijon mustard
2 tsp. minced green onion
1 tsp. minced parsley
½ tsp. salt
¼ tsp. cayenne pepper
6-8 small crepes
6 whole chives, blanched

1. Gently mix together all ingredients except crepes and whole chives.
2. Place heaping tablespoon of crabmeat salad in center of each crepe. Draw up crepe as though making a bundle, twisting the crepe gently to enclose the crabmeat. Tie a chive around the top of the bundle to close.
3. Serve immediately or store in refrigerator, tightly wrapped, for no longer than an hour.

Note: The crab mixture can also be used as a salad, served on top of lettuce leaves, as a dip on small snack bread slices or crackers, or as a spread on thinly sliced baguettes.

Shrimp Hors D'oeuvres

Nancy Perkins

Makes 36 servings

1 lb. fresh shrimp, cleaned and cooked
1 Tbsp. minced onion
1 tsp. minced celery
1 tsp. minced green pepper
2 tsp. lemon juice
½ tsp. grated lemon rind
¼ tsp. salt
4 or 5 drops Tabasco sauce
dash of pepper
¾ cup mayonnaise
36 snack bread slices, or full-sized bread slices
fresh parsley

1. Cut shrimp into very fine pieces. (A food processor works well with the shrimp and fresh vegetables.)
2. Combine all ingredients except bread and parsley.
3. If using full-sized bread slices, cut a round from each slice about the size of a half dollar. Pile a heaping teaspoon of shrimp mix on each round or snack bread slice. Garnish with parsley.

Mushrooms Oregano

Makes 10-12 appetizer servings

50 small mushrooms
2 cloves garlic, minced
1½ Tbsp. olive oil
1 tsp. salt
1 Tbsp. Romano cheese
1 tsp. dried oregano
snack bread or crackers

1. Wash mushrooms and pat dry.
2. In frying pan, heat minced garlic, olive oil, salt, Romano cheese, and oregano until warm. Add mushrooms.
3. Cover and simmer for 15-20 minutes.
4. Serve on top of snack bread slices or crackers.

Italian-Style Finger Sandwiches

Rina Mckee

Makes 20-25 appetizer servings

focaccia
½ lb. Genoa salami, sliced
1 lb. Provolone cheese, sliced
½ lb. pepperoni, sliced
2 medium tomatoes, cut into half slices
Italian dressing or mayonnaise, optional

1. Split focaccia in half lengthwise; then cut into 2-inch squares.
2. Layer meat, cheeses, and tomatoes on focaccia. Drizzle with dressing or dollops of mayonnaise.
3. Serve at room temperature.

Sweet and Sour Turkey Balls

Doris Harvey

Makes 8-10 appetizer servings

1 lb. ground turkey
½ cup Italian bread crumbs
1 egg
1 cup ketchup
2 tsp. cider vinegar
¾ cup brown sugar

Optional Sauce Ingredients:
8-oz. can pineapple chunks with juice
green peppers, chopped
red peppers, chopped
mushrooms, sliced

1. Combine turkey, bread crumbs, and egg. Form into 1-inch balls. Place on cookie sheet.
2. Bake at 350° for 20-30 minutes.
3. In large saucepan, combine ketchup, vinegar, and brown sugar. (Add pineapple chunks, peppers, and mushrooms, if desired.) Bring to boil. Pour over meatballs and serve.

Note: Serve with rice as a main dish.

I can remember my mom taking peach skin and making peach wine and peach brandy in the yard. The bees would be around so you had to strain it, oh yes! It was potent!
— Betty Cunningham,
a member of Bethel AMEC,
Lancaster, PA

Meatballs in Sweet and Sour Sauce

Alice Dabney

Makes 10-15 appetizer servings

1½ lbs. lean ground beef
1½ cups cornflake crumbs
⅓ cup dried parsley flakes
¼ tsp. pepper
3 Tbsp. soy sauce
¾ tsp. garlic powder
⅓ cup ketchup
2 Tbsp. minced onions
9-oz. can whole cranberry sauce
butter or bacon drippings

Sauce
½ cup brown sugar
12-oz. bottle chili sauce
1½ tsp. lemon juice

1. Combine ground beef, cornflake crumbs, parsley flakes, pepper, soy sauce, garlic powder, ketchup, onions, and cranberry sauce.
2. Roll into walnut-sized balls. Brown in batches in skillet in butter or bacon drippings. Place browned meatballs in baking dish; continue until all meatballs are browned.
3. Combine sauce ingredients. Pour over meatballs.
4. Bake uncovered at 350° for 30 minutes.

Southwest Cheesecake

Makes 8-12 appetizer servings

1 cup finely crushed tortilla chips
3 Tbsp. butter or margarine, melted
2 8-oz. pkgs. cream cheese, softened
2 eggs
1 pkg. dry taco seasoning
8 ozs. shredded Colby or Monterey Jack cheese
4-oz. can chopped green chilies, drained
1 cup sour cream
1 cup chopped bell pepper
½ cup sliced green onions
⅓ cup chopped tomatoes
¼ cup pitted ripe olive slices

1. Stir chips and butter together in small bowl. Press into 9" springform pan.
2. Bake at 350° for 15 minutes.
3. Beat cream cheese, eggs, and taco seasoning in large bowl at medium speed until well blended.
4. Fold in shredded cheese and chilies. Pour over crust.
5. Bake at 350° for 30 minutes.
6. Spread sour cream over cheesecake.
7. Loosen cake from rim of pan. Cool before removing rim.
8. Refrigerate for at least 30 minutes.
9. Top with remaining ingredients just before serving.

Sara's Cheese Ball

Sara Flack

Makes 8-10 servings

2 1/4-oz. jar dried beef
2 8-oz. pkgs. cream cheese, softened
1 Tbsp. mayonnaise or salad dressing
1/4 tsp. dry mustard
1/4 tsp. cayenne pepper
4 green onions, chopped
1/4 cup chopped nuts, optional

1. Drain dried beef and tear into shreds.
2. Combine all ingredients except nuts. Refrigerate until very firm.
3. Form into ball.
4. Roll in nuts. Chill until ready to serve. Bring to table with a variety of snack crackers.

Cheese Ball

Makes 12-14 servings

2 8-oz. pkgs. cream cheese, softened
5-oz. jar bleu cheese, softened
5-oz. jar Old English cheese, softened
1 Tbsp. Worcestershire sauce
crushed pecans
parsley

1. Combine cream cheese, bleu cheese, Old English cheese, and Worcestershire sauce with fork until well blended.
2. Refrigerate until very firm.
3. Shape into ball.
4. Mix together crushed pecans and parsley; then roll cheese in mixture until well coated.

Vegetable Spread

Cormylene Williams

Makes 1 1/2 cups

2 carrots
half a sweet red pepper
1 rib celery
1/2 cup walnuts
1 tsp. freshly grated ginger
1 tsp. freshly grated lemon rind
3-4 Tbsp. mayonnaise

1. In food processor, grate carrots. Remove and set aside. Then chop red pepper, celery, and walnuts until of a coarse consistency.
2. Stir in grated carrots, ginger, lemon rind, and enough mayonnaise to hold mixture together.
3. Chill before serving.
4. Spread on snack crackers, celery sticks, or bread squares.

> . . . One universal Father hath given being to us all, and that he hath not only made us all of one flesh, but that he hath also without partiality afforded us all the same sensations and endued us all with the same faculties, and that however variable we may be in society or religion, however diversified in situation or colour, we are all of the same family, and stand in the same relation to Him.
>
> — Benjamin Banneker, excerpt from letter to Thomas Jefferson

Southern Caviar

Mrs. Margaret Bailey

Makes 4 to 6 servings

1/2 lb. dried black-eyed peas
3/4 cup oil
1/4 cup vinegar
1 whole clove garlic, smashed
half an onion, chopped
ground black pepper to taste

1. Rinse peas under cold water. Place in saucepan and cover with water. Boil for 2 minutes. Remove from heat. Let soak for 60 minutes.
2. Drain peas. Rinse well. Cover with water and cook until peas are tender but still whole, about 15 minutes. Drain. Place peas in bowl.
3. Add oil, vinegar, garlic, onion, and pepper. Mix well. Cover and refrigerate for 3 days. Remove garlic after first day. Drain before serving.

We ate so much apple butter that I won't eat it now. My children don't even know what it tastes like.
— Doris Johnson

Anchovy Spread

Makes spread for 16-20 snack crackers

3-oz. pkg. cream cheese, softened
2 tsp. capers
1/2 tsp. grated onion
1 tsp. anchovy paste
few drops Worcestershire sauce
2 Tbsp. mayonnaise, approximately

1. Mash cream cheese.
2. Stir in capers, onion, anchovy paste, and Worcestershire sauce. Mix well.
3. Stir in mayonnaise until thin enough to spread.

Note: Add 1/2 tsp. of your favorite herb to add color and flavor.

Oriental Salmon Dip

Mrs. Margaret Bailey

Makes 1 3/4 cups

1 Tbsp. sesame seeds
1 scant tsp. oil
7 3/4-oz. can salmon, drained and flaked
2 Tbsp. minced green onions
1/2 cup sour cream
1/2 cup mayonnaise
1 Tbsp. soy sauce
1/4 tsp. freshly grated, peeled, fresh ginger
raw broccoli florets
sliced zucchini, celery, and carrots
fresh pea pods

1. Toast sesame seeds by heating in oil in skillet until light brown, or by placing on tray in 350° toaster oven for 2 minutes or until light brown.

2. Combine all ingredients, except raw vegetables and pea pods. Mix well. Refrigerate for at least an hour.

3. Serve with vegetables.

Shrimp Dip

Hester Prince

Makes 6-8 servings

8-oz. pkg. cream cheese, softened
1/2 cup mayonnaise
1 Tbsp. lemon juice
1 Tbsp. ketchup
one-quarter of a medium onion, grated
1/2 tsp. seasoned salt
1/2 lb. cooked shrimp

1. Cream together cheese and mayonnaise.
2. Stir in lemon juice, ketchup, onion, and seasoned salt.
3. Fold in shrimp. Chill.
4. Serve with chips.

Notes:

1. To reduce calories, substitute Neufchatel in place of cream cheese, and light mayonnaise or salad dressing instead of regular mayonnaise.

2. You can use small salad shrimp in place of larger cooked shrimp.

Taco Dip

Bernadette Zone

Makes 10-12 servings

16 ozs. cottage cheese
8-oz. pkg. cream cheese, softened
1 pkg. dry taco seasoning
Mexican cheese, shredded
lettuce, shredded
tomatoes, chopped
taco chips

1. Combine cottage cheese, cream cheese, and taco seasoning. Pour into dish.
2. Top with a layer of Mexican cheese, followed by a layer of lettuce, and then a layer of tomatoes.
3. Serve with taco chips.

Cracklins

fresh pork skin, or 1 cup salt pork or
    slab bacon
salt

1. Cut pork skin into small pieces. Cook in heavy pot until skin is crispy. Stir frequently so the skin doesn't burn.
2. Drain drippings. (Reserve for browning chopped onions or minced garlic or other vegetables.)
3. Sprinkle cracklins with salt. Cool.

Garlic Spread

Nancy Perkins

Makes spread for one loaf Italian bread

1¼ cups (1½ sticks) butter
3 Tbsp. grated Parmesan cheese
½ tsp. garlic powder
loaf of Italian bread, sliced

1. Warm butter to room temperature.
2. Combine all ingredients except bread.
3. Spread on slices of Italian bread.
4. Wrap bread in foil and heat in 350° oven for 15-20 minutes.

Caramel Popcorn

Makes 12-15 servings

1 cup (2 sticks) margarine, or butter
½ cup white corn syrup
2 cups brown sugar
¼ tsp. cream of tartar
1 tsp. salt
1 tsp. baking soda
6 qts. popped popcorn
peanuts, optional

1. In saucepan, combine butter, syrup, and sugar. Boil for 6 minutes, stirring constantly. Remove from heat.
2. Stir in cream of tartar, salt, and baking soda. In large mixing bowl, pour over popcorn and peanuts and stir well. Spread on greased cookie sheet.
3. Bake at 200° for 60 minutes.
4. Allow to cool; then break apart into bite-sized pieces.

Cranberry Fruit Punch

Makes 8-12 servings

1 qt. cranberry juice cocktail
2 cups orange juice
½ cup lemon juice
1 cup pineapple juice
½ cup sugar
1-2 cups water

1. Combine all ingredients.
2. Serve over crushed ice or cubes.

Hot Cranberry Punch

Makes about 24 6-oz. servings

½ cup packed brown sugar
1 cup water
½ tsp. ground cinnamon
½ tsp. ground nutmeg
¼ tsp. ground cloves
2 16-oz. cans jellied cranberry sauce
6 cups water
12-oz. can frozen orange juice concentrate
2 Tbsp. fresh lemon juice

1. Combine brown sugar, 1 cup water, cinnamon, nutmeg, and cloves in Dutch oven. Heat over high heat until mixture boils, stirring constantly. Cook and stir until sugar is dissolved. Remove from heat.
2. Stir in cranberry sauce. Mix well.
3. Stir in remaining water, orange juice, and lemon juice. Heat to boiling. Reduce heat. Simmer, uncovered, for 5 minutes.
4. Serve hot.

Party Punch

Makes 24 servings

3 cups orange juice
fresh whole small strawberries
1 qt. apple juice
1 qt. orange soda
1 qt. ginger ale
2 cups cranberry juice
2 cups pineapple juice
3 cups orange juice

1. Combine 3 cups orange juice and strawberries. Freeze in container to make large ice cube.
2. Chill apple juice, orange soda, ginger ale, cranberry juice, pineapple juice, and 3 cups orange juice.
3. Combine chilled ingredient in punch bowl. Add orange juice-strawberry ice cube.

Hawaiian Fruit Punch

Makes 45 6-oz. servings

2 46-oz. cans unsweetened pineapple juice
2 2/3 cups orange juice
1 1/2 cups lemon juice
2/3 cup lime juice
2 cups sugar
2-liter bottle ginger ale, chilled
2-liter bottle club soda, chilled
orange and lemon slices

1. Combine fruit juices and sugar. Chill.
2. Pour over ice in punch bowl. Slowly pour ginger ale and club soda down the side of the bowl.
3. Garnish with orange and lemon slices.

Wedding Punch

Makes 25 servings

3-oz. pkg. gelatin, any flavor for desired color
3/4 cup sugar
1 gallon hot water
1 small can frozen lemonade
1 large can unsweetened pineapple juice

1. Dissolve gelatin and sugar in hot water. Freeze.
2. When ready to serve, partially thaw punch and stir until slushy. Add frozen lemonade and pineapple juice.

Mock Champagne Punch

Makes 18-20 servings

32 ozs. white grape juice
sliced fruit — lemon, lime, oranges,
    cherries
25.4 ozs. non-alcoholic sparkling white
    grape juice
2 liters ginger ale
32 ozs. white grape juice
6-oz. can frozen lemonade, undiluted

1. Make ice ring with sliced fruit and 32
ozs. white grape juice.
2. Chill remaining ingredients.
3. Combine sparkling grape juice, ginger
ale, 32 ozs. grape juice, and lemonade in
punch bowl. Add ice ring just before serving.

*Note: If you prefer a less sweet beverage,
substitute sparkling water in place of the ginger
ale.*

Instant Russian Tea

Makes many servings

18-oz. jar Tang instant breakfast drink
2 3-oz. pkgs. instant lemonade mix
2 tsp. ground cinnamon
2 tsp. ground cloves
3/4 cup instant dry tea
2 1/2 cups sugar

1. Mix all ingredients together thoroughly.
2. Place in tightly covered jar or plastic
container and use as needed.
3. To make a cup of hot tea, place 2
heaping Tbsp. dry mix in cup and add boiling
water. Stir well.

Peach Tea

Makes 6-8 servings

3 cups chilled iced tea
6 Tbsp. sugar
1/2 cup lemon juice
2 12-oz. cans peach nectar
orange slices
whole cloves
fresh mint sprigs

1. Combine all ingredients and chill.
2. Just before serving remove whole
cloves.

Dried Peach (or Apricot) Wine

3 pounds dried peaches (or apricots)
1½ gallons cold water
4½ lbs. sugar
1 pkg. wine yeast, or one ¼-oz. pkg. active
  dry yeast

1. Soak peaches in cold water overnight.
2. Place peaches and water in large cooking vessel. Bring to boil. Simmer for 5 minutes. Cool mixture until it is just cool enough to handle.
3. Strain through cheesecloth bag into a crock, using your hands to press out as much liquid as possible.
4. Stir in sugar while liquid is still warm. Cool to room temperature.
5. Sprinkle yeast on top. Cover. Let stand for 12 hours.
6. Stir yeast into mixture.
7. Let stand for 7 days, stirring daily.
8. Transfer to gallon jugs. Place fermentation locks or corks on the jugs and allow wine to continue fermentation undisturbed.
9. Rack after 3 months.
10. Bottle when wine has cleared and fermentation has ceased. Age for 9-12 months.

Vanilla Coke

Makes 1 serving

scoop of ice cream
2 ozs. vanilla syrup
cola soda
maraschino cherry

1. Place scoop of ice cream in mason jar.
2. Combine vanilla syrup and cola soda. Pour over ice cream.
3. Garnish with cherry.
4. Serve immediately.

Note: Multiply as often as you want to make more servings.

Every year in the summertime my mother and father would make root beer. We would pour it into the bottles and close them with metal caps. It was my job to squeeze the caps on. Then we'd take them down in the yard and lay them in the sun. When they were ready to drink, the caps would pop off. If you didn't put the caps on right they wouldn't pop off.

— Nelson Polite, Sr.,
a member of Bethel AMEC,
Lancaster, PA

Etc.

Dusting Powder

Sandy Cornish

2 cups cornstarch
1 cup baking soda
20 drops essential oil of any fragrance (no
    substitutes)
wooden boxes or containers of any size
powder puffs

1. Mix cornstarch and baking soda
together.
2. Add drops of essential oil and mix.
3. Place powder in containers.
4. Give as gifts with powder puffs.

Bath Salts

Sandy Cornish

box of Epsom salts or rock salt
1 drop food coloring, optional
15 drops essential oil per cup of salt
empty jars or containers of any size

1. Mix Epsom salts with choice of food
coloring.
2. Add drops of essential oil and mix.
3. Pour salts into jars or containers.

Bath Oil

Sandy Cornish

12-oz. or 16-oz. bottle baby oil
15 drops essential oil
empty jars or containers of any size

1. Place drops of essential oil inside baby
oil bottle and shake.
2. Pour bath oil mixture into jars or
containers. Seal and enjoy.

A wise person speaks carefully and
with truth, for every word that passes
between one's teeth is meant for
something.

— Molefikete Asante

Story and Song

by Reverend Edward M. Bailey

Oh! This is my story, this is my song,
  Praising my Savior all the day long;
This is my story, this is my song,
  Praising my Savior all the day long.

As a youngster I was very proud of my knowledge of history. I read books and pamphlets, attended seminars, and took history courses in college. I felt competent discussing American history, especially the history of my people, sun-kissed African Americans. In fact, I was downright arrogant and insufferably rude in my assessment of how bright and knowledgeable I was about African history and about how ignorant others were.

But in 1987, in a workshop facilitated by Dr. Leroy Hopkins, a student of local African and German history, I began hearing a story of the Africans of America that I knew nothing about. I could not believe my ears nor my ignorance. I learned for the first time that there were African Civil War soldiers, scouts, and nurses. I also discovered that underneath my bravado I carried shame about my people and my history, because I had never heard of the full-scale resistance by Africans. I realized that my knowledge was based on half-truths and untruths.

I wondered how many other African Americans were as limited in their knowledge and as filled with shame about their history as I was. From my conversations with folk who looked like me, I began to realize that others were suffering under these same delusions.

Bethel Harambee Historical Services was born out of this personal struggle. In the Bible the word Bethel means "house of God." For Richard Allen, an enslaved African who helped to found the African Methodist Episcopal Church in the early 19th century, Bethel also meant "a place of refuge and comfort." Harambee comes from the Swahili language and means "Let's pull together."

Reverend Bailey

That is exactly what Richard Allen and the founding parents of the African Methodist Episcopal Church did when they formed the denomination. They pulled together and provided a house of God that was a place of refuge and comfort for both free Africans and enslaved Africans. Almost all of the churches founded by Allen and others in Pennsylvania were called Bethel. These Bethels were active in the fight for freedom, and by their locations were strategically placed milestones on the trail to freedom. In fact, many who "followed the drinking gourd" and traveled the Underground Railroad in Pennsylvania stopped at stations called Bethel.

Bethel Harambee, a not-for-profit corporation, has a vision for freeing those of African descent who have no

Many who followed the drinking gourd *and traveled the Underground Railroad in Pennsylvania stopped at stations called Bethel.*

knowledge of the real African story in America.

Many who are captives of old assumptions also do not know about the triumphs of an ordinary people who trusted in the God of Abraham, Isaac, and Jacob. Through Him and by Him ordinary people did extraordinary acts. Rev. Steven Smith, an African Methodist preacher, was a conductor on the Underground Railroad. William Whipper, a wealthy businessman, helped fund the work of the Africans' underground resistance. These and many others are virtually unknown and until recently were not mentioned in school textbooks.

Bethel Harambee produces "Living the Experience," a spiritual reenactment of the Underground Railroad, which includes the lives and times of enslaved Africans. Along with telling the story, we sing the songs of freedom, without which the story would be incomplete.

Fannie Crosby, in the chorus of "Blessed Assurance," a beloved hymn, captures a profound truth:

This is my story, this is my song,
Praising my Savior all the day long.

The Christian walk is both a song and a story. Having one without the other is being, as Paul of the Bible wrote, "a resounding gong or a clanging cymbal." No one wants to hear the testimony or the song of a Christian who does not have a story and a life that are in agreement. For we not only want to hear a sermon preached, we want to see the sermon lived, with full evidence that both are real.

We at Bethel Harambee find it necessary to hear the story and the song of Africans who have experienced the God who does deliver. It is essential for those of us who have been sun-kissed and who trace our heritage back to a lost time, to lost shores, and to a lost culture.

Our best and our most popular preachers were those who could tell the story—with the rhythm of the song. Those preachers who gave the "whoop" or the song *without* the story found out very quickly during the "call and response" that this was unacceptable. Someone in the congregation would say, "Bring it on in, Rev." That meant, "It is time to sit down and shut up because all you're doing is making noise." In other words, you're singing but you don't have a story.

The old favorite Negro spirituals had both song and story. "Go Down Moses," "Ezekiel Saw a Wheel Way Up in the

"Living the Experience," a spiritual interactive reenactment, was developed to share the story of free and enslaved Africans who lived, pioneered, and carved out a place for themselves in the Americas. Told from the point of view of Africans of the 1800s, it highlights the contribution Africans made in demanding, obtaining, and securing their freedom. Using the first person, "Living the Experience" focuses on individuals who were seeking freedom, and on those who tirelessly and unselfishly participated in the Underground Railroad.

The spirituals throughout the reenactment are sung in homage to the creativity and the ability of Africans to use something ordinary to carry out extraordinary efforts.

A scene from "Living the Experience."

The cast and staff of "Living the Experience" invite you to "live the experience" at the historic Bethel African Methodist Episcopal Church, located in ChurchTowne of Lancaster, Pennsylvania, where the pastors and congregation of old provided a safe house and a community for escaping Africans. Make reservations for the reenactment by visiting the website: www.livingtheundergroundrailroad.com or by calling 800/510-5899.

Middle of the Air," "Joshua Fought the Battle of Jericho," and many others, are biblical stories set to the rhythm of song.

The spirituals that endured are those Bible stories that became the songs and stories of enslaved Africans.

Enslaved Africans adapted the stories of the Bible to tell their story. These songs and stories became their way of communicating and relating with one another. These folks were taken captive from the continent of Africa, where there are more languages and dialects than any of the other continents. Yet these Africans met, sent messages, asked for help, and gave warning to each other through these stories and songs.

Bethel Harambee Historical Services produces the reenactment "Living the Experience" and provides space for the Leroy Taft and Mary Ella Hopkins Research and Study Center. The Hopkins Center fosters research about local African families, businesses, and homes, and the dissemination of stories from the African history of Lancaster. The Center has a growing collection of artifacts and documents, toward its goal of being a hub for African history that spans from Africa to the present by filling in answers about the time between.

These songs endured because the people who sang the songs also lived their stories. They identified with the bondage of the children of Israel so much that they could tell their Moses to go down to Egypt, a place of bondage—the plantation—to tell old Pharaoh—the old Massa—to let "my people" go.

The story and the song were also giving praise all the day long to the God who sits high, but looks low and fights the battle for the least, the last, and the lost.

At Bethel Harambee we are committed to singing the song that tells the story of an historically oppressed people. Because of their song and story they were able to say with conviction, "Before I'll be a slave I'll be buried in my grave and go home with my Lord and be free."

The beauty of these songs and stories is that they have no expiration date, they are never outmoded, and they work no matter the situation. When we look around today—and see the plight of many African Americans, and think about the future—we believe that we need to learn the songs and the story. These songs and stories will help us hear that it was not the goodness of folk that brought us out of the miry clay, but the goodness of God.

In the past our story has not been told by us but by others. We have been allowed to sing the songs while others took the glory with a false story, the story of the deliverance of Africans in America. The true story is about how a good God, who is good all the time, did good things for folk in a no-good situation. The story is also about those folk who walked with God and who did so much with so little with so much against them. "If God be for us, who can be against us." This story, for too long, has not been told.

I believe that the reason so many young African Americans are walking around in a fog, and so many older African Americans are walking in denial, is because they do not know the real story behind the song. Today in our churches we have turned to songs that have no historical meaning for us or for generations to come. And we no longer tell our story. We act as if nothing is happening to our people, all the while many of us are being taken captive, being placed in all types of bondage, and no

Bethel AME Church of ChurchTowne, Lancaster, Pennsylvania.

longer determining our own future. These lost Africans are now singing songs that demean themselves, our mores, and our morals. They are convinced—because of where they were born and the environment in which they live—that there is no way out, except through means that do not bring deliverance, but rather the acceptance and celebration of bondage. To understand this is to listen to their songs that sing of no hope and deny a story of deliverance.

We believe that the hope of our future is in our past. The stories were the perspiration for our fight for freedom, and the songs were our inspiration. Our people lived what they sang about. They were not only dancers and dreamers, but they were workers and thinkers.

In the past these qualities worked against all odds and we became free. To

> "Living the Experience," Bethel Harambee Historical Services, and the Hopkins Research and Study Center are all part of the effort to revive ChurchTowne, a community in Lancaster, Pennsylvania, where businesses, homes, and a one-room school once thrived. The goal is to offer ways for the people now living in this historic community to establish a strong economic, educational, evangelical, responsibly environmental, and enterprising base. This commitment comes from Bethel AME Church's past, and its current vision: to serve as Christ-centered, African-centered leadership for holistic community-building.

stay free we need to live the life we sing about. We do not need new songs; we just need to live our story while we sing our song. And it must be our story and our song if it is to work for our people.

When we sing our song and live our own story, others become inspired to seek freedom and live free. So it was during our sojourn in the past. As we sang and lived our story, women, in part because of our example, fought to be full citizens, and others began to demand their full rights as Americans. Our fight has helped to fulfill the American dream, the dream that states that all persons are created equal and are granted inalienable rights by God. Those who live for this dream, as Martin Luther King has said, are not rabble-rousers, but are American freedom-fighters.

Come sing with us our song and hear our story, and you will find that it is a miracle event within the miracle experiment called America.

Reverend Edward M. Bailey, is pastor of Bethel African Methodist Episcopal Church, ChurchTowne of Lancaster, Pennsylvania.

Reverend Bailey in front of the Bethel AME Cultural Center, home of Harambee Historical Services and the Hopkins Research and Study Center in ChurchTowne of Lancaster, PA.

Index

A

Anchovy Spread, 220
Appetizers (see Snacks and Appetizers)
Apple
  Apple Dumplings, 174-175
  Applesauce Bread, 147
  Applesauce Cake, 200-201
  Baked Apple Pudding, 175
  Fresh Apple Squares, 176
  Fried Apples, 170
  Glazed Apple Rings, 170
  Jewish Apple Cake, 199
  Johnny Appleseed Coffee Cake, 200
  Old-Fashioned Applesauce Cake, 200
  One Bowl Apple Nut Cake, 199
Apple Dumplings, 174-175
Applesauce Bread, 147
Applesauce Cake, 200-201
Artichoke
  Risotto with Spring Veggies, 22
Asparagus
  Asparagus Casserole, 110
  Asparagus Frittata, 109
  Asparagus with Parmesan Cheese, 110
  Creamed Asparagus, 110
  Linguini with Asparagus & Pesto, 20
  Shrimp and Rice Salad, 122
  Stir-Fried Asparagus with Snow Peas, 109
Asparagus Casserole, 110
Asparagus Frittata, 109
Asparagus with Parmesan Cheese, 110
Avocado
  Southwestern Potato Salad, 119

B

Bacon
  Black-Eyed Peas, 92
  Cajun Cassoulet, 32
  Collard Greens, 10
  Cracklins, 221
  Fried Cabbage and Bacon, 97
  Okra Gumbo, 8
  Spanish Rice, 23-24
  Washington Chowder, 154
Bake Sale Pineapple Bread, 145
Baked Apple Pudding, 175
Baked Beans Brewster-Style, 27
Baked Cherries and Custard, 172
Baked Flounder Fillets in Cheese Sauce, 85
Baked Ham, 79
Baked Honey Pears, 169
Baked Lasagna, 25
Baked Oysters Italian Style, 88
Baked Pears, 169
Baked Salmon, 86
Baked Turkey Wings, 64
Banana Bread, 146
Banana Split Delight, 176
Bananas
  Banana Bread, 146
  Banana Split Delight, 176
  Frosted Fruit Salad, 125
  Sunshine Loaf, 146
Barbecued Chicken, 48
Barbecued Chicken Wings, 61
Barbecued Spareribs, 77
Basic Tempura, 47
Batter-Fried Okra, 95
Bean Soup, 157
Bean Sprouts
  Pork Fried Rice, 31
  Shrimp Stir-Fry, 38
Beans, Baked
  Baked Beans Brewster-Style, 27

Beans, Butter
  Bean Soup, 157
  Southern Cooked Butter Beans, 95
Beans, Chili
  Two-Bean Beef Mix, 26
Beans, Fava
  Risotto with Spring Veggies, 22
Beans, Great Northern
  Bean Soup, 157
Beans, Green
  Chicken and Vegetables, 34
  Chicken in White Wine, 53
  Crab Soup, 160
  Italian Green Beans with Mushrooms, 107
  Minestrone with Tortellini, 156
Beans, Kidney
  Bean Soup, 157
  Minestrone with Tortellini, 156
  Two-Bean Beef Mix, 26
Beans, Lima
  Bean Soup, 157
  Crab Soup, 160
  Dry Lima Beans, 95
  Southern Cooked Dried Lima Beans, 96
  Succotash, 100
Beans, Navy
  Bean Soup, 157
Beans, Pinto
  Bean Soup, 157
Beans, Red
  Cajun Cassoulet, 32
Beans, String
  Boiled String Beans with Ham, 14
Beef Barley Minestrone, 155
Beef Stroganoff, 70

Index

Beets
    Harvard Beets, 99
    Pickled Beets, 125
    Pickled Eggs and Beets, 126
Beets with Onions and Tomatoes,
    113
Best Yet Pound Cake, 209
Beverage
    Cranberry Fruit Punch, 222
    Dried Peach (or Apricot)
        Wine, 225
    Hawaiian Fruit Punch, 223
    Hot Cranberry Punch, 222
    Instant Russian Tea, 224
    Mock Champagne Punch, 224
    Party Punch, 223
    Peach Tea, 224
    Vanilla Coke, 225
    Wedding Punch, 223
Big Batch No-Cook Fudge, 190
Biscuits
    Buttermilk Biscuits, 132
    Herby Biscuits, 140
    Yogurt and Chives Biscuits,
        141
    Yogurt and Onion Biscuit
        Squares, 140
Black-Eyed Peas
    Black-Eyed Peas with Ham,
        13
    Hoppin John, 92
    Southern Caviar, 220
Black-Eyed Peas with Ham, 13
Bleu Cheese, 219
    Cheese Ball, 219
Blueberry
    Blueberry and Peach
        Shortcake, 201
    Blueberry Delight, 176
    Blueberry Muffins, 141
Blueberry and Peach Shortcake,
    201
Blueberry Delight, 176
Blueberry Muffins, 141
Boiled String Beans with Ham,
    14
Bombay Rice Dressing, 105

Braided Easter Bread, 136
Braised Veal in Cider, 74
Brandy
    Baked Honey Pears, 169
    Leiths Roast Duck, 66
    Poached Pears, 169
Bread and Butter Pickles, 127
Bread Pudding, 181
Bread, Sweet
    Applesauce Bread, 147
    Bake Sale Pineapple Bread,
        145
    Banana Bread, 146
    Carrot Bread, 146
    Frontier Nut Bread, 148
    Hobby-Bakers Coffee-
        Breakers, 148
    Monkey Bread, 149
    Nutty Pumpkin Bread, 145
    Pumpkin Nut Bread, 144
    Sunshine Loaf, 146
    Zucchini Nut Bread, 147
Breads — Other Favorites
    Applesauce Bread, 147
    Bake Sale Pineapple Bread,
        145
    Banana Bread, 146
    Blueberry Muffins, 141
    Braided Easter Bread, 136
    Carrot Bread, 146
    Cheesy Muffins, 142
    Cornbread, 136
    Country Cinnamon Rolls, 138
    French Toast, 149
    Frontier Nut Bread, 148
    Gift Muffs, 143
    Granola Muffins, 142
    Ham, Cheese, & Raisin Sticks,
        143
    Herby Biscuits, 140
    Hobby-Bakers Coffee-
        Breakers, 148
    Hobo Bread, 144
    Jam Dandies, 140
    Monkey Bread, 149
    Mother's Bread, 137
    Nutty Pumpkin Bread, 145

Party Crescents, 139
Pumpkin Nut Bread, 144
Southern Style Cornbread,
    136
Sunday Brunch Cherry Nut
    Rolls, 138
Sunshine Loaf, 146
Supermuffs, 143
Whole Wheat Muffins, 142
Yankee Doughnuts, 139
Yogurt and Chives Biscuits,
    140
Yogurt and Onions Biscuit
    Squares, 141
Yummy Healthy Muffins, 142
Zucchini Nut Bread, 147
Breads — Traditional
    Biscuits, 131
    Buttermilk Biscuits, 132
    Buttermilk Cornbread, 130
    Buttermilk Rolls, 132
    Cracklin Cornbread, 131
    Homemade Rolls, 134
    Hush Puppies, 135
    Old South Hush Puppies, 135
    Old-Fashioned Cornbread,
        130
    Raisin Bread, 134
    Tasty White Bread, 133
    Whole Wheat Bread, 133
    Whole Wheat Rolls or Bread,
        133
Broccoli
    Broccoli and Rice Casserole,
        106
    Broccoli Casserole, 106
    Broccoli Soup, 158
    Broiled Shrimp Au Porto, 81
    Chicken Divan, 35
    Pasta Primavera, 19
    Primavera Pizza, 20
    Wild Rice, Chicken, and
        Broccoli Bake, 35
Broccoli and Rice Casserole, 106
Broccoli Casserole, 106
Broccoli Soup, 158
Broiled Shrimp Au Porto, 81

Browned Brussels Sprouts, 112
Brownies, Moist 'n Chewy, 183
Brunswick Stew, 9
Brussels Sprouts, Browned, 112
Buffalo Chicken Drumsticks, 60
Buffalo Wings, 61
Butter Beans with Ham Hocks, 13
Butter Cake, 206
Buttermilk Biscuits, 132
Buttermilk Cornbread, 130
Buttermilk Pound Cake, 195
Buttermilk Rolls, 132
Butterscotch Delight, 177

C
Cabbage
    Beef Barley Minestrone, 155
    Cabbage and Smoked
      Neckbones, 12
    Chinese Pot-Au-Feu, 34
    Cold Crab Salad, 123
    Corned Beef and Cabbage, 28
    Creamed Vegetable Dish, 111
    Fried Cabbage and Bacon, 97
    Ground Beef and Cabbage, 29
    Ham and Cabbage Dinner, 30
    Vegetable Broth, 159
Cabbage and Smoked
    Neckbones, 12
Cabbage, Napa
    Chinese Pot-Au-Feu, 34
Cajun Cassoulet, 32
Cajun Chops, 74
Cakes — Other Favorites
    Applesauce Cake, 201
    Best Yet Pound Cake, 209
    Blueberry and Peach
      Shortcake, 201
    Butter Cake, 206
    Cherry Zip Up, 206
    Chocolate Chip Peanut Butter
      Cake, 197
    Chocolate Swirl Coffee Cake,
      198
    Chocolate Texas Sheet Cake,
      197

Coconut Pound Cake, 208
Cool Whip Pound Cake, 211
Cowboy Coffee Cake, 201
Cranberry Orange Butter
    Cake, 203
Cream Cheese Icing, 202
Devil's Food Cake, 196
Dieters' Chocolate
    Cheesecake, 198
Dump Cake, 204
Easy Two-Egg Cake, 206
Five-Flavor Pound Cake, 209
Gingerbread, 212
Gold Rush Coffee Cake, 203
Grand Champion Sponge
    Cake, 212
Hershey's Chocolate Cake,
    196
Hester's Cake, 204
Jello Cake, 213
Jewish Apple Cake, 199
Johnny Appleseed Coffee
    Cake, 200
Million Dollar Pound Cake,
    207
Old-Fashioned Applesauce
    Cake, 200
Old-Fashioned Shortcake, 207
One Bowl Apple Nut Cake,
    199
Pecan Cake, 205
Pineapple Pound Cake, 210
Rum Cake, 213
7-Up Pound Cake, 210
Sour Cream Pound Cake, 208
Spice Cake, 211
Surprisin' Carrot Cake, 202
Tossed Butter Pecan Cake,
    205
Watergate Cake, 204
Williamsburg Orange Cake,
    202
Wine Cake, 213
Cakes — Traditional
    Buttermilk Pound Cake, 195
    Pound Cake, 194
    Shortbread, 195

Candied Yams, 96
Cantaloupe, 67
    Roast Cornish Hens with
      Melon Sauce, 67
Caramel Popcorn, 222
Carolina Red Rice, 15
Carrot Bread, 146
Carrots
    Braised Veal in Cider, 74
    Chicken Marsala, 53
    Chinese Pot-Au-Feu, 34
    Chuck Roast with Vegetables,
      69
    Creamed Vegetable Dish, 111
    Glazed Carrots and Turnips,
      105
    Glazed Honey Carrots, 99
    Harvest Salmon Chowder, 163
    Minestrone with Tortellini,
      156
    Oven-Baked Pot Roast, 70
    Pasta Primavera, 19
    Pot Roast, 68
    Surprisin' Carrot Cake, 202
    Vegetable Broth, 159
Cauliflower Cheese Casserole,
    112
Caviar, 220
    Southern Caviar, 220
Celery
    Chicken Marsala, 53
    Creamed Vegetable Dish, 111
    Vegetable Broth, 159
Chafing Dish A La Newburg, 84
Champagne & Mushroom
    Chicken, 57
Cheese
    Feather-Light Cheese
      Casserole, 18
    Italian-Style Finger
      Sandwiches, 217
    Macaroni and Cheese,
      Home-style, 18
    Southwest Cheesecake, 218
Cheese Ball
    Cheese Ball, 219
    Sara's Cheese Ball, 219

Index

Cheese Garlic Grits, 101
Cheesecake, Dieters' Chocolate, 198
Cheesecake Cookies, 179
Cheesy Muffins, 142
Cherries
    Baked Cherries and Custard, 172
    Cherries and Cream Roll, 172
Cherries and Cream Roll, 172
Cherry Zip Up, 206
Chicken
    Barbecued Chicken, 48
    Barbecued Chicken Wings, 61
    Buffalo Chicken Drumsticks, 60
    Buffalo Wings, 61
    Champagne & Mushroom Chicken, 57
    Chicken Cobbler, 63
    Chicken in White Wine, 53
    Chicken Lemonaise, 56
    Chicken Marsala, 53
    Chicken Parmesan, 56
    Chicken Piccata, 54
    Chicken Teriyaki, 52
    Chinese Pot-Au-Feu, 34
    Fargo a Portuguese, 58
    Fried Chicken, 42-43
    Grilled Chinese Five-Spice Skewered Chicken, 59
    Gumbo Feast, 6
    Hawaiian Chicken, 58
    Honey Baked Chicken, 50
    Honey Buffet Chicken, 49
    Hot Chicken Salad, 62
    Italian-Style Fried Chicken Wings, 61
    Jambalaya, 37
    Lemon Barbecued Chicken, 55
    Lemony Chicken Thighs, 50
    Low-Fat Chicken Salad, 120
    Mexican Chicken, 57
    New Orleans Gumbo, 8
    Orange Baked Chicken, 51
    Orange Ginger Chicken, 51
    Parmesan Baked Chicken Legs, 48
    Pork Mu Shu Burritos, 31
    Rosy Glazed Chicken, 54
    Sesame Fried Chicken, 49
    Smoked-Almond Crusted Chicken, 55
    Sunshine Chicken, 58
    Sweet & Sour Chicken, 60
    Sweet N' Sour Chicken, 59
    Teriyaki Sauce, 52
    Wild Rice, Chicken, and Broccoli Bake, 35
    Wings Teriyaki, 62
Chicken and Rice Soup, 153
Chicken and Vegetables, 34
Chicken Cobbler, 63
Chicken Divan, 35
Chicken in White Wine, 53
Chicken Lemonaise, 56
Chicken Marsala, 53
Chicken Parmesan, 56
Chicken Piccata, 54
Chicken Salad, Hot, 62
Chicken Soup, 159
Chicken Teriyaki, 52
Chicken Wings
    Barbecued Chicken Wings, 61
    Buffalo Wings, 61
    Italian-Style Fried Chicken Wings, 61
    Wings Teriyaki, 62
Chickpeas,
    Three-Bean Soup, 156
Chinese Beef with Broccoli, 29
Chinese Pot-Au-Feu, 34
Chitlins and Maw, 46
Chocolate,
    Big Batch No-Cook Fudge, 190
    Chocolate Chip Peanut Butter Cake, 197
    Chocolate Covered Strawberries, 171
    Chocolate Fudge, 189
    Chocolate Peanut Butter Fudge, 190
    Chocolate Swirl Coffee Cake, 198
    Chocolate Texas Sheet Cake, 197
    Chocolatey Coconut Squares, 179
    Devil's Food Cake, 196
    Dieters' Chocolate Cheesecake, 198
    Hershey's Chocolate Cake, 196
    Opera Fudge, 190
    Peanut Butter Easter Eggs, 191
    Pear Au Chocolate, 170
    Toll House Cookies, 185
Chocolate Chip Peanut Butter Cake, 197
Chocolate Covered Strawberries, 171
Chocolate Fudge, 189
Chocolate Peanut Butter Fudge, 190
Chocolate Swirl Coffee Cake, 198
Chocolate Texas Sheet Cake, 197
Chocolatey Coconut Squares, 179
Chop Suey Vegetables
    Pork Mu Shu Burritos, 31
Chow Chow, Green Tomato, 126
Chuck Roast with Vegetables, 69
Chuck Wagon Roast, 68
Cider, Braised Veal in, 74
Cinnamon Rolls, Country, 138
Coconut
    Chocolatey Coconut Squares, 179
    Dump Cake, 204
    Hester's Cake, 204
    Lassers Cookies, 186
Coconut Pound Cake, 208
Cod, 161
    Seafood Bisque, 161
Coffee Cake
    Chocolate Swirl Coffee Cake, 198
    Cowboy Coffee Cake, 201
    Gold Rush Coffee Cake, 203

Johnny Appleseed Coffee Cake, 200
Cold Crab Salad, 123
Collard Greens, 10
    Quick(er) Collard Greens, 11
Collard Greens Sauteed, 101
Collard Greens with Ham Hocks, 10
Cookies
    Cheesecake Cookies, 179
    Chocolatey Coconut Squares, 179
    Czechoslovakian Cookies, 180
    Danish Cookies, 187
    English Semis, 184
    French Cremes, 187
    Holiday Squares, 178
    Italian Sweets, 188
    Lassers Cookies, 186
    Lemon Squares, 178
    Moist 'n Chewy Brownies, 183
    Molasses Crumbles, 184
    Monster Cookies, 185
    Rum Balls, 186
    Sand Tarts, 186
    Sugar Cookies, 183
    Toll House Cookies, 185
Cool Whip Pound Cake, 211
Corn
    Corn Pudding, 100
    Crab Soup, 160
    Harvest Salmon Chowder, 163
    Individual Baked Pork Chop Dinner, 75
    Salmon Corn Chowder, 162
    Succotash, 100
Corn Pudding, 100
Cornbread
    Buttermilk Cornbread, 130
    Cracklin Cornbread, 131
    Old-Fashioned Cornbread, 130
    Southern Style Cornbread, 136
Cornbread Dressing, 33
Cornbread Sausage Stuffing, 32

Corned Beef and Cabbage, 28
Cornish Hens, Roast with Melon Sauce, 67
Cornmeal,
    Roast Turkey with Oyster Cornbread Stuffing, 36
    Turnip Greens and Cornmeal Dumplings, 12
Country Cinnamon Rolls, 138
Cowboy Coffee Cake, 201
Crab
    Beggars Purses with Crabmeat, 216
    Chafing Dish A La Newburg, 84
    Cold Crab Salad, 123
    Crab Cakes, 87
    Crab Salad, 123
    Crab Soup, 160
    Deviled Crab, 88
    Green Pepper Surprise, 38
    New Orleans Gumbo, 8
    Seafood Gumbo, 7
    Seafood Salad, 122
    Seafood Soup, 162
Crab Cakes, 87
Crab Salad, 123
Crab Soup, 160
Cracklin Cornbread, 131
Cracklins, 221
Cranberry
    Cranberry Fruit Punch, 222
    Cranberry Jewel Salad, 124
    Cranberry Salad, 123
    Fruity Gelatin Salad, 124
    Hot Cranberry Punch, 222
    Meatballs in Sweet and Sour Sauce, 218
Cranberry Fruit Punch, 222
Cranberry Jewel Salad, 124
Cranberry Orange Butter Cake, 203
Cranberry Pork Chops, 76
Cranberry Salad, 123
Cranberry Sauce
    Rosy Glazed Chicken, 54
Cream Cheese Fudge, 190

Cream Cheese Icing, 202
Creamed Asparagus, 110
Creamed Spinach Casserole, 107
Creamed Vegetable Dish, 111
Cregg's Pigs Feet, 46
Crepeselle, 182
Crescents, Party, 139
Cucumbers
    14-Day Sweet Pickles, 127
    Bread and Butter Pickles, 127
Czechoslovakian Cookies, 180

D
Danish Cookies, 187
Dates
    Sunshine Loaf, 146
Deluxe Strawberry Pie, 172
Deviled Crab, 88
Devil's Food Cake, 196
Dieters' Chocolate Cheesecake, 198
Dijon Potato Salad, 118
Dill Potato Salad, 118
Dip
    Oriental Salmon Dip, 220
    Shrimp Dip, 221
    Taco Dip, 221
Dirty Rice, 16
Doughnuts, 139
    Yankee, 139
Dressing (see stuffing)
Dried Beef, 219
    Sara's Cheese Ball, 219
Dried Peach (or Apricot) Wine, 225
Dry Lima Beans, 95
Duck
    Leiths Roast Duck, 66
    Roast Duck with Orange Sauce, 67
Dump Cake, 204
Dumplings, Apple, 174

E
Easy Pilaf, 104
Easy Two-Egg Cake, 206
Eggplant

Eggplant-Beef Medley, 26
Italian Eggplant Parmigiana, 23
Eggplant-Beef Medley, 26
Eggs
Golden Eggs, 126
Pickled Eggs and beets, 126
English Semis, 184
Etc.
Bath Oil, 226
Bath Salts, 226
Dusting Powder, 226

F
Fargo a Portuguese, 58
Favorite Flavors in Layers, 177
Feather-Light Cheese Casserole, 18
Fettuccine Alfredo, 21
Fettuccine and Mixed Fresh Vegetables, 19
Fish
Baked Flounder Fillets in Cheese Sauce, 85
Baked Salmon, 86
Fried Fish, 47
Grilled Salmon with Lemon and Herb Butter, 85
Herring & Rice, 39
Mushroom-Stuffed Flounder, 85
Oven-Fried Fillets of Sole, 84
Salmon Loaf, 87
Salmon or Tuna Loaf, 86
Seafood Batter Dip, 47
Seafood Soup, 162
Five-Flavor Pound Cake, 209
Flavorful Cooked Brown Rice, 104
Flounder
Baked Flounder Fillets in Cheese Sauce, 85
Mushroom-Stuffed Flounder, 85
Fluffy Cream Sauce over Fruit, 171
14-Day Sweet Pickles, 127

French Cremes, 187
French Toast, 149
Fresh Apple Squares, 176
Fresh Strawberry Mousse, 171
Fried Apples, 170
Fried Cabbage and Bacon, 97
Fried Chicken, 42-43
Fried Fish, 47
Fried Green Tomatoes, 98
Fried New Potatoes, 97
Fried Okra, 94
Fried Sweet Potatoes, 96
Frontier Nut Bread, 148
Frosted Fruit Salad, 125
Frosting (see Icing)
Fruit Pizza Cookies, 171
Fruit Salad, 124
Fruity Gelatin Salad, 124
Fudge
Big Batch No-Cook Fudge, 190
Chocolate Fudge, 189
Chocolate Peanut Butter Fudge, 190
Cream Cheese Fudge, 190
Opera Fudge, 190

G
Garlic Herb Lamb Kabobs, 80
Garlic Shrimp, 81
Garlic Spread, 222
Gelatin
Cranberry Jewel Salad, 124
Cranberry Salad, 123
Fresh Strawberry Mousse, 171
Frosted Fruit Salad, 125
Fruity Gelatin Salad, 124
Jello Cake, 213
Orange Pineapple Delight, 176
Giblets, Chicken
Dirty Rice, 16
Gift Muffs, 143
Gingerbread, 212
Glazed Apple Rings, 170
Glazed Carrots and Turnips, 105

Glazed Honey Carrots, 99
Gold Rush Coffee Cake, 203
Golden Eggs, 126
Grand Champion Sponge Cake, 212
Grand Marnier
Chocolate Covered Strawberries, 171
Granola Muffins, 142
Grapefruit Tuna Salad, 121
Grapes
Fruit Salad, 124
Grecian Lamb, 80
Green Goddess Salad Dressing, 120
Green Pepper Surprise, 38
Green Tomato Chow Chow, 126
Grilled Chinese Five-Spice Skewered Chicken, 59
Grilled Lamb Chops, 79
Grilled Meat Sticks, 89
Grilled Salmon with Lemon and Herb Butter, 85
Grits
Cheese Garlic Grits, 101
Grits Souffle, 17
Hominy Grits, 93
Grits Souffle, 17
Ground Beef
Baked Beans Brewster-Style, 27
Baked Lasagna, 25
Eggplant-Beef Medley, 26
Hamburger Casserole, 27
Indian Meat Loaf, 72
Italian Meat Loaf, 73
Meat Loaf, 72
Meatballs in Sweet and Sour Sauce, 218
Shepherd's Pie to Feed a Crowd, 28
Stately Meat Loaf, 72
Stuffed Bell Peppers, 37
Stuffed Shells, 25
Sweet and Sour Meatballs, 73
Two-Bean Beef Mix, 26
Ground Beef and Cabbage, 29

Gumbo Feast, 6

H

Halibut, 161
  Seafood Bisque, 161
Ham
  Baked Ham, 79
  Bean Soup, 157
  Black-Eyed Peas, 92
  Black-Eyed Peas with Ham,
    13
  Boiled String Beans with
    Ham, 14
  Butter Beans with Ham
    Hocks, 13
  Carolina Red Rice, 15
  Collard Greens, 10
  Collard Greens with Ham
    Hocks, 10
  Creamed Vegetable Dish, 111
  Ham and Cabbage Dinner, 30
  Ham Barbecue, 89
  Ham, Cheese, & Raisin Sticks,
    143
  Jambalaya, 37
  Mustard Greens and Ham
    Hocks, 11
  New Orleans Gumbo, 8
  Red Beans and Rice, 15
  Seafood Gumbo, 7
  Talmadge Ham and Red-Eye
  Gravy, 45
  Turnip Greens and Cornmeal
    Dumplings, 12
Ham and Cabbage Dinner, 30
Ham Barbecue, 89
Ham, Cheese, & Raisin Sticks,
  143
Hamburger Casserole, 27
Harvard Beets, 99
Harvest Salmon Chowder, 163
Hawaiian Chicken, 58
Hawaiian Fruit Punch, 223
Hearty Sausage Bake, 33
Herbed Pork Roast, 77
Herby Biscuits, 140
Herring & Rice, 39

Hershey's Chocolate Cake, 196
Hester's Cake, 204
Hobby-Bakers Coffee-Breakers,
  148
Hobo Bread, 144
Hog's Head, 9
  Brunswick Stew, 9
Holiday Squares, 178
Homemade Rolls, 134
Homemade Tomato Soup, 152
Hominy Grits, 93
Honey Baked Chicken, 50
Honey Buffet Chicken, 49
Honey Ice Cream, 189
Hoppin John, 92
Horseradish Mashed Potatoes,
  102
Hot Chicken Salad, 62
Hot Cranberry Punch, 222
Hush Puppies, 135
  Old South Hush Puppies, 135

I

Ice Cream, 225, 166, 168, 170,
  175, 189, 194, 206, 210
  Honey Ice Cream, 189
  Vanilla Coke, 225
Icing, 138, 202, 211
  Butter Frosting, 202
  Cream Cheese Icing, 202
Indian Meat Loaf, 72
Individual Baked Pork Chop
  Dinner, 75
Instant Russian Tea, 224
Italian Eggplant Parmigiana, 23
Italian Green Beans with
  Mushrooms, 107
Italian Meat Loaf, 73
Italian Sweets, 188
Italian-Style Finger Sandwiches,
  217
Italian-Style Fried Chicken
  Wings, 61

J

Jam Dandies, 140
Jambalaya, 37

Jello Cake, 213
Jewish Apple Cake, 199
Johnny Appleseed Coffee Cake,
  200

K

Kidney Beans
  New Orleans Red Beans and
    Rice, 16
  Red Beans and Rice, 15
  Three-Bean Soup, 156
Kielbasa
  Gumbo Feast, 6

L

Lamb
  Garlic Herb Lamb Kabobs, 80
  Grecian Lamb, 80
  Grilled Lamb Chops, 79
  Marinated Lamb Chops, 80
Lassers Cookies, 186
Leeks
  Chinese Pot-Au-Feu, 34
  Risotto with Spring Veggies,
    22
Leiths Roast Duck, 66
Lemon Barbecued Chicken, 55
Lemon Squares, 178
Lemony Chicken Thighs, 50
Lentils
  Bean Soup, 157
Linguini with Asparagus & Pesto,
  20
Liver and Onions, 44
Livers, Chicken
  Dirty Rice, 16
Lobster
  Chafing Dish A La Newburg,
    84
Low-Fat Chicken Salad, 120
Lunch Meat
  Grilled Meat Sticks, 89

M

Macaroni & Tuna Pasta Salad,
  121

Index

Macaroni and Cheese, Home-style, 18
Macaroni Salad, 120
Main Dishes — Other Favorites,
Baked Beans Brewster-Style, 27
Baked Lasagna, 25
Cajun Cassoulet, 32
Chicken and Vegetables, 34
Chicken Divan, 35
Chinese Beef with Broccoli, 29
Chinese Pot-Au-Feu, 34
Cornbread Dressing, 33
Cornbread Sausage Stuffing, 32
Corned Beef and Cabbage, 28
Eggplant-Beef Medley, 26
Feather-Light Cheese Casserole, 18
Fettuccine Alfredo, 21
Fettuccine and Mixed Fresh Vegetables, 19
Green Pepper Surprise, 38
Ground Beef and Cabbage, 29
Ham and Cabbage Dinner, 30
Hamburger Casserole, 27
Hearty Sausage Bake, 33
Herring & Rice, 39
Italian Eggplant Parmigiana, 23
Jambalaya, 37
Linguini with Asparagus & Pesto, 20
Macaroni and Cheese, Home-style, 18
Pasta Mexicana, 24
Pasta Primavera, 19
Pork Fried Rice, 31
Pork Mu Shu Burritos, 31
Primavera Pizza, 20
Risotto with Spring Veggies, 22
Roast Turkey with Oyster Cornbread Stuffing, 36
Shepherd's Pie to Feed a Crowd, 28

Shrimp Fried Rice, 39
Shrimp Stir-Fry, 38
Smoked Turkey & Black-Eyed Peas, 36
Spanish Rice, 23-24
Spinach Manicotti, 21
Stuffed Bell Peppers, 37
Stuffed Shells, 25
Stuffed Yellow Squash with Cheese Sauce, 22
Succulent Veal Stew, 30
Two-Bean Beef Mix, 26
Wild Rice, Chicken, and Broccoli Bake, 35
Main Dishes — Traditional
Black-Eyed Peas with Ham, 13
Boiled String Beans with Ham, 14
Brunswick Stew, 9
Butter Beans with Ham Hocks, 13
Cabbage and Smoked Neckbones, 12
Carolina Red Rice, 15
Collard Greens, 10
Collard Greens with Ham Hocks, 10
Dirty Rice, 16
Grits Souffe, 17
Gumbo Feast, 6
Mustard Greens and Ham Hocks, 11
New Orleans Gumbo, 8
New Orleans Red Beans and Rice, 16
Okra Gumbo, 8
Quick(er) Collard Greens, 11
Red Beans and Rice, 15
Red Beans, Sausage, and Rice, 14
Seafood Gumbo, 7
Turnip Greens and Cornmeal Dumplings, 12
Mandarin Oranges Fruit Salad, 124
Marinated Lamb Chops, 80

Mashed Sweet Potatoes, 101
Maw, Chitlins and, 46
Meat Loaf
Indian Meat Loaf, 72
Italian Meat Loaf, 73
Stately Meat Loaf, 72
Meatballs, Sweet and Sour, 73
Meatballs in Sweet and Sour Sauce, 218
Meats — Other Favorites
Baked Flounder Fillets in Cheese Sauce, 85
Baked Ham, 79
Baked Oysters Italian Style, 88
Baked Salmon, 86
Baked Turkey Wings, 64
Barbecued Chicken, 48
Barbecued Chicken Wings, 61
Barbecued Spareribs, 77
Beef Stroganoff, 70
Braised Veal in Cider, 74
Broiled Shrimp Au Porto, 81
Buffalo Chicken Drumsticks, 60
Buffalo Wings, 61
Cajun Chops, 74
Chafing Dish A La Newburg, 84
Champagne & Mushroom Chicken, 57
Chicken Cobbler, 63
Chicken in White Wine, 53
Chicken Lemonaise, 56
Chicken Marsala, 53
Chicken Parmesan, 56
Chicken Piccata, 54
Chicken Teriyaki, 52
Chuck Roast with Vegetables, 69
Chuck Wagon Roast, 68
Crab Cakes, 87
Cranberry Pork Chops, 76
Deviled Crab, 88
Fargo a Portuguese, 58
Garlic Herb Lamb Kabobs, 80
Garlic Shrimp, 81

Grecian Lamb, 80
Grilled Chinese Five-Spice
    Skewered Chicken, 59
Grilled Lamb Chops, 79
Grilled Meat Sticks, 89
Grilled Salmon with Lemon
    and Herb Butter, 85
Ham Barbecue, 89
Hawaiian Chicken, 58
Herbed Pork Roast, 77
Honey Baked Chicken, 50
Honey Buffet Chicken, 49
Hot Chicken Salad, 62
Indian Meat Loaf, 72
Individual Baked Pork Chop
    Dinner, 75
Italian Meat Loaf, 73
Italian-Style Fried Chicken
    Wings, 61
Leiths Roast Duck, 66
Lemon Barbecued Chicken,
    55
Lemony Chicken Thighs, 50
Marinated Lamb Chops, 80
Meat Loaf, 72-73
Mexican Chicken, 57
Mexican-Style Pot Roast, 68
Mushroom-Stuffed Flounder,
    85
Orange Baked Chicken, 51
Orange Baked Pork Chops, 76
Orange Ginger Chicken, 51
Oven-Baked Pot Roast, 70
Oven-Fried Fillets of Sole, 84
Parmesan Baked Chicken
    Legs, 48
Pepper Steak, 68
Pork Chops and Rice, 75
Pot Roast, 68-70
Roast Cornish Hens with
    Melon Sauce, 67
Roast Duck with Orange
    Sauce, 67
Rosy Glazed Chicken, 54
Salmon Loaf, 87
Salmon or Tuna Loaf, 86
Sesame Fried Chicken, 49

Shrimp and Mushrooms with
    Paprika Sauce, 83
Shrimp Bake, 82
Shrimp Newburg, 83
Smoked Almond Crusted
    Chicken, 55
Spareribs, 77-78
Spicy Ribs, 78
Stately Meat Loaf, 72
Steak Tartare, 71
Stuffed Pork Chops, 76
Sunshine Chicken, 58
Sweet & Sour Chicken, 60
Sweet & Sour Shrimp, 82
Sweet and Sour Meatballs, 73
Sweet and Sour Short Ribs, 71
Sweet N' Sour Chicken, 59
Teriyaki Sauce, 52
Turkey Croquettes, 66
Turkey Loaf, 65
Turkey Scallopini Piccata, 63
Turkey Supreme, 65
Turkey Wings and Gravy, 64
Wings Teriyaki, 62
Meats — Traditional
    Basic Tempura, 47
    Chitlins and Maw, 46
    Cregg's Pigs Feet, 46
    Fried Chicken, 42-43
    Fried Fish, 47
    Liver and Onions, 44
    Oxtails, 43
    Pig's Feet, 45
    Pork Sausage and Gravy, 44
    Seafood Batter Dip, 47
    Talmadge Ham and Red-Eye
        Gravy, 45
Mexican Chicken, 57
Mexican-Style Pot Roast, 68
Million Dollar Pound Cake, 207
Minestrone Soup, 155
Minestrone with Tortellini, 156
Mock Champagne Punch, 224
Moist 'n Chewy Brownies, 183
Molasses Crumbles, 184
Monkey Bread, 149
Monster Cookies, 185

Mother's Bread, 137
Muffins
    Blueberry Muffins, 141
    Cheesy Muffins, 142
    Gift Muffs, 143
    Granola Muffins, 142
    Supermuffs, 143
    Whole Wheat Muffins, 142
    Yummy Healthy Muffins, 142
Mushroom Soup, 157
Mushroom-Stuffed Flounder, 85
Mushrooms
    Chinese Pot-Au-Feu, 34
    Fettuccine and Mixed Fresh
        Vegetables, 19
    Italian Green Beans with
        Mushrooms, 107
    Mushrooms Oregano, 217
    Primavera Pizza, 20
    Shrimp and Mushrooms with
        Paprika Sauce, 83
Mushrooms Oregano, 217
Mustard Greens and Ham
    Hocks, 11

N

Neckbones, Cabbage and
    Smoked, 12
Nectarine Pie, 182
New Orleans Gumbo, 8
New Orleans Red Beans and
    Rice, 16
Nutty Pumpkin Bread, 145

O

Oak Hill Potatoes, 103
Okra
    Batter-Fried Okra, 95
    Black-Eyed Peas with Ham,
        13
    Butter Beans with Ham
        Hocks, 13
    Fried Okra, 94
    Okra Gumbo, 8
    Pan-Fried Okra, 95
    Peas and Okra, 94
    Seafood Gumbo, 7

Index

Shrimp and Vegetable Gumbo, 160
Succotash, 100
Okra Gumbo, 8
Old South Hush Puppies, 135
Old-Fashioned Applesauce Cake, 200
Old-Fashioned Cornbread, 130
Old-Fashioned Shortcake, 207
One Bowl Apple Nut Cake, 199
Opera Fudge, 190
Orange
    Cranberry Orange Butter Cake, 203
    Gold Rush Coffee Cake, 203
    Williamsburg Orange Cake, 202
Orange Baked Chicken, 51
Orange Baked Pork Chops, 76
Orange Ginger Chicken, 51
Orange Pineapple Delight, 176
Oriental Salmon Dip, 220
Oven-Baked Pot Roast, 70
Oven-Fried Fillets of Sole, 84
Oxtails, 43
Oysters
    Baked Oysters Italian Style, 88
    Roast Turkey with Oyster Cornbread Stuffing, 36
    Seafood Gumbo, 7

P

Pan-Fried Green Tomatoes, 98
Pan-Fried Okra, 95
Parmesan Baked Chicken Legs, 48
Party Crescents, 139
Party Punch, 223
Pasta
    Baked Lasagna, 25
    Fettuccine Alfredo, 21
    Fettuccine and Mixed Fresh Vegetables, 19
    Linguini with Asparagus & Pesto, 20

Macaroni and Cheese, Home-style, 18
Macaroni & Tuna Pasta Salad, 121
Macaroni Salad, 120
Minestrone with Tortellini, 156
Pasta Mexicana, 24
Pasta Primavera, 19
Risotto with Spring Veggies, 22
Seafood Salad, 122
Spinach Manicotti, 21
Stuffed Shells, 25
Pasta Mexicana, 24
Pasta Primavera, 19
Peach, Blueberry and Shortcake, 201
Peach Cobbler, 168
Peach Tea, 224
Peanut Butter, Chocolate Chip Cake, 197
Peanut Butter Easter Eggs, 191
Peanut Brittle, 191
Pear Au Chocolate, 170
Pears
    Baked Honey Pears, 169
    Baked Pears, 169
    Pear Au Chocolate, 170
    Poached Pears, 169
Peas
    Minestrone Soup, 155
    Pasta Primavera, 19
    Peas and Okra, 94
    Risotto with Spring Veggies, 22
    Shepherd's Pie to Feed a Crowd, 28
    Southern Cooked Green Peas, 93
Peas and Okra, 94
Peas, Smoked Turkey & Black-Eyed, 36
Pecan
    Pecan Cake, 205
    Tossed Butter Pecan Cake, 205

Pecan Cake, 205
Pecan Pie, 167, 182
Pepper Steak, 68
Pepper, Green
    Green Pepper Surprise, 38
    Stuffed Bell Peppers, 37
Pepperoni
    Italian-Style Finger Sandwiches, 217
Perch
    Seafood Bisque, 161
Pickled Beets, 125
Pickled Eggs and Beets, 126
Pickles
    14-Day Sweet Pickles, 127
    Bread and Butter Pickles, 127
Pie
    Nectarine Pie, 182
    Pecan Pie, 167, 182
Pig Knuckles
    Dry Lima Beans, 95
Pigs Feet
    Cregg's Pigs Feet, 46
    Pig's Feet Soup, 153
Pineapple Pound Cake, 210
Pineapples
    Bake Sale Pineapple Bread, 145
    Banana Split Delight, 176
    Blueberry Delight, 176
    Dump Cake, 204
    Frosted Fruit Salad, 125
    Fruit Salad, 124
    Hester's Cake, 204
    Orange Pineapple Delight, 176
Pizza, Primavera, 20
Poached Pears, 169
Popcorn, Carmel, 222
Pork Chops
    Cajun Chops, 74
    Cranberry Pork Chops, 76
    Individual Baked Pork Chop Dinner, 75
    Orange Baked Pork Chops, 76
    Pork Chops and Rice, 75
    Pork Mu Shu Burritos, 31

Stuffed Pork Chops, 76
Pork Chops and Rice, 75
Pork Fried Rice, 31
Pork Mu Shu Burritos, 31
Pork Sausage and Gravy, 44
Pork Skin, 221
  Cracklins, 221
Pork, Salt
  Hoppin John, 92
  Peas and Okra, 94
  Southern Cooked Dried Lima
    Beans, 96
  Southern Cooked Green Peas,
    93
  Southern Cooked Rutabagas,
    99
Pot Roast, 68-70
Potato Pancakes, 104
Potato Salad, 116
Potato Salad for a Crowd, 117
Potatoes
  Chuck Roast with Vegetables,
    69
  Dijon Potato Salad, 118
  Dill Potato Salad, 118
  Harvest Salmon Chowder, 163
  Horseradish Mashed Potatoes,
    102
  Individual Baked Pork Chop
    Dinner, 75
  Minestrone with Tortellini,
    156
  Oak Hill Potatoes, 103
  Oven-Baked Pot Roast, 70
  Potato Pancakes, 104
  Potatoes Pizziola, 102
  Red-Skin Potato Salad, 119
  Scalloped Potatoes, 103
  Seafood Soup, 162
  Southwestern Potato Salad,
    119
  Washington Chowder, 154
Potatoes Pizziola, 102
Pound Cake
  Best Yet Pound Cake, 209
  Coconut Pound Cake, 208
  Cool Whip Pound Cake, 211

Five-Flavor Pound Cake, 209
Million Dollar Pound Cake,
  207
Pineapple Pound Cake, 210
7-Up Pound Cake, 210
Sour Cream Pound Cake, 208
Primavera Pizza, 20
Prune Tarts in Egg Pastry, 174
Pudding
  Bread Pudding, 181
  Butterscotch Delight, 177
  Favorite Flavors in Layers,
    177
Pumpkin
  Nutty Pumpkin Bread, 145
  Pumpkin Cheese Roll, 173
  Pumpkin Nut Bread, 144
Pumpkin Cheese Roll, 173
Pumpkin Nut Bread, 144
Pumpkin Pie, 168

Q
Quick(er) Collard Greens, 11

R
Raisin Bread, 134
Red Beans and Rice, 15
Red Beans, Sausage, and Rice, 14
Red Snapper, 161
  Seafood Bisque, 161
Red-Skin Potato Salad, 119
Ribs
  Barbecued Spareribs, 77
  Spareribs, 78
  Spicy Ribs, 78
  Sweet and Sour Short Ribs, 71
Rice
  Bombay Rice Dressing, 105
  Broccoli and Rice Casserole,
    106
  Carolina Red Rice, 15
  Chicken and Rice Soup, 153
  Dirty Rice, 16
  Easy Pilaf, 104
  Flavorful Cooked Brown Rice,
    104
  Herring & Rice, 39

New Orleans Red Beans and
  Rice, 16
Pork Chops and Rice, 75
Pork Fried Rice, 31
Red Beans, Sausage, and Rice,
  14
Shrimp and Rice Salad, 122
Shrimp and Vegetable
  Gumbo, 160
Shrimp Fried Rice, 39
Shrimp Gumbo with Rice,
  161
Spanish Rice, 23-24
Tomato and Rice Soup, 154
Wild Rice, Chicken, and
  Broccoli Bake, 35
Risotto with Spring Veggies, 22
Roast Cornish Hens with Melon
  Sauce, 67
Roast Duck with Orange Sauce,
  67
Roast Turkey with Oyster
  Cornbread Stuffing, 36
Roast, Beef
  Brunswick Stew, 9
  Chuck Roast with Vegetables,
    69
  Chuck Wagon Roast, 68
  Mexican-Style Pot Roast, 68
  Oven-Baked Pot Roast, 70
  Pepper Steak, 68
  Pork Mu Shu Burritos, 31
  Pot Roast, 68-70
  Tomato and Rice Soup, 154
Roast, Pork
  Herbed Pork Roast, 77
  Pork Fried Rice, 31
Rolls
  Buttermilk Rolls, 132
  Country Cinnamon Rolls, 138
  Homemade Rolls, 134
  Sunday Brunch Cherry Nut
    Rolls, 138
  Whole Wheat Rolls or Bread,
    133
Rosy Glazed Chicken, 54
Rum Balls, 186

Index

Rum Cake, 213
Rutabagas, Southern, Cooked, 99

S

Salad Dressing, Green Goddess, 120
Salads — Other Favorites
  14-Day Sweet Pickles, 127
  Bread and Butter Pickles, 127
  Cold Crab Salad, 123
  Crab Salad, 123
  Cranberry Jewel Salad, 124
  Cranberry Salad, 123
  Dijon Potato Salad, 118
  Dill Potato Salad, 118
  Frosted Fruit Salad, 125
  Fruit Salad, 124
  Fruity Gelatin Salad, 124
  Golden Eggs, 126
  Grapefruit Tuna Salad, 121
  Green Goddess Salad
    Dressing, 120
  Green Tomato Chow Chow,
    126
  Low-Fat Chicken Salad, 120
  Macaroni & Tuna Pasta Salad,
    121
  Macaroni Salad, 120
  Pickled Beets, 125
  Pickled Eggs and Beets, 126
  Red-Skin Potato Salad, 119
  Seafood Salad, 122
  Shrimp and Rice Salad, 122
  Shrimp Salad, 121
  Southwestern Potato Salad,
    119
  Tuna Salad, 121
  Turkey Salad, 120
Salads — Traditional
  Potato Salad, 116
  Potato Salad for a Crowd, 117
Salami, 217
  Italian-Style Finger
    Sandwiches, 217
Salmon
  Baked Salmon, 86

Grilled Salmon with Lemon
  and Herb Butter, 85
Harvest Salmon Chowder, 163
Oriental Salmon Dip, 220
Salmon Corn Chowder, 162
Salmon Loaf, 87
Salmon or Tuna Loaf, 86
Salt Pork
  Cracklins, 221
  Red Beans, Sausage, and Rice,
    14
Sand Tarts, 186
Sara's Cheese Ball, 219
Sausage
  Baked Lasagna, 25
  Cajun Cassoulet, 32
  Cornbread Sausage Stuffing,
    32
  Gumbo Feast, 6
  Hearty Sausage Bake, 33
  New Orleans Gumbo, 8
  Pork Sausage and Gravy, 44
  Red Beans, Sausage, and Rice,
    14
  Sausage & Cheese Omelet, 33
Scalloped Potatoes, 103
Scotch Shortbread, 188
Seafood Batter Dip, 47
Seafood Bisque, 161
Seafood Gumbo, 7
Seafood Salad, 122
Seafood Soup, 162
Sesame Fried Chicken, 49
7-Up Pound Cake, 210
Shepherd's Pie to Feed a Crowd,
  28
Sherry
  Beef Stroganoff, 70
  Chicken Divan, 35
  Chinese Pot-Au-Feu, 34
  Succulent Veal Stew, 30
Shortbread, Scotch, 188
Shortcake
  Blueberry and Peach
    Shortcake, 201
  Old-Fashioned Shortcake, 207

Shrimp
  Broiled Shrimp Au Porto, 81
  Chafing Dish A La Newburg,
    84
  Garlic Shrimp, 81
  Jambalaya, 37
  New Orleans Gumbo, 8
  Seafood Batter Dip, 47
  Seafood Gumbo, 7
  Seafood Soup, 162
  Shrimp and Mushrooms with
    Paprika Sauce, 83
  Shrimp Bake, 82
  Shrimp Newburg, 83
  Stuffed Bell Peppers, 37
  Sweet & Sour Shrimp, 82
Shrimp and Mushrooms with
  Paprika Sauce, 83
Shrimp and Rice Salad, 122
Shrimp and Vegetable Gumbo,
  160
Shrimp Bake, 82
Shrimp Bisque, 161
Shrimp Dip, 221
Shrimp Fried Rice, 39
Shrimp Gumbo with Rice, 161
Shrimp Hors D'oeuvres, 216
Shrimp Newburg, 83
Shrimp Salad, 121
Shrimp Stir-Fry, 38
Smoked Almond Crusted
  Chicken, 55
Smoked Turkey & Black-Eyed
  Peas, 36
Snacks and Appetizers — Other
  Favorites
  Anchovy Spread, 220
  Beggars Purses with
    Crabmeat, 216
  Caramel Popcorn, 222
  Cheese Ball, 219
  Cracklins, 221
  Cranberry Fruit Punch, 222
  Dried Peach (or Apricot)
    Wine, 225
  Garlic Spread, 222
  Hawaiian Fruit Punch, 223

Hot Cranberry Punch, 222
Instant Russian Tea, 224
Italian-Style Finger
    Sandwiches, 217
Meatballs in Sweet and Sour
    Sauce, 218
Mock Champagne Punch, 224
Mushrooms Oregano, 217
Oriental Salmon Dip, 220
Party Punch, 223
Peach Tea, 224
Sara's Cheese Ball, 219
Shrimp Dip, 221
Shrimp Hors D'oeuvres, 216
Southern Caviar, 220
Southwest Cheesecake, 218
Sweet and Sour Turkey Balls,
    217
Taco Dip, 221
Vanilla Coke, 225
Vegetable Spread, 219
Wedding Punch, 223
Snow Peas
    Shrimp Stir-Fry, 38
    Stir-Fried Asparagus with
        Snow Peas, 109
Sole, Oven-Fried Fillets of, 84
Soups — Other Favorites
    Bean Soup, 157
    Beef Barley Minestrone, 155
    Broccoli Soup, 158
    Chicken Soup, 159
    Crab Soup, 160
    Harvest Salmon Chowder, 163
    Minestrone Soup, 155
    Minestrone with Tortellini,
        156
    Mushroom Soup, 157
    Salmon Corn Chowder, 162
    Seafood Bisque, 161
    Seafood Soup, 162
    Shrimp and Vegetable
        Gumbo, 160
    Shrimp Gumbo with Rice,
        161
    Stracciatella, 160
    Three-Bean Soup, 156

Tomato and Rice Soup, 154
Vegetable Broth, 159
Washington Chowder, 154
Zucchini Soup, 158
Soups — Traditional
    Chicken and Rice Soup, 153
    Homemade Tomato Soup, 152
    Pig's Feet Soup, 153
    Turkey Soup, 152
Sour Cream Pound Cake, 208
Southern Caviar, 220
Southern Cooked Butter Beans,
    95
Southern Cooked Dried Lima
    Beans, 96
Southern Cooked Green Peas, 93
Southern Cooked Rutabagas, 99
Southern Style Cornbread, 136
Southwest Cheesecake, 218
Southwestern Potato Salad, 119
Spanish Rice, 23-24
Spareribs, 77-78
Spice Cake, 211
Spicy Ribs, 78
Spinach
    Chinese Pot-Au-Feu, 34
    Creamed Spinach Casserole,
        107
    Salmon Corn Chowder, 162
    Spinach Manicotti, 21
    Stir-Fry Cabbage, 107
Spinach Manicotti, 21
Sponge Cake, Grand Champion,
    212
Spread
    Anchovy Spread, 220
    Garlic Spread, 222
    Vegetable Spread, 219
Squash
    Stuffed Yellow Squash with
        Cheese Sauce, 22
    Yellow Squash and Onions,
        108
Stately Meat Loaf, 72
Steak
    Beef Barley Minestrone, 155
    Beef Stroganoff, 70

Minestrone Soup, 155
    Steak Tartare, 71
Steak Tartare, 71
Stir-Fried Asparagus with Snow
    Peas, 109
Stir-Fry Cabbage, 107
Stracciatella, 160
Strawberries
    Chocolate Covered
        Strawberries, 171
    Deluxe Strawberry Pie, 172
    Fresh Strawberry Mousse,
        171
    Frosted Fruit Salad, 125
    Strawberry Roll, 173
Strawberry Roll, 173
Stuffed Bell Peppers, 37
Stuffed Pork Chops, 76
Stuffed Shells, 25
Stuffed Yellow Squash with
    Cheese Sauce, 22
Stuffed Zucchini, 108
Stuffing, Cornbread Sausage, 32
Succotash, 100
Succulent Veal Stew, 30
Sugar Cookies, 171, 183
Sunday Brunch Cherry Nut
    Rolls, 138
Sunshine Chicken, 58
Sunshine Loaf, 146
Supermuffs, 143
Surprisin' Carrot Cake, 202
Sweet & Sour Chicken, 60
Sweet & Sour Shrimp, 82
Sweet and Sour Meatballs, 73
Sweet and Sour Short Ribs, 71
Sweet and Sour Turkey Balls, 217
Sweet N' Sour Chicken, 59
Sweet Potatoes
    Candied Yams, 96
    Fried Sweet Potatoes, 96
    Mashed Sweet Potatoes, 101
    Sweet Potato Pancakes, 102
    Sweet Potato Pie, 166
    Sweet Potato Pone, 180
    Sweet Potato Pudding, 166
    Sweet Potato Soufflé, 181

Index

Sweets — Other Favorites
Apple Dumplings, 174
Baked Apple Pudding, 175
Baked Cherries and Custard, 172
Baked Honey Pears, 169
Baked Pears, 169
Banana Split Delight, 176
Big Batch No-Cook Fudge, 190
Blueberry Delight, 176
Bread Pudding, 181
Butterscotch Delight, 177
Cheesecake Cookies, 179
Cherries and Cream Roll, 172
Chocolate Covered Strawberries, 171
Chocolate Fudge, 189
Chocolate Peanut Butter Fudge, 190
Chocolatey Coconut Squares, 179
Cream Cheese Fudge, 190
Crepeselle, 182
Czechoslovakian Cookies, 180
Danish Cookies, 187
Deluxe Strawberry Pie, 172
English Semis, 184
Favorite Flavors in Layers, 177
Fluffy Cream Sauce over Fruit, 171
French Cremes, 187
Fresh Apple Squares, 176
Fresh Strawberry Mousse, 171
Fried Apples, 170
Fruit Pizza Cookies, 171
Glazed Apple Rings, 170
Holiday Squares, 178
Honey Ice Cream, 189
Italian Sweets, 188
Lassers Cookies, 186
Lemon Squares, 178
Moist 'n Chewy Brownies, 183
Molasses Crumbles, 184

Monster Cookies, 185
Nectarine Pie, 182
Opera Fudge, 190
Orange Pineapple Delight, 176
Peanut Butter Easter Eggs, 191
Peanut Brittle, 191
Pear Au Chocolate, 170
Pecan Pie, 167, 182
Poached Pears, 169
Prune Tarts in Egg Pastry, 174
Pumpkin Cheese Roll, 173
Rum Balls, 186
Sand Tarts, 186
Scotch Shortbread, 188
Strawberry Roll, 173
Sugar Cookies, 171, 183
Sweet Potato Pone, 180
Sweet Potato Soufflé, 181
Toll House Cookies, 185
Sweets — Traditional
Peach Cobbler, 168
Pecan Pie, 167, 182
Pumpkin Pie, 168
Sweet Potato Pie, 166
Sweet Potato Pudding, 166

T

Taco Dip, 221
Talmadge Ham and Red-Eye Gravy, 45
Tasty White Bread, 133
Tea
Dried Peach (or Apricot) Wine, 225
Instant Russian Tea, 224
Peach Tea, 224
Teriyaki Sauce, 52
Three-Bean Soup, 156
Toll House Cookies, 185
Tomato and Rice Soup, 154
Tomato Bake, 113
Tomatoes
Chicken and Vegetables, 34
Fried Green Tomatoes, 98
Homemade Tomato Soup, 152

Pan-Fried Green Tomatoes, 98
Tortellini, 156
Minestrone with Tortellini, 156
Tortillas
Pork Mu Shu Burritos, 31
Tossed Butter Pecan Cake, 205
Tuna
Grapefruit Tuna Salad, 121
Macaroni & Tuna Pasta Salad, 121
Salmon or Tuna Loaf, 86
Tuna Salad, 121
Tuna Salad
Turkey
Baked Turkey Wings, 64
Pork Mu Shu Burritos, 31
Roast Turkey with Oyster Cornbread Stuffing, 36
Smoked Turkey & Black-Eyed Peas, 36
Sweet and Sour Turkey Balls, 217
Turkey Croquettes, 66
Turkey Loaf, 65
Turkey Salad, 120
Turkey Scallopini Piccata, 63
Turkey Supreme, 65
Turkey Wings and Gravy, 64
Turkey Croquettes, 66
Turkey Loaf, 65
Turkey Salad, 120
Turkey Scallopini Piccata, 63
Turkey Soup, 152
Turkey Supreme, 65
Turkey Wings
Collard Greens, 10
Turkey Wings and Gravy, 64
Turnip Greens and Cornmeal Dumplings, 12
Turnips
Chicken Marsala, 53
Glazed Carrots and Turnips, 105
Two-Bean Beef Mix, 26

V

Vanilla Coke, 225
Veal
  Braised Veal in Cider, 74
  Succulent Veal Stew, 30
Vegetable Broth, 159
Vegetable Spread, 219
Vegetables Au Gratin, 111
Vegetables — Other Favorites
  Asparagus Casserole, 110
  Asparagus Frittata, 109
  Asparagus with Parmesan
    Cheese, 110
  Beets with Onions and
    Tomatoes, 113
  Bombay Rice Dressing, 105
  Broccoli and Rice Casserole,
    106
  Broccoli Casserole, 106
  Browned Brussels Sprouts,
    112
  Cauliflower Cheese Casserole,
    112
  Cheese Garlic Grits, 101
  Collard Greens Sauteed, 101
  Corn Pudding, 100
  Creamed Asparagus, 110
  Creamed Spinach Casserole,
    107
  Creamed Vegetable Dish, 111
  Easy Pilaf, 104
  Flavorful Cooked Brown Rice,
    104
  Glazed Carrots and Turnips,
    105
  Horseradish Mashed Potatoes,
    102
  Italian Green Beans with
    Mushrooms, 107
  Mashed Sweet Potatoes, 101
  Oak Hill Potatoes, 103
  Potato Pancakes, 104
  Potatoes Pizziola, 102
  Scalloped Potatoes, 103
  Stir-Fried Asparagus with
    Snow Peas, 109
  Stir-Fry Cabbage, 107

Stuffed Zucchini, 108
Succotash, 100
Sweet Potato Pancakes, 102
Tomato Bake, 113
Vegetables Au Gratin, 111
Yellow Squash and Onions,
  108
Zucchini Provencal, 108
Vegetables — Traditional, 92-99
  Batter-Fried Okra, 95
  Black-Eyed Peas, 92
  Candied Yams, 96
  Dry Lima Beans, 95
  Fried Cabbage and Bacon, 97
  Fried Green Tomatoes, 98
  Fried New Potatoes, 97
  Fried Okra, 94
  Fried Sweet Potatoes, 96
  Glazed Honey Carrots, 99
  Harvard Beets, 99
  Hominy Grits, 93
  Hoppin John, 92
  Pan-Fried Green Tomatoes, 98
  Pan-Fried Okra, 95
  Peas and Okra, 94
  Southern Cooked Butter
    Beans, 95
  Southern Cooked Dried Lima
    Beans, 96
  Southern Cooked Green Peas,
    93
  Southern Cooked Rutabagas,
    99

W

Washington Chowder, 154
Watergate Cake, 204
Wedding Punch, 223
Whole Wheat Bread, 133
Whole Wheat Muffins, 142
Whole Wheat Rolls or Bread, 133
Wild Rice, Chicken, and Broccoli
  Bake, 35
Williamsburg Orange Cake, 202
Wine
  Champagne & Mushroom
    Chicken, 57

Chicken in White Wine, 53
Chicken Marsala, 53
Chicken Piccata, 54
Dried Peach (or Apricot)
  Wine, 225
Glazed Apple Rings, 170
Turkey Scallopina Piccata, 63
Wine Cake, 213
Wine Cake, 213
Wings Teriyaki, 62

Y

Yams,
  Rosy Glazed Chicken, 54
Yams (also see Sweet Potatoes)
Yankee Doughnuts, 139
Yellow Squash
  Pasta Primavera, 19
Yellow Squash and Onions, 108
Yogurt and Chives Biscuits,
  140
Yogurt and Onions Biscuit
  Squares, 141
Yummy Healthy Muffins, 142

Z

Zucchini
  Minestrone Soup, 155
  Minestrone with Tortellini,
    156
  Pasta Primavera, 19
  Primavera Pizza, 20
  Stuffed Zucchini, 108
  Zucchini Provencal, 108
Zucchini Nut Bread, 147
Zucchini Provencal, 108
Zucchini Soup, 158

About the Author

Phoebe M. Bailey was born to John Cornelius and Margaret Marie Bailey, the youngest of 15 children, in Huntington, Long Island, New York. Phoebe currently resides in ChurchTowne of Lancaster, Pennsylvania, with her son Piindamon. Phoebe has been encouraged by her father's strength and courage as a black man, and inspired by her mother's faith in God and undeniable intelligence as a black woman, to embrace herself and her African heritage.

Phoebe began her career with Bethel Harambee Historical Services as a call from God. She left the corporate world to work closely with her brother, the Reverend Edward M. Bailey, and the congregation of Bethel African Methodist Episcopal Church, to preserve and tell the stories of those Africans who have been discounted and left out of traditional American history and to restore and rebuild a community of promise.

Phoebe is the executive director of "Living The Experience," a spiritual Underground Railroad reenactment. She is also one of the reenactors. Her ministry is to sing the song of an awesome God, who continues to deliver His people.

Group Discounts for *An African American Cookbook*
(see other side)

METHOD OF PAYMENT

❏   Check or Money Order
(payable to Good Books in U.S. funds)

❏   Please charge my:
❏ MasterCard   ❏ Visa   ❏ Discover   ❏ American Express

\# _____

exp. date _____

Signature _____

Name _____

Address _____

City _____

State _____

Zip _____

Phone _____

Email _____

SHIP TO: (if different)

Name _____

Address _____

City _____

State _____

Zip _____

Mail order to:
Good Books
P.O. Box 419 • Intercourse, PA 17534-0419
Call toll-free: 800/762-7171 • Fax toll-free: 888/768-3433

Prices subject to change.

Group Discounts

An African American Cookbook
ORDER FORM

If you would like to order multiple copies of *An African American Cookbook* for groups you are a part of, use this form. (Discounts apply only for more than one copy.)

Photocopy this page as often as you like.

The following discounts apply:

1 copy	$15.95
2-5 copies	$14.35 each (a 10% discount)
6-10 copies	$13.55 each (a 15% discount)
11 or more copies	$12.76 each (a 20% discount)

Prices subject to change.

Quantity   *Price*   *Total*

_____ copies of *An African American Cookbook* @ _____ _____

PA residents add 6% sales tax _____

Shipping & Handling
(add 10%, $3.00 minimum) _____

TOTAL _____

(Please fill in the payment and shipping information on the other side.)